SILVER BURDETT PROFESSIONAL PUBLICATIONS

Changing Behavior: How and Why

**The Cooperative Classroom:
Styles and Strategies for Teaching**

The Craft of Music Teaching

**Handicapped People in Society:
Ideas and Activities for Teachers**

Hints for Classroom Teachers

Hints for Teaching Social Studies

Mathematics Games for Classroom Use

Music: Materials for Teaching

Science: Its Social Significance

Sense and Humanity in Our Schools

**Social Science
in the Contemporary Classroom**

Teaching Science: Grades 5 to 9

Understanding Science Fiction

Practical

Techniques for TEACHING HISTORY

Myra Hayes Severance
Social Studies Teacher
Brecksville Junior High School
Brecksville, Ohio

SILVER BURDETT COMPANY
Morristown, New Jersey
Glenview, Ill. • San Carlos, Calif. • Dallas • Atlanta

Cover: Silver Burdett

Art: Kathy Hughes

Photos, page 251, courtesy of Thomas Lamphier

PRACTICAL TECHNIQUES FOR TEACHING HISTORY

Printed in the United States of America.

Published simultaneously in Canada.

ISBN 0-382-29060-7

Library of Congress Card Number: 80-53714

DEDICATION

Nothing is as important to a classroom teacher
as a cooperative and supportive school principal.
I owe my own professional growth
to three outstanding principals
who have guided me throughout my teaching career.
Gratefully, I dedicate this book to

Hugh Meaborn

Sam Cappas

Steve Vargo

ACKNOWLEDGEMENTS

The author is indebted to the following:

Mr. Sam Cappas, assistant principal, Brecksville Junior High School—consultant on mechanics, educational philosophy, and classroom techniques. He also served as a critic reader.

Mrs. Ruth Stoddard, librarian, Brecksville Junior High School—consultant on resources, particularly library materials. She also served as a consultant on educational philosophy and as a critic reader.

Mrs. Joan Scharff—typist. She typed the entire manuscript with skill and assisted in determining the structure of charts and tables.

Mr. Wesley Severance—husband of the author, whose patience and support were essential to this endeavor.

Interact, Lakeside, California—publishers who generously granted permission for the use of their material in Chapter 8.

CONTENTS

1

What's It All About?

I HAVE SPENT THIRTY-FIVE YEARS OF MY LIFE AS A teacher in several fields of study and in a number of situations. It has been a very satisfying career, and I am not yet ready to lay it aside. Both my files and my head are bulging with materials and programs and good ideas that I feel are worth sharing with others.

The process of sharing such information is, in fact, the purpose of this book. I direct this writing toward young teachers who are just starting their careers. It is my intention to present in this book some practical and workable teaching techniques, as well as specific and detailed projects and programs, which might be useful. I would like to pass on to all who read this some of my driving enthusiasm for teaching. I would also hope to inspire teachers to become truly creative in setting up their teaching programs.

In terms of subject matter, the focus of this book will be primarily on American history. In terms of grade level, my experience in the Social Studies field has been entirely at the junior high school level. It is my belief, however, that this book would be useful to the senior high school teacher as well. Both the teaching techniques and the detailed programs in this book can be adapted to various age levels and to several fields of study.

It would be appropriate at this point to tell you what this book is NOT. It is not a textbook on Educational Theory. I will not concern myself with "values clarification," "student rap sessions," "humanistic education," "student directed learning," "open classrooms," etc. Such theoretical material should be explored in college education courses.

Perhaps this book should not properly be called a textbook. Rather, it is a supplement, a reference, a manual to be found on the reading list of a Professor of Education or on the teachers' shelf of a school library. It should be, I believe, a source of aid to anyone involved in practice teaching.

This book should begin where the Education textbook stops. I intend it to be concerned with very practical suggestions that will help the teacher to cope with the day to day realities of classroom life.

PHILOSOPHY

Any educator who has spent many years in the field of teaching develops certain principles, beliefs, and prejudices that are usually quite well defined. It seems advisable to explore some of my own convictions so that the reader may understand the frame of reference from which I write.

I am one of the many teachers who vigorously supports and applauds the current hue and cry for a "back to the basics" movement in education. I am seriously concerned about the gradual decline in basic learning skills and study habits that I have observed in my own classroom as I meet new groups of students each year. I am equally concerned with the passive approach to learning characteristic of many of today's students. Most students expect to be entertained in the classroom. This is often accompanied by the expectation that the teacher should take the only active role in the educational process and "spoon-feed" the knowledge to the students. It leads one to question the impact of TV viewing (certainly a passive activity) on our young people.

In educational terms I have come to view the words "new" and "change" and "innovation" with suspicion. We have so readily embraced sweeping changes such as "New Math," or "New Reading," or "New Alphabet," and have found in such cases that the performance seldom lives up to the promise. I find myself advocating "change with caution."

In recent years many secondary schools have eliminated American history as such and have replaced it with a series of "mini-courses," each four to six weeks in length and each with a different teacher. Such courses are often taught out of sequence and without a textbook. They generally include a broad selection of choices ranging from a study of the United States constitution to the history of sports. I do not approve of this change. I believe in the sequential orderly approach to the teaching of American history—i.e., start in the eleventh century in Europe and progress steadily through to the twentieth century. I also believe in the use of a well-constructed text as the backbone of the course. Junior high school students are still young enough that they need the security of a sequential course, a good text, and one teacher for a subject.

There has been considerable controversy in recent years about "tracking" or homogenous grouping in the classroom. I believe that heterogeneous grouping is the most effective in teaching American history. All of the students have so much to give to one another in terms of ideas and opinions. I do believe, however, that the very slowest students, the ones who would be totally lost in a fast paced course with high standards, should be put in a special course. I am referring to those students with reading problems, neurological difficulties, slow maturation, and similar problems. These students can learn so much in a specially prepared course and achieve the feeling of success that so many of them badly need. This is another example of my policy of "change with caution." I am quietly resisting the recent trend to "mainstream" our very slow learners.

Educational theorists have been telling us for years that we must "teach students, not subjects." The students, of course, must be the primary concern of the classroom teacher, and if this is not the case, the teacher should change to another line of work. But I object strongly to the implication in that quotation that we should not teach subjects. My task in the classroom is to do the very best possible job of teaching American history to eighth graders. My challenge to myself, and to all who read this, is to teach the subject with such enthusiasm, creativity, thorough preparation, and plain hard work that the result is an exciting, exhilarating experience in learning for both the students and the teacher.

While I confess to being a traditionalist in many ways, I wish for our children the best of both worlds. I do not shrink from such terms as drill, study, memorize, practice, work hard, think, and learn. But at the same time, I endorse and embrace with great enthusiasm any kind of program that will get students actively involved in a learning process that is exciting. It is my hope that this book may help young teachers to produce such learning situations in their classrooms.

WHO'S IN CHARGE?

I am! And, if you are a teacher, so are you! Naturally, I recognize that I am accountable to my school principal, and to the Superintendent of Schools, and, less directly, to the Board of Education and to the community. But the youngsters in the classroom need to know that there is an adult in the room with full control. I will not be a "buddy" to my students; they are not my pals, my peers, nor my contemporaries. I would submit to you that most young people are not really comfortable with a teacher who attempts to enter the teenage world.

Nor do I approve of the premise that students should help to plan and develop their own curriculum and choose the direction of their own learning process. A look ahead to Chapter 7, "Individualized Instruction," may seem to present a contradiction in this regard. A closer look at that chapter, however, will reveal the fact that while the student does have many choices, the unit is highly structured. In addition, all work in this unit is completed under the close supervision of the teacher.

During my lifetime I have witnessed a veritable revolution in terms of rights, privileges, and freedoms given to our young people. Perhaps this is preferable to the old authoritarian approach to children that was a part of my own childhood. I would submit, however, that the pendulum has swung too far. In my view, permissiveness fostered in schools in recent years by both parents and teachers can result in more freedom than the students can comfortably handle. Such permissiveness fails to provide the disciplined orderly classroom atmosphere so important to education and to growth.

Let me hasten to assure you that my emphasis on control and discipline does not indicate that I am suggesting a harsh, cold, dreary classroom atmosphere. Quite the contrary, I consider the establishment of good teacher-student rapport to be the single most important factor in classroom teaching. There needs to be ample opportunity for humor, fun, change of pace, and downright nonsense. Students need to feel that the teacher really knows them as individuals and cares about what happens to them. They need to feel comfortable with their peers and with the teacher. Students need to feel safe from ridicule and embarrassment—free to express and defend their own opinions, knowing they will be respected, even when disagreeing with the teacher. They need to feel a sense of accomplishment and to experience success.

I usually find that it takes from September to December to develop to the fullest that kind of feeling in the classroom.

It is my opinion that, in developing this good learning atmosphere, the single greatest asset that a teacher can bring to the job is enthusiasm—enthusiasm for the students and for the subject. Enthusiasm is contagious, and it's a marvelous "disease" to have in the classroom. Nurture it and sustain it in every possible way.

2

Hints, Tips, and Techniques

I HAVE ALWAYS THOUGHT THAT TEACHING IS AN ART, not a science. I also believe that those who teach well not only possess a gift, but have worked very diligently to utilize that gift fully. Each one of us needs to develop his own individual style, approach to students, and methods of organizing materials and programs.

In this chapter I offer a potpourri of unrelated hints, tips, and techniques that may help young teachers as they establish their professional identities. Some of the topics will be dealt with rather superficially, others in more detail. The solutions and suggestions that I offer here are probably far less important than the questions raised for the beginning teacher to think about.

OBJECTIVES FOR THE YEAR

For several years each teacher in our school system was required to fill out a paper at the beginning of the school year stating the "targets for the year." The suggested choices were so theoretical and wordy that I was tempted several times to state defiantly and ungrammatically that my target was "to learn 'em history." I have come to feel, however, that setting annual goals or targets for the classroom teacher is an idea with merit. We all need to work constantly to improve our teaching performances, to face our weaknesses, and to improve generally the educational process.

These goals need not be numerous. They can be stated very simply. The important thing is that they should reflect thoughtful sincere effort by the teacher to improve his contributions to education.

Setting up goals for the year bears some resemblance to adopting New Year's resolutions on January 1. The results can end up sounding rather pious.and noble. They also can fall by the wayside as the year progresses. But the soul searching required for choosing them can be a positive experience and one that I recommend to all of you, whether or not it is required by your school system.

Course Outline

I begin each school year with a course outline for the year. This outline is mimeographed and distributed to students and parents. I suggest this as a good procedure for any classroom teacher. Such an outline must necessarily be very flexible and subject to changes, but it forces both the teacher and the student to preview the year's work as a whole. A typical outline is shown on the next two pages.

RULES AND REGULATIONS

Establish rules and regulations early in the year. Be sure to explain them very clearly. Then enforce them throughout the year consistently and matter-of-factly. Students are much more comfortable in the classroom when they know exactly what is expected of them.

In setting up rules for your classroom give some thought to the following ideas:

1. Care of property: writing on desks, spit balls on ceilings, paper wads on floors.
2. Materials needed for your class each day: notebooks, texts, pens or pencils, and additional supplies and special equipment.
3. Regulations concerning assignments: policy on late work, information required on each—name, date, class period.
4. Makeup work due to absence.
5. A miscellaneous grab bag of rules concerning behavior: talking, paper airplanes, chewing gum, squirt guns, and other typical types of student mischief.
6. Cheating and plagiarism.

No matter what the regulations are, the important thing is to be sure that they are well thought out and clearly explained. These rules also should help to set the tone for the classroom as a purposeful and businesslike atmosphere.

FREE WHEELING IN THE CLASSROOM

Some of the very best learning in the school takes place without the active participation of the teacher. This is especially true if the teacher provides the time and the materials to facilitate enrichment learning.

AMERICAN HISTORY—TENTATIVE OUTLINE FOR THE YEAR

THE FIRST SEMESTER

Time Allowed and Chapters Covered	***Current Events***	***Other***
First 6 weeks Chapters 1–4 Discovery and Exploration The English Colonies French and Indian War	The 1960's and 1970's (the students' own history) Survey of current affairs involving foreign news only Both background and up-to-date news of various regions of the world	Review of U.S. geography—especially topography and resources Map work of the Western Hemisphere Establishment of work habits—good reading note taking, listening, discussion, etc.
Second 6 weeks Chapters 5–7 Events leading to the Revolution The American Revolution The Constitution of the United States	Domestic issues of current importance. Each student writes a paper on a specific topic on domestic news. Very little library research—mostly from newspapers and news magazines and TV	Special emphasis on thorough base on the Constitution, Bill of Rights, and the Law Simulation exercise—Supreme Court Cases involving the Bill of Rights*
Third 6 weeks Chapters 8–12 The First Five Presidents Industrial and Social Growth Jackson and the West Our Territorial Expansion	Term papers on the following topics: The United Nations Any Military Alliance Any Economic Alliance Any Civil Rights Group Any Activist Movement Library Research Essential	At least three days to be devoted to reporting on and discussion of the topics covered in the term papers

THE SECOND SEMESTER

First 4 weeks Chapters 13–14–15 Buildup to the Civil War Events and Results of the War	The Political Cartoon* Students will collect, discuss, and analyze political cartoons—will also make original cartoons	Civil War Debates* Mock Congress set up (year 1858) to let students really get involved in War issues
Second 4 weeks Chapters 16–19 The Growth of the U.S. in the Post-Civil War Period Agriculture, Railroads, Indians, Labor, Big Business, and Immigration	NONE	A specially planned unit that centers around individualized instruction*
The next 6 weeks Chapters 22–26 America and the World World War I The 20's, depressions, and the New Deal	Special study of the ISMS Nazism, Fascism, Communism, Capitalism, Socialism	A very special unit using simulation (role playing)—living thru the period of the 1920's and 1930's—ending with a "Twenties Costume Day"*
The last 4 weeks Chapters 27 and 28 and parts of 29–32— World War II Review of 60's and 70's	Editorials—one-page papers with personal opinions on current issues	Emphasis on group discussion
Throughout the entire year emphasis will be placed on the following: Vocabulary words that apply to history—people in American history—work habits, study skills, ability to talk before a group, ability to use a library, cultivation of interest in history and world affairs—importance of education		

*These items are a must.

There is a wealth of materials in my classroom for the students to use. There are two sets of history maps, one set of geography maps, a globe, and two study tables. The study tables hold about 25 different junior high school history texts as well as an assortment of booklets and pamphlets related to American history. Over a period of many years, I have put together a very complete picture file. Two large bulletin boards are in use constantly, and they are changed about once a week.

All of this is not there simply to decorate the room. Such materials need to be an integral and important part of the course. Our class periods are approximately 50 minutes in length. Each day I allow the students the last 10 to 15 minutes of the period for free-wheeling study on their own. They are permitted at this time to move about the room, discuss the things they see with other students, help one another, or start on their homework. This privilege is extended to the students only as long as they do not abuse it. If it deteriorates into a social period, I withdraw this privilege for several days and then try it again. I have found that an amazing amount of good discussion takes place during these informal exchanges at the wall maps and bulletin boards. In addition, the students get interested in increasing my supply of enrichment materials.

This free-wheeling learning period will not be successful unless the limits are set and enforced. Properly handled, this approach benefits most students.

DAILY BOARD

Each morning I write an outline on the blackboard (always in the same place) for the day's lesson. This includes the day and date, several things that happened in history on that date (just for fun), a list of things to be covered in the lesson for the day, and the assignment for the next day.

Students quickly form the habit of reading this board each day as soon as they arrive, and many of them even "pop in" before homeroom to take a look. A sample Daily Board is shown on the opposite page.

WORKING WITH THE SUBSTITUTE TEACHER

Each school system will offer rules, procedures, and guidelines to be followed when it is necessary to have a substitute teacher.

Tuesday, September 20
- 1519—Magellan starts trip around the world
- 1797—Old Ironsides launched
- 1850—Congress banned slave trade in Washington, D.C.

Today's Lesson—Spanish Empire in the New World
1. Colonies—Florida, New Mexico, Texas, Arizona, California, Central and South America
2. Five ways of life in New Spain
3. Government in the Spanish Empire
4. Class structure in New Spain
5. Spanish institutions brought to the New World

Assignment
1. Study pages 12 to 18 for tomorrow
2. Unit review next Monday
3. Unit test on Tuesday

You will find that you will rarely know ahead of time when a substitute must take your place. An illness or family emergency seldom gives warning. It is essential that clear directions be ready at all times. This should start, obviously, with good lesson plans written as far in advance as possible. The best of lesson plans may not provide the substitute with everything he or she needs to know—location of materials, tests, quizzes, handouts, teacher's notes, etc.

Each year I tape a paper on the inside front cover of my lesson plan book. This paper contains directions of a general nature for my courses and my room. I include a sample copy for your consideration.

INSTRUCTIONS FOR SUBSTITUTE TEACHERS —MYRA SEVERANCE

Please note that there are two daily preparations, that is, two separate subjects—Regular 8th grade American history and Adjusted 8th grade American history. The texts for both subjects will be found on my desk, along with the lesson plan book.

1. ***Schedule***—You will find it taped to the front of the lesson plan book.

2. ***Seating charts***—Are available at the office. However, you will also find seating charts for each class in the grade book. You may find these more convenient to use.
3. ***Organization of the lesson plan book***—The proper place in the book usually will be marked with a marker of some kind. Dates for the plans are in the *margins of the pages*. The left-hand white page will have the plans for the Regular history classes. The right-hand white page will have the plans for the Adjusted 8th grade class in American history. The yellow pages may have extra notes or corrections of some kind.
4. ***Desk file***—On top of the small file cabinet to the right of the desk, you will find a wooden file with six slots in it. Each slot is labeled. This is used for storing papers and materials for each class.
5. ***Quizzes***—These will be prepared well in advance for both courses. They are labeled according to subject and can be identified by a number on the top of the quiz card. They are referred to in the plan book by this number. Quizzes are kept in the top right-hand desk drawer.
6. ***Notes***—These have been prepared in detail for the Regular American history course. Feel free to use them if they seem to be helpful to you. They are in the top right-hand desk drawer. Please note that sections typed in red type is material *not* found in the text. Material typed in black is a review of material in the textbook.
7. ***Other materials***—If the lesson plan calls for mimeographed sheets or tests, these materials may be in the second left-hand desk drawer, if I have managed to prepare far enough ahead. If they are not there, it will probably be productive to look in the large files in the rear of the room. (Keys or answer sheets for the tests are often inside the back cover of the lesson plan book.)
8. ***Files***—These can be found in the rear of the room. The left-hand file as you face them is for Regular American history; materials are ready for the entire year. They are well labeled and are in chronological order. You will find materials for the Adjusted American history course in either the second or third drawer of the right-hand file.

9. ***Enrichment materials***—On top of the files there is a large cardboard carton with bulletin board materials, these materials are in labeled folders in chronological order. On the study table at the rear of the room there are books and pamphlets, these are available to the students for their use, but may not be taken out of the room. Note that there is a whole set of dictionaries in the bookcase.
10. ***Assistance***—If there is any question whatsoever, feel free to phone me at my home. I won't mind a bit being disturbed, even if I am ill. The number is 524-5769. If I'm out for a long period of time, would you please water my plants?

Thank you,
Myra Severance

Unfortunately, substitutes are considered to be fair game by many young people. I have absolutely no tolerance for students who give substitute teachers a hard time. My students are cautioned about this early in the year, and they find retribution to be swift and strong if they choose to ignore the warning.

The substitute deserves total cooperation from both the staff and the students. The classroom teacher should do everything possible to ensure this. It is important that the substitute be able to function effectively as a teacher, not as a baby sitter.

THE PARENTS' ROLE IN THE LEARNING PROCESS

Obviously, parents have a unique role of their own at home. My interest here, however, centers on the role of the parent in relation to the child's school experience.

I strongly emphasize to my students my eagerness to make contact with their parents in any possible way—the school open house program, visits to the classroom during National Education Week (or any other time), or personal conferences. I've found it necessary to reassure junior high students that my purpose in making such contacts is a positive one. In no case do I wish contact with parents for the purpose of "tattling" on students.

I want very much to have an opportunity to share with the parents my program for the year. I wish them to know what I am trying to accomplish in the classroom. I wish them to know the reasons for various major assignments.

Most of my major assignments are given to students in writing. I urge them to share such papers with their parents. I also ask the students to share with their parents any long range project or program in which we are involved.

The parents can offer to the students so much in terms of reinforcement, enrichment, and support. The mere fact that they are interested is decidedly helpful.

Every so often I deliberately intrude into the family dinner hour. I may casually suggest to the students ''Tonight at dinner ask your parents what they thought of Franklin D. Roosevelt,'' or ''Tonight at dinner ask your parents how they feel about the Panama Canal Treaty.'' Occasionally, classroom feedback lets me know that my ploy has succeeded. I hear about lively dinner table discussions and the fact that both parents and students were surprised to find out how much the other knew.

We must face the fact that parent support can go too far. When I give an assignment to a student and receive a paper worthy of a college graduate in both substance and form, I have to face a situation that must be handled carefully and firmly. Parents who actually do their children's homework are hurting their children in many ways, and it must not be tolerated.

Another problem arises with the parent who pushes the child to achieve. This is the parent who expects a youngster of average ability to get all *A*'s. Such pressure on a student can be very damaging. Parent problems such as these are often best solved by the teacher working together with guidance counselors and/or school psychologists.

There are other ways in which parents create problems for the educator, but that is another book. For my purposes here, I wish to stress again the positive progress that can come from a good parent-teacher relationship.

WORKING WITH THE SCHOOL LIBRARIAN

In this section I shall plead guilty to charges of female chauvinism. I have the great good fortune to work with a truly superb librarian. I am extremely grateful for her skills, her diligence, and her cooperation. I wish that all teachers could have the same blessing. I insist on referring to a librarian as ''she.''

School librarians are the unsung heroes of the public school system. There is no way that I can overstate the value of a skillful and cooperative librarian to the social studies teacher. In an ideal situation she becomes a teaching partner in the fullest sense of the word.

Each school librarian will have her own rules and procedures. These will be made known to all of you in your various teaching situations. Beyond these rules, several suggestions stated here may help to promote this teaching partnership between the library and the classroom from which both you and the students benefit.

On any major assignment that you plan to give:

1. Plan it well in advance. Request a conference with the librarian and discuss the assignment thoroughly. If the assignment is mimeographed, give her several copies. Encourage her to make suggestions on the assignment based on her knowledge of the materials available.
2. Inform the librarian of the value of the assignment in terms of grades. Also be sure that she knows the due date.
3. Discuss with the librarian the library skills that might be strengthened by this assignment. How much help should students receive with the card catalogue? Will it involve the *Readers' Guide*? How about a pamphlet file? Should limits be put on the use of encyclopedias? Are there any new books in the reference section that should be called to the attention of the students?
4. Consider the possibility of setting aside one day in the library and have your classes meet there for the entire period. This period can be used for getting the assignment off the ground. There is value in explaining the assignment in the presence of both the teacher and the librarian. There is further merit in having the librarian speak about the assignment as well as the teacher.
5. Be sure to arrange for the librarian to receive feedback on each assignment. Share with her the skills and the knowledge dem-

onstrated by the students in fulfilling the assignment. She will probably be interested in reading some of the papers. She often will become as interested as the teacher in the project in question, and it is gratifying to see results that have come from her efforts as well as from yours.

6. Under no circumstances should a teacher give a library assignment to a large group of students without first consulting the librarian. Consider the poor librarian who is suddenly confronted with 120 students, for example, all assigned to do a report on the same topic. Suppose the topic is "The United Nations." In this case, there simply is not enough material in the best equipped school library to meet the needs. Such an assignment is sheer lunacy.

   If the major thrust of your classroom work centers around the United Nations at any given time, why not broaden the topic to include several kinds of peace-keeping efforts? Assign each row of students in each class a different subject, such as:

   a. The United Nations
   b. The League of Nations
   c. The Palace of Peace in the Hague (and various courts that have used it)
   d. The United States as a peacemaker
   e. Neutral Switzerland and its role in keeping the peace.

   Thus, instead of 120 students doing one topic, you will have 20 students doing one of five topics. This makes much more efficient use of library materials and provides for more stimulating classroom discussion when students are prepared on a variety of topics relating to the central theme.

CLASSROOM CONTROL

Proper control in the classroom can present a real challenge to the new teacher. It is difficult to find the middle of the road approach that is so essential to good teaching. If the atmosphere is too strict, the class will be stifled and lose its spontaneity. If it is too lax, however, the result can be chaos.

Ideally, discipline should never be a problem. If there were such a thing as a perfect teacher, he or she would constantly have the students so very interested and absorbed in their work that there would never be a problem. I would suggest that all of us need to work toward that ideal as far as possible. Good control, easily achieved, is a bonus that comes with well-planned, interesting lessons.

In the best of situations, discipline does occasionally become a problem. Here are some suggestions:

1. Make sure that students are fully aware of your particular classroom rules.
2. Be consistent in enforcing those rules.
3. If it becomes necessary to impose a punishment on a student, do so calmly and matter-of-factly. Avoid anger or emotion in such a case.
4. Avoid raising your voice. A loud angry voice can be very effective if it is used once or twice a year. If such a voice is used repeatedly, it only serves to point up the frustration that you must feel, and often leaves the students in command.
5. Avoid repetitious nagging. Students learn very quickly to "tune it out."
6. In facing a rowdy or unruly group, try simply standing and waiting (with a stern look on your face) until complete silence settles over the room. Then proceed to express your displeasure in a slow, quiet voice—so very quiet that students must strain to hear. An "edge of steel" in a quiet tone is much more effective than any bellowing or hollering.
7. Try a light touch first when possible. If you enter a classroom where the kids are talking up a storm, your opening comment might be, "You people sound like an old ladies' sewing circle," rather than "Hey, cut out the noise!"
8. Do not punish the entire class for the actions of a few. Fairness is very important to the junior high school student.
9. Do not tolerate any student who is a constant disruption in your classroom. No matter how anxious you are to help that student,

> the entire class must not suffer because of him. Send him to the school office and insist that he may not return until there is some guarantee of improved behavior. Be firm about this, even if it means doing battle with the powers that be.

The real base for a good classroom atmosphere must be mutual respect. If you like and respect your students, they will usually like and respect you.

I feel that another word is necessary. Inner city school teachers, please forgive me if I seem to be simplistic on this topic in terms of your needs. I realize that you face many difficult and special problems. I can only hope that some of the above suggestions may be of some small help.

I would like to examine one last aspect of discipline. Be aware of the fact that a young person of this age who misbehaves, or feels that he has done something "wrong," often feels miserable. It is important to him to set things right, and he usually doesn't know quite how to go about it.

I'm reminded of an incident that happened many years ago and left a lasting impression on me. Two ninth-grade boys came back from the high school to visit me one evening after school. I happened to be out of my room at the time, and when I returned I found the boys there. Under ordinary circumstances, I'd have welcomed them cordially and enjoyed a visit with them. However, they were busily going through my grade book as I entered the room. I hit the ceiling, and by the time I finished talking, there could be no doubt that I was definitely displeased.

One of these boys I never saw again. The other one returned one evening a couple of weeks later with a bucket of water in one hand and cleanser and rags in the other. Without saying a word, he proceeded to scrub every desk in my room, thoroughly and carefully. There was no doubt that he found it awkward to discuss the unfortunate incident with me and had chosen his own penance.

I played it his way and quietly kept busy at my desk. When he had finished I simply thanked him, and we both went home. Little did he know that he had kept me after school that evening; I had planned to leave rather promptly for an appointment.

I'm pleased to add that this young man and his wife (another of my favorite students) visited me last year during the Christmas holidays and brought their newborn baby with them.

QUESTIONING TECHNIQUES

There are many different approaches or procedures that can be used in teaching social studies. It is my observation that there are three methods that are used most frequently at the secondary school level.

The first approach is the lecture by the teacher. I would suggest that this should be used sparingly at the junior high school level. If a twelve- or thirteen-year-old youngster faces four to six teachers daily who "talk at him," he is destroyed by the end of the day. Students at this age need to be very actively involved in the learning process. There are occasions, however, when a lecture of reasonable length is appropriate. Perhaps the teacher feels a need to add some material that is not covered by the text. Another valid reason for giving occasional lectures is to help develop note-taking skills for the student. There is also the possibility that the teacher has something quite unique to bring to the class through a lecture because of travel, special study, hobbies, etc.

The second approach is small group discussion or "buzz sessions." These can and should be introduced at the junior high school level, and are even more useful at the senior high school. This topic will be covered in a later chapter.

The third, and I suspect most common approach, is through general class discussion led by skillful questioning on the part of the teacher. It takes a long time and a lot of practice for a teacher to develop good questioning skills. Give some thought to the following suggestions:

1. Ask an introductory question that sets the stage and "tells the story" of the incident to be discussed.

Q. *Susie, tell me everything you know about the Whiskey Rebellion. What was it?*

2. Ask questions that provide an opportunity for the students to give opinions or make judgments.

Q. *Bill, you are George Washington—you've just heard about this rebellion in Pennsylvania. How are you going to handle the problem? How did Washington actually handle it? Would you have done anything differently?*

3. Ask questions that invite comparisons.

Q. *Joan, does this incident remind you of another rebellion that you have studied recently? If so, how did they differ? (I'm thinking of Shays' Rebellion.)*

4. Ask questions that call for analysis and independent thinking.

   Q. *Can anyone tell us why the story of the Whiskey Rebellion is in all of the history books? Why do we burden you with it? Why is it important?*

   Q. *What does this rebellion tell us about the nature of the American people in those days?*

5. Ask questions that allow for speculation. (Junior high students like these and often raise "what if" questions themselves.)

   Q. *What if Washington had decided to ignore the Whiskey Rebellion? How might this have affected our history?*

Sometimes it is helpful to lead the class step by step to an important conclusion by asking a whole series of questions that are addressed to one student. I refer to this in the classroom as "putting a student on the griddle." The students come to enjoy this. For the sake of brevity I've deliberately shortened both questions and answers:

Q. Bob, a fellow by the name of Eli Whitney invented a gadget called the cotton gin. What did this machine do?

A. *Separated the seeds from the cotton.*

Q. What did this do to the time required for this operation?

A. *Reduced it—it was much faster than hand labor.*

Q. How did this affect the amount of raw cotton produced?

A. *They were able to produce much more cotton in the same amount of time.*

Q. How did this affect the price of cotton?

A. *Lowered it—there was more cotton available.*

Q. What happened to the market for cotton?

A. *It grew—more people could afford it.*

Q. Did this have any effect on the westward movement?

A. *Spurred it on—plantation owners needed to expand to keep up with the demand.*

Q. Now we come to the nitty-gritty. If plantations were expanding, what happened to the need for slaves in the South?

A. *It grew. More slaves were needed for labor as the cotton industry expanded.*

Q. All right, class. Here is the big question. Can you explain why many historians state, "The invention of the cotton gin was a cause of the Civil War"?

Bob works very hard in dealing with this whole set of questions. Other class members are not only interested, but pitch in to help him think his way through. And by the time the discussion has ended, the students have some understanding of the commitment of the south to "King Cotton" and the slavery system.

Another technique that not only adds to understanding, but provides fun in the classroom as well, is role playing. It often can be a part of the questioning process. This is a very useful tool for getting the students truly involved. Their feelings are affected by pretending that they actually lived through the experience being discussed.

The subject is Alexander Hamilton and his financial program as first Secretary of the Treasury. We have already laid foundation in terms of his two major aims—to establish credit and build up capital for the nation. We have discussed the terms—capital, credit, bonds, interest. At this point I turn to Dick:

> Dick, you are a southern plantation owner. You are trying to expand your plantation and you face serious financial problems. Your business suffered during the Revolutionary War and you are short of capital. You are holding bonds issued by the state of Virginia during the war in the amount of $25,000. You try to cash in the bonds and are told that the state of Virginia has no funds.
>
> John, you are a Boston merchant. You have made a fortune by getting involved in the China trade and have surplus capital to invest. You decide that you might make good money by buying up state bonds held by southerners for a cheap price. You are taking a trip through the South for that purpose. You and Dick are sharing mint juleps on the veranda of his plantation. Both of you take it from there.

After some negotiation that may need to be guided a bit by the teacher, Dick sells his bonds to John for 25¢ on the dollar. The teacher steps in again:

> Now, along comes a man by the name of Alexander Hamilton who proposes to have the national government assume the debts of the states and pay them in full from tax money collected from all of the people. Dick, how do you feel about this? John, how do you feel about this?

By the time this role playing is complete, the students not only have an increased knowledge of the fact that differences between the North and South surfaced early in our history, but can also identify a bit with the feelings that people must have had when facing these problems.

Role playing can be equally important and interesting when explanations are a big part of the lesson. Each year we go through the Bill of Rights in detail. The process takes at least two days. When we come to amendments five, six, seven, and eight, we personalize this experience by having a full cast of characters—a murder victim, the accused, the defense attorney, the prosecutor, etc.

I offer a few more thoughts about questioning in general. Avoid questions that can be answered with a simple "yes" or "no," they leave the teacher pulling teeth. Think out your questions in advance as a part of a carefully planned lesson. Be sure that your questions are stated very clearly. In the question and discussion process, always make each student feel that he has contributed something positive to the class, no matter what his answer. Use honest praise wherever possible. Use a quietly spoken "good," or, "that is a sample of some really fine thinking," or, an occasional "great!" in response to student contributions. Such praise can truly be a help in motivating students.

One final comment on questions—be sure to allow ample opportunity for students to raise questions and treat each question with respect. Every question raised by a student deserves a patient and thorough answer from the teacher.

FRAME OF REFERENCE

There is no such thing as a history teacher without bias. It is impossible to handle a subject that deals with people, issues, and emotionally charged events in a totally objective fashion. This applies to the past as well as to the present.

Each of us teaches from a "frame of reference" that should be acknowledged and explained to the students. So many things in your life have helped to shape that frame of reference—your religion, political party, family upbringing, college professors, schools attended, racial or ethnic background, and many more. Did you do your growing up during the conservative 50's or the radical 60's? Was your father a union worker or a company executive? Was your mother a D.A.R. or a member of the feminist movement or both? Such things certainly affect your viewpoints.

In your teaching be very certain that you separate historical fact from historian's opinions. It is quite unfair to impose your views on your students as the ''Gospel according to teacher.''

You can state, ''I believe that Andrew Jackson was an exceptionally good president,'' or, ''It is my opinion that Herbert Hoover was underrated by our historians'' as long as you make it clear that you are expressing opinions, not facts.

It is not only important that you refrain from imposing your values on your students; it is equally important that you encourage them to form opinions of their own. Then listen to those opinions and treat them with the utmost respect, no matter how much they may differ from yours.

HUMOR IN THE CLASSROOM

In spite of the education courses that provide a good background in ''child development,'' the new teacher finds that junior high school students ''take some getting used to.''

Students of this age are strange creatures. In general they are noisy and giggly and squirmy, open and honest and friendly, enthusiastic and excitable. They are also often ill-poised and clumsy, frequently worried and insecure, very mature one minute and childish the next. In short, they are quite unpredictable, but fun to be with in the classroom. I enjoy teaching them more than I can say, but I could never endure living with them. I commend their parents for being able to survive!

The humor of junior high school students, especially the boys, ranges from wild to weird. At times it will test your patience and staying power most severely.

Expect to find on your desk or chair all kinds of plastic goodies that are devised to represent vomit, snakes, spiders, and all manner of frightening things. Be ready to accept the fact that boys of this age think that it is terribly funny to hide the teacher's chalk, erasers, waste baskets, or anything else in the room that isn't nailed down. Various articles of clothing as well as book covers will display all kinds of funny sayings. They laugh hilariously when some poor soul trips or stumbles or drops all of his or her books.

Much of the humor of these youngsters is directed at the teachers and often reflects their affection as well as a sense of fun. They are most responsive to a teacher who not only permits some fun and banter and teasing but also adds some humor to the classroom.

Every teacher has to come to grips with the question of fun in the classroom and make their own decision about policies on this matter. I offer the following thoughts on classroom humor for your consideration:

1. These kids have a long day (too long!) and a fairly heavy schedule. There must be some lighter moments along the way.
2. Even if a bit of nonsense occasionally interferes somewhat with the lesson, it provides a change in the routine, a welcome change of pace.
3. Shared humor does strengthen student-teacher rapport.
4. A few words of caution are in order. Be very careful to see to it that nonsense never causes you to lose control of your class. Allow only as much fun as you can comfortably handle. Students must respond immediately when you decide it is time to stop. Be equally careful not to disturb the adult-student relationship that I stressed in Chapter 1.
5. Remember that students do not possess the good judgment demonstrated by most adults. Student humor can, and sometimes does, go too far. The teacher has a responsibility to be watchful and prevent this.

A classroom without humor is deadly. A teacher who enjoys the work and enjoys young people will find it easy to provide a certain amount of fun in the classroom.

3

Handouts

THERE'S AN OLD QUOTATION, AND I CANNOT REMEMBER the source, "Give me a room full of students, a blackboard, and a piece of chalk. That's all I need to be a good teacher." Such a quote must have come from an old-fashioned "basic" school teacher, but it is overdoing the "back to the basics" movement quite a bit. In order to get into the twentieth century, I would add a typewriter and a duplicating machine at the very least. Most of us would be seriously handicapped in our teaching efforts if we could not use mimeographed sheets.

As you put together a year long course in American history, there are countless opportunities for you to enrich the course with well-designed handouts. These serve many useful purposes. Handouts can take the form of lists, outlines, charts, maps, questions, stories, or assignments. They can demonstrate to the student better methods of taking notes, or organizing material, or reviewing for tests. They can, and should, reflect the creativity and originality of the teacher.

This chapter will deal with various types of mimeographed sheets that can be valuable teaching tools. Descriptions, explanations, and samples will be included.

VOCABULARY

If I were asked to choose the single most important skill that can be given to students in the educational process, there would be no contest. I would choose the use of words. I would like to see our students able to write clearly, concisely, and effectively, using proper grammar, sentence structure, spelling, and punctuation. I would like to see our students infected with a respect for our language and a curiosity about the origins, meanings, variations, and uses of any new words introduced to them. I would like to hear our students speaking with poise, communicating with each other and with their teachers, fully at ease with the spoken word. My desire to have all students develop the ability to communicate in both speech and writing in an articulate and skillful fashion surely must sound like the impossible dream. But we owe it to our students, to our profession, and to ourselves to give it a try.

Teaching verbal skills should never be solely the role of the English department. Each teacher, no matter what his field, should assume some responsibility for promoting competency in the use of our language. The most obvious place to start is with the vocabulary of the subject being taught.

I have designed a set of vocabulary word sheets that apply to American history. Each student is given one of these sheets at the beginning of each unit. The assignment is explained carefully at the beginning of the year, and it is described as an "automatic, year long assignment." Students are required to bring the current sheet to class each day. The first time that any one of the words is used in class, students are encouraged to interrupt to point out to everyone that the word is on the list and to identify it by number. At that point we stop whatever we are doing to talk about the new word. It is not enough to define it; we literally dissect it. We talk about the origin of the word, the various meanings of the word, other words that come from the same root, the importance of the word in history. In this way students come to appreciate and utilize the richness and variety of their language.

For example, the first time that we use the word "capital," the following information might be put together in class:

1. Source—Latin—*caput*, head

2. Various meanings
Capital punishment (relating to the head)—a crime punishable by "losing one's head"
capital letter (standing at the head)
capital city (standing at the head)
capital property or money (standing at the head)

3. Variations
capitol (building at the head)
cap (worn on the head)
capitalize, capitalist, capitulate, captain

A full understanding of some of these words is very important in establishing certain social studies concepts. The first time that I have a need to use the word "radical" (at the time of the American Revolution), I spend an entire class period on the four words "radical," "liberal," "conservative," and "reactionary." In studying these words, all of the following need to be considered:

1. Establish the definitions.
2. Use the words in examples that relate to the lives of the students. For instance, supposing a student asks his parents for a change of rules to provide for a later bedtime. What response from a parent would be radical? Liberal? Conservative? Reactionary?
3. Establish the fact that it is difficult to decide which of the four terms best fits the situations or people under discussion. Use a continuum on the blackboard to illustrate this. Have the students try to place leaders of our Revolution on the proper place on this continuum. Disagreements will surface quickly.
4. Apply the terms to modern leaders. Where would the students place Kennedy, Eisenhower, Nixon, Goldwater, etc.?
5. Point out that the terms have different meanings in different places. Which of the four words would describe a procommunist speech in Washington, D.C.? In Moscow?
6. Demonstrate the fact that the same idea would be classified differently in terms of these four words at different times in history. What kind of an idea would Jefferson have considered Social Security to be? F. D. Roosevelt? Carter?
7. Introduce the terms "left" and "right" and apply them to the four words being studied.

Careful thought and preparation can make the study of words interesting and exciting. The vocabulary assignment, however, must go beyond the classroom discussion. Once the word is introduced and discussed, the students are responsible for writing a definition of the word (in ink, on notebook paper, with the words numbered). The complete list is automatically due on the day the unit is completed. This is an assignment that can be graded with a check, check plus, or check minus (see Chapter 4, Testing and Grading).

I urge all students to keep these completed vocabulary assignments, not only through the eighth grade course, but also for use as a refresher before the start of the eleventh grade American history course.

At the beginning of the year students usually view this assignment as a tiresome chore, but they soon become quite comfortable with their vocabulary sheets and generally give them a favorable rating at the end of the year on evaluation sheets.

Along with the vocabulary lists for each unit, I also prepare a sheet listing the people whom we will "meet" in that unit. This sheet is intended primarily as a helpful tool to use in the classroom. Students can refer to it to check spelling. They can earn extra credit by identifying or defining each item. I include here all the lists I use.

AMERICAN HISTORY—NAMES AND VOCABULARY
Exploration and Settlement of the New World

1. Renaissance
2. Medieval
3. urban
4. optimism
5. nationalism
6. feudalism
7. monarchy
8. Protestant Reformation
9. individualism
10. Crusade
11. serf
12. dissenters
13. Inquisition
14. mercantilism
15. autocratic
16. immigration
17. mission
18. viceroy
19. presidio
20. *coureur de bois*
21. troika
22. Magna Carta
23. common law
24. canon law
25. feudal law
26. statute law
27. limited monarchy
28. precedents
29. Huguenots
30. peers
31. parliament
32. legislature
33. joint-stock company
34. aristocracy
35. merchant marine
36. Tudors
37. compromise
38. moderate
39. Pilgrims
40. Quakers
41. Separatists
42. Puritans
43. Anglicans
44. pacifists
45. reformers
46. Stuarts
47. royal colony
48. proprietary colony
49. salutary neglect
50. burgess
51. freeman
52. patroon
53. indentured servant
54. charter
55. director general
56. armada
57. frontier
58. diversified economy
59. pure democracy
60. representative democracy
61. bicameral
62. Glorious Revolution
63. census

AMERICAN HISTORY—NAMES AND VOCABULARY
Exploration and Settlement of the New World

1. Christopher Columbus
2. Marco Polo
3. Leif Ericson
4. Gutenberg
5. Amerigo Vespucci
6. Ponce de Leon
7. Balboa
8. Hernando de Soto
9. Francisco de Coronado
10. Ferdinand Magellan
11. Cortez
12. Montezuma
13. Pizarro
14. Atahualpa
15. Francisco Orellano
16. John Cabot
17. Francis Drake
18. Henry Hudson
19. Giovanni Verrazano
20. Jacques Cartier
21. Champlain
22. Father Marquette
23. Louis Joliet
24. LaSalle
25. Vasco da Gama
26. Diaz
27. Cabral
28. Sir Humphrey Gilbert
29. Sir Walter Raleigh
30. John Smith
31. John Rolfe
32. Sir William Berkeley
33. Nathaniel Bacon
34. Lord Baltimore
35. James Oglethorpe
36. Edmund Andros
37. Peter Stuyvesant
38. William Bradford
39. Miles Standish
40. John Winthrop
41. Thomas Hooker
42. Roger Williams
43. John Mason
44. Sir Ferdinand Gorges
45. Benjamin Franklin
46. Governor Dinwiddie
47. William Pitt
48. Edward Braddock
49. General Forbes
50. General Montcalm
51. General Wolfe
52. John Peter Zenger

Know the following monarchs

Spain
Isabella and Ferdinand

Portugal
Prince Henry the Navigator

France
Louis XIV

England
Henry VII
Henry VIII
Elizabeth I
James I
Charles I
Charles II
James II
William and Mary
Anne
George I
George II

AMERICAN HISTORY—NAMES AND VOCABULARY
The American Revolution and the United States Constitution

1. favorable balance of trade
2. triangular trade routes
3. minister
4. writs of assistance
5. boycott
6. tyranny
7. taxation without representation
8. repeal
9. customs
10. import
11. export
12. treason
13. smuggling
14. act
15. Loyalist
16. Tory
17. Patriot
18. privateer
19. revolution
20. commander-in-chief
21. strategy
22. Olive Branch Petition
23. minuteman
24. traitor
25. intellectuals
26. Hessians
27. alliance
28. neutral
29. requisition
30. voluntary militia
31. ratify
32. executive
33. Bill of Rights
34. Critical Period
35. public domain
36. central government
37. federal government
38. national government
39. judicial
40. amendment
41. unanimous
42. depression
43. tariffs
44. ordinance
45. revenue
46. convention
47. constitution
48. Federalist
49. states' rights
50. electoral college
51. impeach
52. bill
53. veto
54. candidate
55. liberal
56. conservative
57. radical
58. reactionary
59. mercenaries
60. anarchy
61. slander
62. libel
63. enumerated
64. implied
65. quorum
66. extradition
67. levy

AMERICAN HISTORY—NAMES AND VOCABULARY
The American Revolution and the United States Constitution

1. King George III
2. Pontiac
3. James Otis
4. Patrick Henry
5. John Dickinson
6. Sam Adams
7. Paul Revere
8. John Hancock
9. Crispus Attucks
10. Ethan Allen
11. William Dawes
12. Colonel William Prescott
13. General Howe
14. General Richard Montgomery
15. General Benedict Arnold
16. Thomas Paine
17. Nathan Hale
18. General Johnny Burgoyne
19. Colonel St. Leger
20. General Cornwallis
21. General Gates
22. Robert Morris
23. Haym Solomon
24. Lafayette
25. Baron Von Steuben
26. Pulaski
27. Kosciusko
28. John Paul Jones
29. John Barry
30. Major Andre
31. General Clinton
32. George Rogers Clark
33. Tom Sumter
34. Francis Marion
35. General Nathanael Greene
36. General Rochambeau
37. John Jay
38. Robert Gray
39. Alexander Hamilton

AMERICAN HISTORY—NAMES AND VOCABULARY
The First Five Presidents

1. cabinet
2. inauguration
3. credit
4. assumption of states' debts
5. funding the debt
6. bond
7. strict construction
8. loose construction
9. protective tariff
10. alien
11. sedition
12. deportation
13. republic
14. impressment of seamen
15. isolationism
16. embargo
17. Industrial Revolution
18. spinning jenny
19. power loom
20. standardization of parts

21. Doctrine of Nullification
22. tribute
23. states' rights
24. blockade
25. labor union
26. packet ship
27. flat boat
28. westward expansion
29. sectionalism
30. internal improvements
31. reform movements
32. suffrage
33. abolition
34. temperance
35. excise tax
36. doctrine
37. Edmund Randolph
38. Henry Knox
39. Citizen Genêt
40. George Clinton
41. Aaron Burr
42. Thomas Pinckney
43. Stephen Decatur
44. Robert Livingston
45. Henry Clay
46. John Calhoun
47. Tecumseh
48. Captain John Lawrence
49. Napoleon Bonaparte
50. General William Hull
51. Oliver Hazard Perry
52. Commodore Thomas McDonough
53. Francis Scott Key
54. Simon Bolívar
55. Jose de San Martín
56. Horace Greeley
57. John Fitch
58. Robert Fulton
59. Henry Shreve
60. John Ericsson
61. Governor DeWitt Clinton
62. George Stephenson
63. Peter Cooper
64. James Watt
65. Eli Whitney
66. Elias Howe
67. Charles Goodyear
68. Cyrus McCormick
69. Horace Mann
70. James Fenimore Cooper
71. Washington Irving
72. Edgar Allan Poe
73. Nathaniel Hawthorne
74. Henry Wadsworth Longfellow
75. James Whittier
76. Ralph Waldo Emerson
77. Henry David Thoreau
78. Richard Hoe
79. Dorothea Dix
80. Susan B. Anthony

AMERICAN HISTORY—NAMES AND VOCABULARY
Andrew Jackson and the New West

1. Spoils System
2. Specie Circular
3. Kitchen Cabinet
4. Whigs
5. annexation
6. dictator

7. Manifest Destiny
8. Forty-niners
9. siege
10. "Remember the Alamo"
11. "54-40 or fight"
12. clipper ship
13. Daniel Boone
14. James Robertson
15. John Sevier
16. Robert Hayne
17. Santa Anna
18. Moses Austin
19. Stephen Austin
20. William Travis
21. Davy Crockett
22. Marcus and Narcissa Whitman
23. James Gadsden
24. John Slidell
25. John Fremont
26. Stephen Kearny
27. John Sutter
28. Winfield Scott
29. James Bowie
30. Sam Houston
31. John Marsh

AMERICAN HISTORY—NAMES AND VOCABULARY
The Civil War

1. secession
2. popular sovereignty
3. underground railroad
4. fugitive slave law
5. Omnibus Bill
6. Confederacy
7. yeoman
8. blockade
9. draft
10. ironclads
11. blockade runners
12. sea raiders
13. frontal assault
14. flanking movements
15. emancipation
16. arbitration
17. Anaconda Policy
18. sharecropper
19. tenant farmer
20. scalawag
21. carpet bagger
22. reconstruction
23. Ku Klux Klan
24. segregation
25. corruption
26. Jim Crow Laws
27. Gabriel Prosser
28. Denmark Vesey
29. Nat Turner
30. Harriet Tubman
31. Frederick Douglass
32. Ben Lundy
33. William Lloyd Garrison
34. Harriet Beecher Stowe
35. William Lovejoy
36. David Wilmot
37. Jefferson Davis
38. Stephen Douglas
39. John Brown

40. Chief Justice Taney
41. Dred Scott
42. William Seward
43. Salmon Chase
44. General Beauregard
45. Major Anderson
46. David Farragut
47. Commander Foote
48. General Albert Sydney Johnston
49. Thaddeus Stevens
50. Charles Sumner
51. General Thomas
52. General Rosecrans
53. General Bragg
54. General Sherman
55. General Sheridan
56. Maximilian
57. General Halleck
58. General McClellan
59. General Meade
60. General Pickett
61. Robert E. Lee

AMERICAN HISTORY—NAMES AND VOCABULARY
Development of the Nation
1865–1900

1. industry
2. commerce
3. natural resources
4. raw materials
5. philanthropist
6. vertical combination
7. monopoly
8. trust
9. corruption
10. generator
11. fractional distillation
12. corporation
13. dividend
14. stock
15. board of directors
16. proxy
17. pools
18. interlocking directorate
19. merger
20. holding company
21. graft
22. grange
23. open range
24. lode
25. reservation
26. cynicism
27. reclamation
28. homestead
29. dry farming
30. recession
31. pork barrel projects
32. injunction
33. Populists
34. Greenbackers
35. fringe benefits
36. lockout
37. yellow dog contract
38. blacklist
39. collective bargaining
40. strike

41. picket
42. closed shop
43. strike breaker
44. feather bedding
45. grievance committee
46. naturalization
47. quota
48. Andrew Carnegie
49. Henry Bessemer
50. William Kelly
51. J. P. Morgan
52. George Bissell
53. Edwin Drake
54. Richard Hoe
55. Otto Mergenthaler
56. John Deere
57. Cyrus McCormick
58. Cyrus Field
59. Alexander Graham Bell
60. Robert Morse
61. Christopher Sholes
62. Thomas Edison
63. F. J. Sprague
64. Charles and Frank Duryea
65. Henry Ford
66. Ransom Olds
67. Wright Brothers
68. John D. Rockefeller
69. John Butterfield
70. William Russell
71. Leland Stanford
72. James Hill
73. Cornelius Vanderbilt
74. George Pullman
75. George Westinghouse
76. Oliver Kelley
77. Uriah Stevens
78. Samuel Gompers

AMERICAN HISTORY—NAMES AND VOCABULARY
Political and Social Reform and the Spanish American War

1. foundation
2. yellow journalism
3. Chautauqua
4. social protest
5. political machine
6. patronage
7. Civil Service Commission
8. muckrakers
9. settlement houses
10. primary election
11. initiative
12. referendum
13. recall
14. prohibition
15. workman's compensation
16. imperialism
17. spheres of influence
18. Open Door policy
19. reparations
20. John Dewey
21. Booker T. Washington
22. William DuBois
23. William Randolph Hearst
24. Joseph Pulitzer

25. Frederick Remington
26. James Whistler
27. John Sargent
28. Winslow Homer
29. George Bellows
30. Grandma Moses
31. Frank Lloyd Wright
32. Jack London
33. Stephen Crane
34. Susan B. Anthony
35. Jane Addams
36. Lillian Wald
37. William Booth
38. P. T. Barnum
39. Mark Hanna
40. William Jennings Bryan
41. Valeriano Weyler
42. Admiral George Dewey
43. Emilio Aguinaldo
44. Admiral Cervera
45. Admiral Sampson
46. John Hay
47. General Wood
48. Walter Reed

AMERICAN HISTORY—NAMES AND VOCABULARY
Teddy Roosevelt through World War II

1. imperialism
2. yellow journalism
3. spheres of influence
4. Open Door policy
5. Square Deal
6. trust buster
7. intervention
8. corollary
9. idealist
10. reparations
11. New Freedom
12. American Expeditionary Force
13. disarmament
14. normalcy
15. prohibition
16. overexpansion
17. margin
18. public utilities
19. New Deal
20. relief, recovery, and reform
21. Social Security
22. Dust Bowl
23. totalitarianism
24. charisma
25. reciprocate
26. communism
27. fascism
28. Nazism
29. socialism
30. capitalism
31. appeasement
32. proletariat
33. bourgeoisie
34. Aryan
35. fifth columnist
36. underground
37. Quisling
38. paratroopers
39. motorized divisions
40. blitzkreig
41. kamikaze
42. Atlantic Charter
43. OPA
44. D-Day
45. VE Day
46. VJ Day
47. Axis
48. rationing
49. WAVES
50. WACS
51. SPARS
52. William Jennings Bryan
53. Alfred T. Mahan
54. Commodore George Dewey

55. John Hay
56. Colonel William Gorgas
57. Colonel George Goethals
58. Pancho Villa
59. General John Pershing
60. Ferdinand Foch
61. Lloyd George
62. Georges Clemenceau
63. Vittorio Orlando
64. Carrie Nation
65. Charles Evans Hughes
66. Albert Fall
67. Al Smith
68. Charles Lindbergh
69. John L. Lewis
70. Vladimir Lenin
71. Joseph Stalin
72. Nikita Khrushchev
73. Karl Marx
74. Benito Mussolini
75. Adolf Hitler
76. Tojo
77. Hirohito
78. Haile Selassie
79. Francisco Franco
80. Winston Churchill
81. Charles DeGaulle
82. Douglas MacArthur
83. George Marshall
84. Chiang Kai-shek
85. Mao Tse-tung

STUDY SHEETS

When it comes to study sheets, I could imitate Mr. Heinz and offer you "57 varieties." There are many types of study sheets, and they can be helpful in a variety of situations. I choose to discuss three kinds of study sheets in this chapter. Each one of these will be related to one of three sample sheets that are included. There is little reason to go beyond these few. An effective study sheet needs to be tailor made for a specific situation with a definite goal in mind. Therefore, it becomes a very individual exercise that each teacher must resolve. Samples can be helpful, however, especially to the beginning teacher.

Study Sheet for Supplemental Information

No matter how carefully you choose a text, it will always have some shortcomings for each teacher who uses it. Occasionally you will find that the author gives no information on some topic that you consider to be very important in American history. You may choose to cover this topic by giving a lecture on it and having the students take notes. Another alternative would be to assign library reports on various aspects of the situation and require the students to report verbally on their findings. A third possibility is to use a study sheet designed to present the information to the students. The form of such a study sheet can take one of several directions—formal outline, paragraph form, numbered lists of facts, story form, etc. In any case, it needs to be clear and concise and right to the point. I generally make it a practice to limit any study sheet to one page in order to curb my tendency to be too wordy.

Let us look at an example. The period under study is the early 1900's. The United States is leaving behind a century of isolationism and developing an internationalist view, acquiring some new territories, and generally exerting its influence on world affairs. Our text describes the Spanish-American War and then goes on to review our relations with the Philippines, Cuba, Puerto Rico, China, Japan, and Europe. The author neglects to review our relationships with Canada and most of Latin America. I take a dim view of this oversight, since I feel that we are prone to minimize foreign affairs in the Western Hemisphere. I want my students to know more about our neighbors. Therefore, I construct a study sheet to fill the void. I also add a summary on the Panama Canal, which I feel has been inadequately covered in the text.

The following study sheet is the result.

STUDY SHEET—SUPPLEMENTAL INFORMATION
Panama Canal—Relations with Latin America and Canada

Panama Canal

1. Reason for a canal—had talked about one since the days of the Gold Rush—growing trade with Asia—and defense needs.
2. Problems to solve—had a treaty with England that we would build a canal with them (this was peacefully set aside). The French had rights in Panama and had tried to build a canal (we bought them out). We needed land that belonged to Colombia. (Couldn't agree on price and Panama revolted from Colombia with the backing of the United States.)
3. Treaty with Panama provided for a 10-mile strip under our control—paid 10 million dollars plus an annual rent. In 1921 we paid Colombia 25 million dollars to recognize our rights.

4. In recent years, Panama demanded the canal—by treaty it was ours in perpetuity! In order to resolve this problem, a new treaty was written. It was signed and ratified by the Senate.

Canada

1. Early relations with us—a common background from the English (but don't forget the early French influence). We tried to take Canada in the American Revolution and the War of 1812. In 1817, the Rush-Bagot Treaty settled the Great Lakes Boundary and provided for an unfortified boundary. Oregon Boundary was settled in 1846 at the 49th parallel. The Maine boundary was settled by the Webster-Ashburton Treaty while Tyler was President.
2. Canada gains self-government—1791 the British formed Upper Canada (English) and Lower Canada (French). Compare to Ontario and Quebec today. In 1840 the Durham Report united these two sections. In 1867, the Dominion of Canada was formed. Provinces were formed that were largely self-governing. Canada is now fully independent, but joined the British Commonwealth in 1926 and still respects the British monarch.
3. Today's government—the Queen has no real authority. Parliament of two houses—House of Commons and the Senate. The real leader is the Prime Minister (Trudeau)—majority leader of the House of Commons. Governor General is appointed to represent the crown—largely honorary position. Senators are appointed for life by the Governor General—this is the lower house of the Parliament. Canada is a federation of ten self-governing provinces plus two federally administered territories.
4. Present relations with Canada—lots of trade, our number one customer. Cooperation on the St. Lawrence Seaway and the Alaskan Highway. Defense—the Distant Early Warning (DEW) line—radar lines across North America to warn us of any attack over the North Pole.
5. Present problems—under population and the English-French conflict.

Latin America

1. There are 25 republics south of the Rio Grande River. Brazil speaks Portuguese—Haiti, French, and the rest mostly Spanish—Catholic religion. Most of these countries got their independence from 1810 to 1825—Governments have been very unstable, many dictatorships, need land reform badly—also need better education and a higher standard of living. Overpopulation promises to be a very big problem. Latin America is growing at a faster rate than any other region on earth.
2. Relations with the U.S.—First, the "Big Brother Policy" started with the Monroe Doctrine. Second, "Big Stick Policy" began under Teddy Roosevelt—policy of intervention that was resented very much. U.S. was called the "Colossus of the North." Third, Good Neighbor Policy started under F. D. Roosevelt. It attempted to improve relations because of the approach of World War II.
3. Unions with the U.S.—Pan American Union set up in 1899—regular meetings to work on social, economic, and political problems. This grew into the Organization of American States in 1948—primarily military. Canada is not a member of this group and Cuba was expelled. Discuss the Alliance for Progress and relations under President Kennedy through President Carter.

Study Sheet as a Teaching Tool

This type of study sheet is designed to help the students master something that is unusually difficult, or requires great concentration, or is particularly important. Let us study an example.

I have a great reverence for the Constitution of the United States and for the 55 men who constructed this document. I want to be certain that my students understand not only the laws therein, but the reasons for each of these laws as well. I also want the students to have some feeling for the long and difficult process experienced by the founding fathers as they worked together.

"Checks and balances" is the topic for the day. I construct a study sheet concisely listing the essential facts on this topic. This immediately serves two useful purposes for this lesson. First, it eliminates for me the need to write this material on the blackboard. Second, it almost eliminates the need for the students to take notes. Thus, the use of this sheet as a "tool" frees all of us to discuss, probe, ask questions, analyze, or debate the material at hand.

Some of my questions to the students as we discuss this sheet might be:

1. Why do you suppose they decided that only the House may start revenue bills?
2. What are the arguments for and against a Federal System?
3. What evidence can you see on this sheet that would justify the term, "A bundle of compromises" as a name for our Constitution?
4. Why did the founding fathers think it necessary to allow the president to call special sessions of Congress?
5. Why can election rules be considered to be a "check on the people?"

A word of caution applies here. If the study sheet is given to the students simply as a list of facts to be memorized, it loses its value as a teaching tool. When the sheet serves its purpose as a catalyst for in-depth discussion, there is little need for memory work.

STUDY SHEET—A TEACHING TOOL
American History—Checks and Balances in the Constitution

NOTE —All italic words, other than the headings, are vocabulary words and must be learned.

Legislative Checks

1. House of Representatives can *impeach* the President. The Senate tries the case. *Majority* vote needed in the House; two-thirds vote in the Senate.
2. A two-thirds vote of the Senate is needed to approve a *treaty* made by the President of the United States.
3. A *majority* vote of the Senate is needed to approve appointments made by the President.
4. *Revenue* bills can start only in the House (a check on the Senate).
5. *Bills* must be passed by both houses to become laws.
6. Only Congress has the power to declare wars.
7. A two-thirds vote of both houses may override a Presidential *veto.*

Executive Checks

1. Laws passed by Congress need the President's signature.
2. The President may *veto bills.*
3. *Federal* judges are appointed by the President.
4. The President has the right to call special sessions of the Congress.
5. Although only the Congress has the power to declare war, the President is the head of the armed forces.

Judicial Checks

1. The Supreme Court can declare a law to be unconstitutional.
2. *Federal* judges are appointed for life.

Checks on the People

1. Elections—House of Representatives, two-year term; Senators, six-year term; President, four-year term; judges, a lifetime. The people cannot upset the Government by throwing everybody out at once. There will always be some experienced people in the *Federal* Government.
2. The *Electoral College*—it was felt that the common people could not properly assume the responsibility of electing the President of the United States.
3. Senators were chosen by the state *legislatures.* Judges were appointed.

Checks Between the Federal Government and the States

1. Certain powers were specifically given to the Federal Government (delegated powers).
2. Certain powers were shared by both the Federal Government and the state governments (concurrent powers).
3. All other powers belonged to the state governments (residual powers).

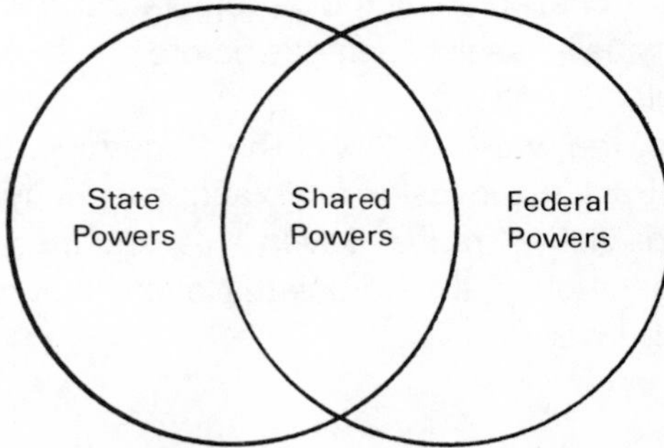

Study Sheet for Review

"I studied two hours for that test and bombed out. You didn't ask any questions on the stuff I studied." This is an old familiar refrain that most teachers hear from their students.

The ability to study for tests is a long time coming to some students, and they need help along the way. Some students simply have no facility for organizing material—in their notes, in their essays, nor in their heads. Others, at the junior high level, are still struggling to adjust to having five or six teachers and the varied testing methods that result. There are also students who lack the necessary self-discipline required for concentrated study for a test.

In all such cases, a well designed study sheet from the teacher can be most helpful. This type of study sheet should not have detailed information in sentence form. This would only encourage the student to "cram." That, of course, would not result in a desirable learning situation.

It is best to list headings, phrases, topics, or single words. Such information gives clues to the things that you as a teacher consider to be important. It is then up to the student to find those items in his text or notes and prepare himself for the test.

A sample study sheet for World War II follows.

STUDY SHEET FOR REVIEW
American History—World War II Unit

1. KNOW—The 13 steps to war, all vocabulary words, all people listed on the vocabulary sheet—all key dates: Sept. 1939; June 1940; June 1941; August 1941; Dec. 7, 1941; June 1944; V-E Day, May 1945; V-J Day, Aug. 1945.
2. KNOW—The characteristics of a totalitarian government; the "economic isms"; Fascist countries before and during World War II; Communist Countries.
3. Early part of the war—KNOW—The Panay Incident, the Nonaggression Pact; the invasion of Poland; the phony war; Dunkirk; Free French; Vichy, France; Seven Axis countries and the leaders of the major ones; the European Nations that remained neutral during the war.

4. Our position—KNOW—Neutrality Acts; American Firsters; Lend Lease; Selective Service; Our occupation of Greenland (Denmark). The "Big Five" of the United Nations and their leaders; elections of 1940 and 1944 in America (Wilkie and Dewey); our preparations; factories; rationing.
5. Later fighting—KNOW—Scorched Earth; "V" for Victory; Africa and the "Desert Fox"; Invasion of Italy (Salerno and Anzio); Stalingrad and the turning point; D-Day and Normandy; Battle of the Bulge.
6. The Pacific—KNOW—Pearl Harbor; Wainwright and the Philippines; names of three major islands in the Philippines; Coral Sea; "I shall return"; Midway (turning point); "Island hopping"; Doolittle Raid; other island groups involved; Iwo Jima and Okinawa; the atom bomb; Hiroshima and Nagasaki; Tokyo Bay and the battleship *Missouri*.

Fill-in Stories[1]

These are such fun to work with in the classroom that they might properly be labeled as sugar coated pills.

The teacher summarizes the important points of an entire chapter in short story form. Blank spaces are substituted for key words in the story. It is helpful to write all the dates in the left-hand margin. They are read right into the story, and certainly should not be memorized. This positioning of the dates allows the student to follow the sequence of events a bit more easily as he reads.

The purpose of using this technique is to reinforce and clarify material that has already been covered. Since I wish to eliminate any sense of pressure on this assignment, I make no attempt to grade this exercise.

I allow about 15 minutes for students to fill in the blank spaces. In doing so, they may not refer to texts or notes. Then I call on a student to start reading. This person is allowed to read only until a mistake is made. A volunteer then takes over and reads until the class catches the reader in an error. Students correct their own papers as the reading progresses. The end result is a review sheet that can be helpful in studying for a unit test. The sample that I include here happens to be on the causes of the American Revolution. Fill-in stories can easily be used with any unit in history.

---

[1]Idea for this activity courtesy of Stewart Bailey, Social Studies teacher, Brecksville Junior High School.

It takes considerable time for the teacher to write up several of these. But once the task is complete, these can be a permanent part of the handout file and be used for many years. The effort is certainly worthwhile, as the students enjoy the game aspect of this review sheet.

FILL-IN STORY

Worksheet—Revolutionary War

In the beginning, the English followed a policy of
Salutary Neglect with their colonies, and the colonies were
pretty free to conduct their business affairs as they pleased.
During the rule of the Puritans under the leadership of
1651 ***Oliver Cromwell*** in ____ a series of laws was passed in
order to make England more prosperous. These were called
the ***Trade and Navigation*** Acts. These laws were not
strictly enforced.

After the French and Indian War, the British, under
King ***George III*** decided to enforce the laws that they had
1764 passed in 1651. In the year ____ they lowered the tax on
sugar and molasses by passing the ***Sugar*** Act. British offi-
cers were given papers called ***Writs of Assistance*** to help
them enforce the new laws. The colonists continued to re-
sent taxation and resisted the law by smuggling. In the year
1765 ____ the British put a tax on papers and documents by passing the ***Stamp*** Act. The colonists resisted this law by refus-
ing to buy British goods. This was called a ***Boycott***. They
also organized a patriotic group called the
Sons of Liberty. A fiery speech against this law was made
by ***Patrick Henry***. The colony of ***Massachusetts*** invited the
other colonies to a meeting to protest against this law. This
meeting was called the ***Stamp Act Congress***. The law was
1765 finally repealed in the year ____ but the ***Declaratory*** Act
was passed stating that the Parliament had the right to make
laws that were binding upon the colonies. The colonies, on

the other hand, felt that they should not have taxation without ***Representation***.

In the same year, the ***Quartering*** Act was passed stating that the colonies had to house British soldiers. The colonial legislature of ***New York*** was disbanded because it
refused to obey this law. In an effort to raise money, the
1767 British passed laws in ____ putting taxes on lead, glass,
paint, tea, etc. These laws were called the ***Townshend*** Acts.
Again the colonists resisted and British troops were sta-
1771 tioned in Boston to preserve order. In the year ____ a clash
between soldiers and colonists where four men were killed was called the ***Boston Massacre***. Refusal to buy British goods finally led to a repeal of these taxes except for the tax on ***Tea***. The people still protested against this single tax, and in December of ____ a group of colonists dumped the cargo of a ship into the sea. This was known as the ***Boston Tea Party***.

The British were determined to punish the colonies,
especially Massachusetts, for the above incident and
1774 passed laws in the year ____ called the ***Intolerable*** Acts,
closing the port of ***Boston***. At the same time, the boundaries of ***Quebec*** were changed. The colony of ***Virginia*** organized a day of ***Mourning***. As a result of this, their legislature was dissolved and a call was sent out for a meeting of the 13 colonies. This meeting was known as the ***First Continental Congress.***

The British responded by sending more troops to America and an order was given for the arrest of ***Sam Adams*** and ***John Hancock***. These two men went to a small town and British troops followed. Shots were fired in two towns, ***Lexington and Concord***, and the Revolutionary War had begun in April 1775.

CHARTS

I plead guilty to being obsessively efficient and well organized—traits that have often driven my family wild. While my tendency to organize those around me can be a problem at home, it seems to be an asset in the classroom. Since the norm for junior high students can be described as scatterbrained or flaky, any exposure to efficiency is a step in the right direction. They sorely need to develop study skills that will help them to master assigned reading material. These skills will help them not only in school but for the rest of their lives as well.

One of the most useful tools in this regard is the chart. It can take many forms and be useful in many different ways. I have many such charts in my files, but I choose to discuss only three, each of which serves a different purpose.

The first one (below) relates to the colonial period of history. It is mimeographed with only the headings and the topics, and the student is expected to complete the chart. The seven things listed on this chart are all discussed in the text. But I have found that students tend to "read right over them" without grasping their importance or significance. Each of these seven things was either an act of autocracy, which the colonists resisted, or an act of democracy, which they promoted. In either case, they reflected the growing spirit of independence in the colonies. The completed chart is helpful in class discussion.

COLONIAL GOVERNMENT		
Plan	***Colony***	***Explanation***
House of Burgesses		
Act concerning religion		
Grand model		
Dominion of New England		
Great Law		
Mayflower Compact		
Fundamental Orders		

The second chart (page 51) is concerned with the events that led to the American Revolution and is given to my students in completed form. We use it as a basis for discussion. It makes it easier for the students to grasp the complicated sequence of events and tends to highlight the inexorable march of events toward this war. When our discussion on this topic has been completed, the chart serves a further purpose as a good review sheet for the entire chapter.

PARLIAMENTARY ACTS

Act	*Date*	*Provisions*	*Results*
Trade and Navigation Acts	1651	1. Goods carried in English ships 2. Certain products sold only to England 3. Certain goods bought only from England 4. Some things could not be made in the colonies 5. Tax on goods from other countries	1. Smuggling 2. Resentment in the colonies 3. Colonial juries would overlook lawbreakers
Sugar Act	1764	1. Lowered tax on sugar and molasses 2. Writs of assistance were used	1. Smuggling 2. Resentment
Proclamation of 1763	1763	1. No settlers west of Appalachians 2. Settlers there had to leave 3. Only the crown could buy more land	1. Anger in the colonies 2. They wanted more land
Stamp Act	1765	1. Certain things had to have a stamp on them—a direct tax	1. Boycott on English goods 2. Fires and riots 3. Sons of Liberty 4. Patrick Henry's speech 5. Stamp Act Congress meets in Massachusetts 6. Stamp Act repealed
Declaratory Act	1765	1. Parliament declared that it had the power to make laws binding on the colonies	1. Colonists were so busy rejoicing over repeal of the Stamp Act that they ignored the warning in the new Act

PARLIAMENTARY ACTS (Cont'd)

Act	***Date***	***Provisions***	***Results***
Quartering Act	1765	1. Colonies had to house and pay the British soldiers	1. New York Assembly refused to pay 2. This assembly was dissolved
Townshend Acts	1767	1. Tax on lead, glass, paint, tea, paper, etc. 2. Writs of assistance were used 3. British officials were tried in England 4. Colonial violaters no longer tried by juries	1. Massachusetts letter to the colonies 2. Massachusetts Assembly dissolved 3. More British soldiers from England 4. Boston Massacre 5. Colonial boycott on British goods 6. Repeal of Townshend Act except for tea 7. Tea sent to colonies 8. Boston Tea Party
Quebec Act	1774	1. Religious freedom to Catholics in Canada 2. Gave the Ohio Valley to Quebec	1. Anger
Intolerable Acts	1774	1. Boston closed as a port 2. Massachusetts charter taken away 3. Law breakers were sent to England	1. Colonies gave aid to Boston 2. Colonies were united 3. Day of mourning for Boston promoted by Virginia 4. House of Burgesses was disbanded 5. Virginia calls for the First Continental Congress

The third chart (page 53) was designed for a different reason. In the study of any war, I like to discuss causes, strengths of both sides, battles, and results. In such a study, I prefer to dwell on the causes and results. Many American history texts cover the battles in so much detail that it becomes confusing to most of the students. The chart shown here on the Civil War condenses many pages of the text into one sheet that is more manageable.

THE CIVIL WAR

Battle	***Location***	***Leaders***	***Won by***	***Other information***
Ft. Sumter	South Carolina	Beauregard Anderson	South	First shots of the war—four more states seceded—border states remain in the Union
Bull Run	Manassas Junction, Virginia	Beauregard McDowell	South	Left the North demoralized and the South overconfident
Ft. Henry Ft. Donelson	Tennessee River	Johnson Grant	North	First step toward taking the Mississippi River
Shiloh	Southern Tennessee	Johnson Grant	North	Extremely bloody battle
New Orleans	Louisiana	Farragut	North	Taken without a shot—Mouth of the Mississippi
Vicksburg	Mississippi	Pemberton	North	Turning point of the war—Union control of the Mississippi completed
Chattanooga Chickamauga Lookout Mountain Missionary Ridge	Southern Tennessee	Johnson Bragg Grant Rosecrans	North	Entire state of Tennessee now in Union hands
Chancellorsville Fredericksburg Cold Harbor 2nd Battle of Bull Run Battle of the Wilderness	Virginia	Mostly Lee and Grant	South	All were unsuccessful attempts of the North to take Richmond—heavy and bloody fighting
Antietam	Maryland	Lee McClellan	North	First attempt by Lee to take Washington, D.C.
Gettysburg	Pennsylvania	Lee Meade	North	Second attempt by Lee to take Washington, D.C.—Pickett's Charge and the Gettysburg Address

THE CIVIL WAR				
Battle	***Location***	***Leaders***	***Won by***	***Other information***
Sherman's march to the sea	Georgia Atlanta to Savannah	Hood <u>Sherman</u>	North	Strategy was to destroy the power of the South to wage war
Petersburg	Virginia	Lee <u>Grant</u>	North	Led to fall of Richmond
Appomattox Court House	Virginia	Lee <u>Grant</u>	North	Final surrender

Know Monitor and Merrimac; all vocabulary words; four commanders-in-chief of the North; Emancipation Proclamation and results; importance of the Shenandoah Valley; leaders' names on chart that are underlined are Union leaders, the others are Southern leaders.

I encourage my students to take notes whenever they can in chart form. Consider the following as examples:

Notes on the exploration period can be organized under these headings.

Explorer	*Date*	*Flag*	*Territory*	*Importance*

A chart of this type can be useful during the study of the colonial period.

Colony	*Date*	*Founded by*	*Purpose*	*Leaders*	*Type of Government*

For further examples of helpful charts, study the Learning Activity lists in Chapter 7 (Individualized Instruction).

MAPS

I have long been aware that my seventh grade geography students refer to me as "map freak." It is at this grade level, and in the geography course, that I stress map work throughout the year. We work with many kinds of maps—physical, political, population, land use, and climate for each region of the world that we study. The students are given experience in various map related skills including map reproduction, map reading, and the use of an atlas. They are taught to recognize and use the five essential elements of a map—title, direction, scale, latitude and longitude, and legend. They are given assignments in original map making that include such titles as "My Home," "My Vacation," and "My Dream Island." By the end of the year, these seventh graders are expected to know thoroughly major topographic regions of the United States, the various climatic areas, and the location of resources and major cities. They must, of course, also know the location and spelling for each of the 50 states. All of this is essential background for an American history course. We have some excellent geography teachers in our school, and I have found that my history students come to me well prepared. Even so, I start the history course each year with a three day review of United States geography, and I strongly recommend such a procedure for any history class. I would suggest that new teachers need to determine what kind of geography background their students have had. It may be necessary to spend considerable time on map skills in the American history course if the background is thin.

My own emphasis on maps in American history focuses on the two sets of historical maps on my walls. Our classroom work is constantly tied to the appropriate map on those sets.

I usually give only three map assignments during the course. One is an explorer's map of North and South America where the students are required to place the explorers in the proper regions. A second one is a Civil War map, locating famous battles of that war. The third one I include on the next page as a sample. It is a map assignment locating islands in the Pacific Ocean and relates to two things—our acquisition of an "empire" around the turn of the century and the battles in the Pacific during World War II.

You may need to include many maps in your handout file. The number and the variety will depend on the background of the students and your emphasis as a teacher.

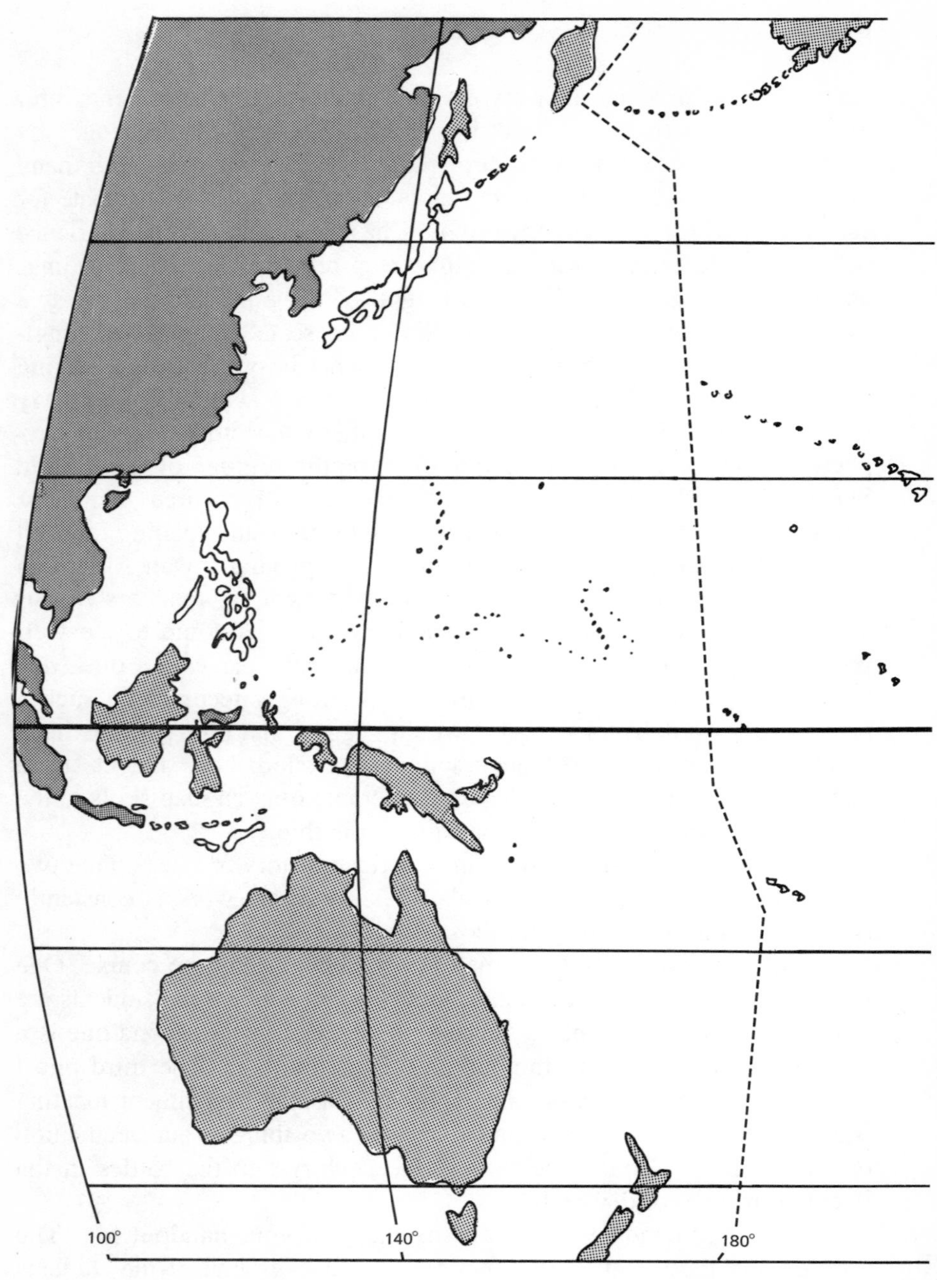
100°
140°
180°

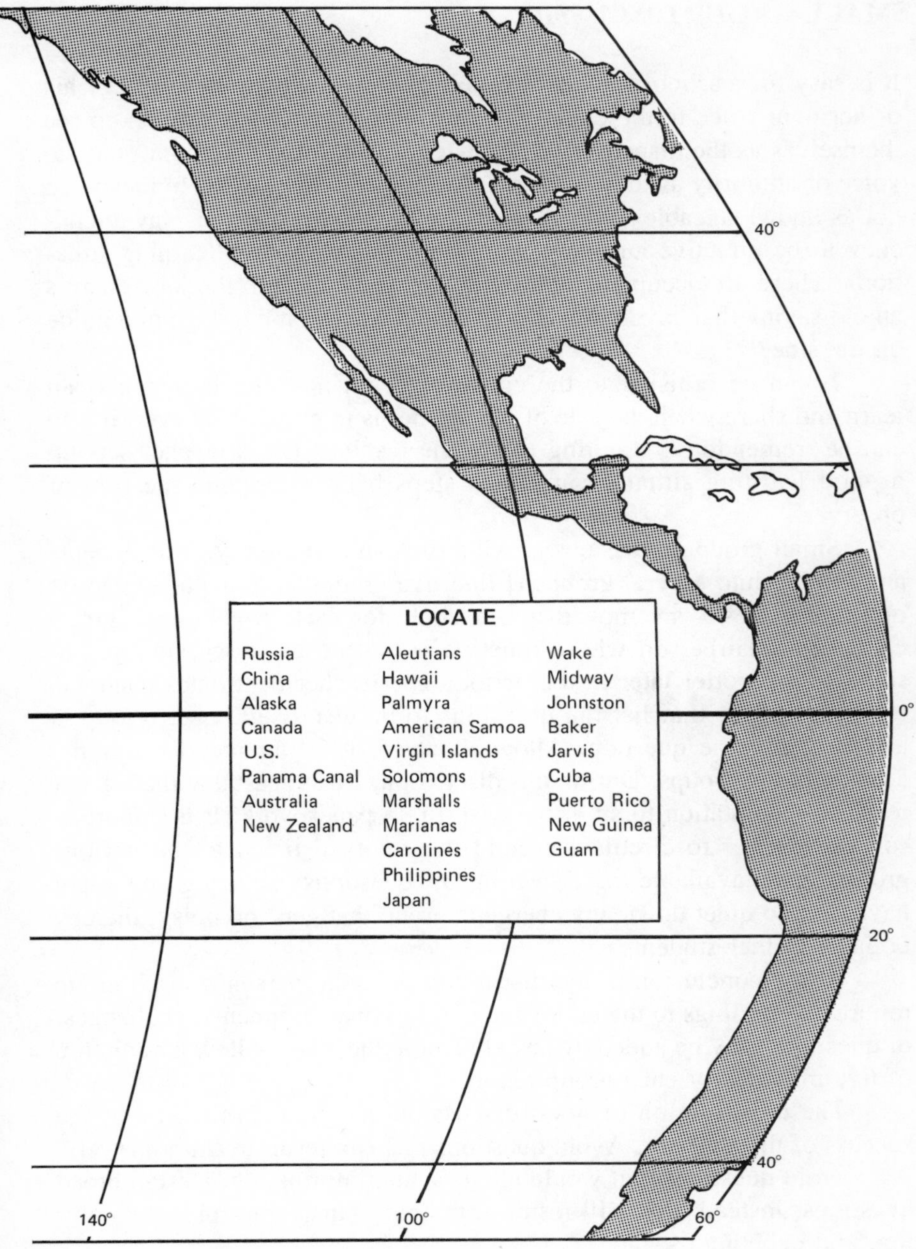
40°
0°
20°
40°
140°
100°
60°
LOCATE
Russia
China
Alaska
Canada
U.S.
Panama Canal
Australia
New Zealand
Aleutians
Hawaii
Palmyra
American Samoa
Virgin Islands
Solomons
Marshalls
Marianas
Carolines
Philippines
Japan
Wake
Midway
Johnston
Baker
Jarvis
Cuba
Puerto Rico
New Guinea
Guam

SMALL GROUP DISCUSSION

It is easy for a school teacher to become enamored with the sound of his or her own voice in the classroom. It is equally easy for teachers to see themselves as the dispensers of knowledge, the font of wisdom, and the voice of authority as they work with young teen-agers who obviously are not as knowledgeable as the teacher. Teachers also often display a tendency to be directive and very involved in all classroom learning situations. These are occupational hazards that are built into the job. There's an old saying that covers it well, "Are you a sage on the stage or a guide on the side?"

It can be bruising to the ego to find out how much students can learn and share when the role of the teacher is minimal. However, it also can be tremendously exciting to see the results when a teacher sets up a good learning situation and then steps back to assume the role of observer.

Small group discussions provide such an opportunity. The students are divided into several groups (I find five groups of five students to be optimum). Desks are moved into a circle for each group. Each group chooses a chairperson whose function is to lead the discussion and to serve as a reporter later in the period. The teacher distributes handouts to each student that list the questions to be discussed. Each group is assigned just one question. Allow about 15 or 20 minutes for the discussion in the groups. During this discussion, I'd suggest that the teacher resist the temptation to sit at the desk to do paper work. It is important for the teacher to circulate around the room to listen to the various groups, to be available for answering any questions that any group might have, and to quiet down any energetic group that gets too noisy, thereby bothering other students.

At the conclusion of the discussion, the chairperson of each group reports the findings to the entire class. Additional comments, challenges, or questions may be added by any student in the class. Allow a minimum of five minutes for each group report.

The construction of good discussion questions is the key to the success of this activity. Avoid questions that can result in short answers. Also avoid questions that would elicit factual information. Design broad questions, instead, that will result in thinking, analyzing, problem solving, and debating.

I have found that seventh graders are not quite comfortable with small group discussions that require the kind of thinking just described.

I use discussion groups in the seventh grade geography course, but in this instance, I focus more on questions that lead the students to locate and compile factual information.

It is interesting to note that I have found this technique to be much more successful with eighth graders at the end of the school year than it is at the beginning. It leads me to suspect that a certain level of maturity is necessary before small group discussion can be used with maximum effectiveness. For a further discussion of this topic, its physiological basis, and the implications for teaching, see Chapter 2 of *Teaching Science: Grades 5 to 9* (Silver Burdett, 1981).

I believe that the greatest advantage of this type of classroom activity is the fact that all students have a real opportunity to express themselves fully. These groups provide a good vehicle for a great deal of student interaction. I also have observed that a youngster who hesitates to speak up before the entire class will often open up in a small group where he may feel more secure. This is definitely an active rather than a passive learning activity.

A word of caution is in order, however. Choose the groups carefully for good balance in ability, participation, and leadership; and, for maximum interpersonal contact, form new groups each time you use small group discussion.

I have found that the unit covering our history from the end of World War II to the present lends itself well to small group discussion. Each year I cover that entire unit through the use of discussion groups. There are several reasons for this choice:

1. My students are already rather well-informed about this period of history because of the year long current events program (see Chapter 5).
2. It is a good change of pace after the World War II Unit.
3. The eighth graders have reached a higher level of maturity by the end of the school year.
4. The active learning situation is more palatable to the students during the warm days of late May and June than general classroom discussion would be.
5. It is a satisfying way in which to end the year.

I include here as examples the lists of questions that I use for this final unit of the year. You will find further samples of questions in Chapter 7.

DISCUSSION QUESTIONS, 1945–1978

1. At the end of any major war in modern times, many adjustments must be made. How does the end of a war affect the following: education; industry; housing; labor unions; the economy in general; morals of the people; politics; welfare measures; anything else?
2. Analyze the term "Iron Curtain" in terms of the following:
    a. The countries involved
    b. List as many restrictions as possible that are imposed by the Iron Curtain.
    c. If the Iron Curtain were to be completely eliminated tomorrow, what effect would this have on the world?
3. The Marshall Plan offered aid to all of Europe and was accepted by 16 nations. Can you think of any American leaders in past times who had similar philosophies? In other words, was the idea "revolutionary" or "evolutionary"? How might history have been different if a "Marshall Plan" had been used after earlier wars that the United States was involved in? How might history have been different if we had <u>not</u> used this plan after World War II?
4. The United States has pledged to protect West Berlin against any attack. Give as many reasons as you can to explain why Berlin is important. Consider geography, politics, economics, world opinion, world peace, etc.
5. You are a historian in the year 2081 writing a book on American History. Which of the following things will you describe in your text as having the greatest effect on history? NATO; Marshall Plan; United Nations; the Cold War. Give reasons for your answers.
6. During the Korean War, General MacArthur wanted permission to launch full scale war against China. Truman insisted that the enemy should only be pushed back to the 38th parallel. Who was right? Give reasons for your answer.
7. We are opposing two huge Communist nations, Russia and China. Which of these do you see as the more dangerous? Give reasons for your answer.
8. Compare the treatment given to Germany with that given to Japan after World War II. Note areas where treatment was similar and where it was different. Account for the differences.

9. Review for the class every commitment, promise, and organization that the United States became involved with in the postwar years. Indicate which of these is worthy of further support by the United States and give reasons why.

10. Imagine that all of the Far East (from India eastward to the Pacific) were to be given to the Communists. List all the advantages that the countries of Asia would bring to the Communist bloc of nations. Would there be any disadvantages?

11. In an armed revolt in Hungary in 1956, the people attempted to break away from Russian control. Why, in your opinion, did we fail to go to the aid of the "Hungarian Freedom Fighters?" Do you approve or disapprove of the American policy on this matter? Give reasons for your answer.

12. The Suez Canal was originally built by private companies from England and France under a 99-year lease. President Nasser of Egypt seized this canal in 1956 by force. As a result, Israel, England, and France attacked Egypt. The United States and the United Nations condemned all three nations. What is your opinion of this incident and its results?

13. The Taft-Hartley Law is heartily disliked by labor leaders because (1) it forbids a "closed shop" and (2) it allows a President to stop a strike for 80 days. What is your opinion of these two provisions? Give reasons for your answer.

14. Discuss fully the reasons for the Senate's unusual action in "censuring" Senator Joseph McCarthy. Do you agree or disagree with the censure? Give reasons for your answer.

15. Civil Rights

- **a.** List all of the "Civil Rights."
- **b.** Name all of the minority groups in our history that have been discriminated against.
- **c.** Review for the class the major Civil Rights groups in the United States. Which of these has been the most effective? Give reasons.
- **d.** What four minority groups in the United States today have the most severe problems?

16. Despite the Good Neighbor Policy, the OAS, and the Alliance for Progress, our relationships with Latin America are far from satisfactory. Analyze the problems of the Latin American Nations, and try to suggest a plan of action that the United States could follow where we might: (1) help solve their problems; (2) improve our relationship with them.

17. The United States and Canada have maintained peaceful relations for many years. Discuss the factors that tend to strengthen this relationship. What kinds of things might tend to divide these two countries?
18. Review the advantages gained by the United States with the addition of our last two states—Alaska and Hawaii. Do these two states pose any problems to us today? Are there any other areas of the world that could possibly be added to our country as states in the future?
19. What problems were created for our country by the "U-2" incident and the "Pueblo" incident? Do you feel that the United States should continue to use spy ships and planes around the world? Give reasons for your answers.
20. What does "prestige" mean? How would you analyze the prestige of the United States during World War II? What do you think has happened to the prestige of the United States since World War II? Do you consider prestige to be important to our country? If so, why? If not, why not? What would you do to improve the prestige of the United States?
21. Name three "firsts" in the election of 1960. From what you know of that election as well as the ones in 1964, 1968, 1972, and 1976, would you suggest any changes in our method of electing Presidents? Any changes in campaign rules?
22. Review what you have already learned about the history of Cuba before 1960. Do you agree that the Bay of Pigs was a mistake? Give reasons for your answer. Analyze Kennedy's actions during the Cuban Missile Crisis. Was he reasonable? Right? Successful? Describe other incidents in our history when American Presidents chose to take a strong stand.
23. Conquest of Distance
    - **a.** Who was the first man to circle the globe? When? How long did it take? How long does it take to circle the globe today?
    - **b.** List every development or invention that has helped the world to "grow smaller."
    - **c.** What effect has the conquest of distance had on each of the following: American foreign policy; world peace; education?
    - **d.** Do you agree with this statement: "The advantages that tel-

evision brings to the public greatly outweigh the disadvantages"? Justify your stand.

e. It is the year 2000. Describe the latest developments in transportation and communication.

24. Conquest of Space

a. Define the following: rocket; atmosphere; Sputnik; satellite; orbit.

b. Compare the space program of the United States with that of Russia.

c. Does the conquest of space present any problems to World Peace? If so, what?

d. Analyze the space program in terms of knowledge gained through it.

e. Describe the progress in space that you expect to see in your lifetime.

25. Identify the following and give the importance:

a. Castro

b. Khrushchev

c. James Meredith

d. Dr. Martin Luther King

e. Yuri Gagarin

f. John Glenn

Which of these people will be remembered the most in history? Why?

26. List the assassinations (or attempted assassinations) of American public figures since 1960. Do we have more of these incidents than other countries do? How do you explain these violent incidents in our American society? Can you think of any steps that we might take to make our public officials more secure?

27. Legislation on Civil Rights—give provisions of the following (Use *Five Centuries in America* as reference):

a. 1948 order issued by Truman

b. 1954 Brown vs. the Board of Education

c. 1957 Civil Rights Law

d. 1964 Civil Rights Law

e. The 24th Amendment

f. 1968 Civil Rights Law

g. Is there any further legislation that you would recommend?

28. What is your opinion of a "welfare state"? Explain each of the following and give your opinion:
    a. Vista
    b. War on Poverty
    c. Medicare
    d. Elementary and Secondary Education Act

    Are the matters listed above properly the concern of the Federal Government or of the states? Does this question raise the issue of "States' Rights"? What do such programs do to American taxes? To the power of the Federal Government?
29. Would you label Barry Goldwater a radical, liberal, conservative, or reactionary?
    a. What was his platform in 1964? Give your own analysis of that platform.
    b. What did the election results demonstrate about the direction that the American people wanted to take?
    c. Goldwater is again in the United States Senate. Can you think of a valuable and useful role that he plays there?
    d. Answer questions a and b above in terms of Ronald Reagan and the election of 1976.
30. Explain the 25th Amendment to the class.
    a. How many times in our history did the Vice President have to take over? Name the people involved.
    b. Give reasons why the 25th Amendment was passed—give specific examples.
    c. Review for the class the line of succession to the Presidency.
31. You are the President of the United States. On the basis of everything that you have heard or read about Indo-China, what plan of action would you set up for solving the problems of Southeast Asia?
32. Review the Arab-Israel conflict from 1948 right up to date:
    a. Israel set up as a nation
    b. United Nations action there
    c. Suez Canal crisis of 1956
    d. The six-day war of 1967
    e. The attempts of Sadat and Begin to secure a peace

    Which side of this conflict do you favor? What action should the United States take, if any? What do you see as the biggest danger in this situation?

33. Automation—define and give examples:
   a. When in our history did automation first occur?
   b. What effect does automation have on employment?
   c. How can we best handle the problems of automation?
   d. Some labor leaders are agitating for a "slow-down" in automation. Would you favor this? Why or why not?

34. Population explosion
   a. Total population of the earth today? Expected by the year 2000?
   b. List, in order, the five most populated countries today and give their approximate populations.
   c. Analyze the problems caused by overpopulation.
   d. Give possible solutions to these problems.
   e. On an outline map of the world, show five areas not fit for food production today. Could any of these be made useful for farming? How?

35. Recent Presidents
   a. Compare and contrast the last five Presidents: Kennedy, Johnson, Nixon, Ford, and Carter. Consider their personalities, background, government experience, political parties, etc.
   b. List some of the problems that all five of these men have had to face while they were in office (problems they had in common).
   c. Which of these five will go down in history as the greatest? Why?

36. Leisure Time
   a. Describe the leisure time activities of the typical American in 1880.
   b. Describe the leisure time activities of the typical American today.
   c. An increasing number of Americans are retiring at age 65. Many are living for 15 or 20 years beyond retirement age. What are some of the ways in which these senior citizens can make their retirement years productive, interesting, and satisfying?

37. List ten goals for the United States that should be accomplished within your lifetime. Choose the two that you would consider to be the most important. Give reasons for your choices.

38. The Atom
   a. Describe the peaceful uses of atomic power today.
   b. What are some of the problems involved in producing and using atomic energy?
   c. Explain the following: fission; fusion; guided missile; ballistic missile; ICBM; IRBM; ABM.

39. Medical Advances
   a. List all of the diseases that you can think of for which we now have a preventative vaccine.
   b. Explain the uses of the following: Sulfa drugs, antibiotics, insulin, cortisone, anti-histamines, blood, any others?
   c. If you had to choose just one medical discovery of the last 100 years, which one would you consider to be the most important?
   d. What would you consider to be the most important target or goal of the medical research people today?

PRESIDENTIAL ELECTIONS

Every four years the entire world watches while Americans put on the three ringed circus known as "The election of a President." In all the world there is nothing quite like it. Somehow, in spite of all the ballyhoo and the wheeling and dealing, we've managed to do pretty well throughout history in choosing our leaders.

When the presidential election year rolls around, the eighth graders are able for the first time to comprehend our electoral process. Whatever they remember from the election held while they were fourth graders is rather superficial. It is a good opportunity, therefore, to explain to our students the manner in which our system works as we actually live through it.

A full scale production is probably the most exciting approach. We did this in our school in 1964 by staging a mock political convention of the Republican Party. This event received coverage by both the *Cleveland Plain Dealer* and the *Cleveland Press*.

In another election year I discovered that our congressman, William Minshall, was to be in town. I phoned and asked if he would consider coming to our junior high school to speak to the students. Much to my surprise, he accepted my invitation. We set up a "Meet the Press" program in which he answered questions posed by a panel of eighth graders.

On a simpler scale, I prepare handouts on presidential elections that we use in class as a basis for class discussion. I prefer to distribute these in the spring of an election year so that students may refer to them during the summer months when the candidates are chosen. I include as a sample the handout from the 1980 election. The questions on the handout in no way constitute a test. Rather, they are used in the discussion. I also include a handout comparing the presidency of George Washington with that of Gerald Ford, just because it is interesting. Never let an election year go by without making good use of it in some fashion.

PRESIDENTIAL ELECTIONS—1980

B **1.** Presidential elections are held every ______.
A. 2 years **B.** 4 years **C.** 6 years **D.** 8 years

even **2.** They are always held in *even* or *odd* years. Choose one.

C **3.** How many Presidents have we had?
A. 30 **B.** 33 **C.** 39 **D.** 42
(Our next President will be number *40*.)

D **4.** How many Presidential elections have we had?
A. 35 **B.** 39 **C.** 42 **D.** 49
(November's election will be number 49.)

A **5.** In our early history, presidential candidates were chosen by ______.
A. congress **B.** party leaders **C.** conventions **D.** the people

B **6.** National party conventions to choose the candidates were first used during the time of ______.
A. Jefferson **B.** Jackson **C.** Wilson **D.** F.D. Roosevelt

C* **7. Primary elections to help choose Presidential candidates are used by what fraction of the states?
A. 1/4 **B.** 1/3 **C.** 1/2 **D.** all fifty

A **8.** Laws for the primary elections are usually set by the ______.
A. states **B.** federal government **C.** political parties **D.** all of these

*In 1980 there were primaries in 35 states, plus the District of Columbia and Puerto Rico.

D **9.** Delegates to nominating conventions are chosen by ______.
A. primary elections **B.** state party conventions **C.** party leaders **D.** all of these

D **10.** Delegates to nominating conventions are committed to a candidate ______.
A. for at least one round of voting **B.** until released by the candidate **C.** who is a "favorite son" **D.** all of these

C **11.** The number of delegates each state may send to a nominating convention is determined by the ______.
A. states **B.** federal government **C.** political parties **D.** all of these

C **12.** Total number of delegate votes at the Democratic convention will be roughly ______.
A. 1000 **B.** 2000 **C.** 3000 **D.** 4000
Number of delegate votes needed to nominate? 1,600 out of 3,331.

B **13.** Total number of delegate votes at the Republican Convention will be roughly ______.
A. 1000 **B.** 2000 **C.** 3000 **D.** 4000
Number of delegate votes needed to nominate? 998 out of 1994.

D **14.** The duty of the national committee of the party is to ______.
A. conduct all party affairs **B.** raise funds for the party **C.** plan nominating conventions **D.** do all of these
This committee consists of one man and one woman from each of the fifty states. Other members are added. A National Chairperson of the party presides over the group.

The Convention Procedures in Sequence

1. Election of a temporary chairperson.
2. Keynote speech—to criticize the other party and to praise their own—to generate spirit, etc.
3. Election of the permanent chairperson of the convention.
4. Setting of the convention rules.

5. Approval of the credentials of the delegates.
6. Presentation of the party platform and voting on this platform.
7. Roll call of the states in alphabetical order to allow for nominations. A state may make a nomination, second a nomination that has already been made, yield to another state that wishes to make a nomination, or pass. The person nominating a candidate makes a speech about the nominee. This is usually followed by a lengthy and noisy demonstration. Such demonstrations are almost always carefully planned and organized in advance.
8. After all of the nominations have been made, comes the first roll call of the states for voting on the candidates. The winner must have a majority of the total vote (more than half).
   - **a.** The Democrats have chosen 21 candidates on the first ballot.
   - **b.** The Republicans have chosen 21 candidates on the first ballot.
   - **c.** It required 49 ballots to nominate Pierce in 1852, 46 ballots for Woodrow Wilson in 1912, 59 for Douglas in 1860; the record: it took 103 ballots to nominate John Davis, a Democrat, in 1924.
9. The voting on a Vice Presidential candidate is usually a formality. He is almost always chosen by the Presidential candidate. Why?
10. Acceptance speeches are made by the chosen candidates for President and Vice President. They generally are "Pep Talks."
11. The National Committee for the next four years is voted on.
12. The convention is adjourned.

The Election

1. The first Tuesday after the first Monday in November.
2. The citizens cast the popular vote (registered voters only).
3. By state law in most states, *all* electoral votes in a state go to the winner in the popular election in that state.
4. Electors in each state are equal to the total number of Senators and Representatives from that state. The District of Columbia has 3 electoral votes (23rd amendment). Thus, there are a total of 538 electoral votes. A majority of the electoral votes is needed to elect a President (270 electoral votes). If a majority is not

reached, the election goes into the House of Representatives, where each state gets one vote. When you watch election results on TV in November, you will find that both the popular votes and the electoral votes are posted as the results come in to the station.

5. Electors meet in each state capital on the first Monday after the second Wednesday in December to cast their official votes. These votes are sent to the Congress. Hence, the President is not officially elected until December.
6. On January 6, the President of the Senate (the Vice President of the United States), in the presence of both houses of Congress, counts the votes and announces the winner. (Thus, in 1961, it was the duty of Richard Nixon to announce that John Kennedy had defeated Nixon in the election of 1960.)
7. The winner is inaugurated on January 20.

TEN KEY STATES TO WATCH IN NOVEMBER

State	Electoral Vote—1960	Electoral Vote—1970
California	40	45
New York	43	41
Pennsylvania	29	27
Illinois	26	26
Ohio	26	25
Texas	25	26
Michigan	21	21
New Jersey	17	17
Florida	14	17
Massachusetts	14	14

A Reminder Seats on the House of Representatives are redistributed every ten years according to the census figures. Thus the electoral votes are also redistributed every ten years. The 1980 census figures will affect the elections of 1984 and 1988.

Note If the above ten states all voted for the same candidate, there would be a total of 259 electoral votes—the majority needed to elect a president is 270. In other words, eleven or twelve states could elect a president.

Important Legislation Dealing with the Presidency

1. What is the President's salary today? How is it determined?
2. What are the provisions of the 20th amendment?
3. What are the provisions of the 22nd amendment?
4. What are the provisions of the 23rd amendment?
5. What are the provisions of the 25th amendment?
6. What article of the Constitution spells out the duties and powers of the President?
7. What is the succession to the Presidency according to the 1947 law?

Vocabulary

1. Convention—a body or assembly of persons met to accomplish a specific purpose.
2. Platform—a declaration of the principles and policies on which a group of people stand and on which they appeal for public support.
3. Credentials—letters and papers proving that a person is entitled to exercise official power.
4. Caucus—Private unofficial meeting of party leaders to decide on candidates or a course of action.
5. Dark horse—Candidate who is not well known nor expected to win the nomination. He is chosen if the convention becomes deadlocked with two candidates. (Polk was the first dark horse and Wendell Willkie was the most famous.)
6. Draft—a movement to nominate a candidate through pressure from the party or a large group of voters. The "office seeks the man."
7. Electorate—Total number of American citizens qualified to vote.
8. Favorite son—One who is nominated in a party convention for his loyal state or regional support, rather than for his national following. He generally releases his delegates to vote for someone he is supporting.
9. Alternate—A person chosen to take the place of a delegate at a party convention when the regular delegate is absent.

Some Interesting Comparisons

The Presidencies of George Washington and Gerald Ford

	Washington	Ford
Executive Staff members	2	535
Cabinet members	4	11
Federal Government Employees	350	2,815,670
Rooms in the official residence	10	132
Salary	$25,000	$200,000 $ 50,000 Expenses $1,695,000 Annual budget for White House

1. In 1860 Lincoln spent $200 for his total campaign expense. Of that amount, $199.25 was for the campaign. $.75 was spent on cider for himself! Today a candidate may spend unlimited amounts if he does not have matching funds from the government. With matching federal funds he may spend $15,000,000. In 1980, Ted Kennedy spent ½ million dollars on a TV and radio campaign in Ohio alone!
2. The oldest man to be elected to the Presidency? Ronald Reagan, born February 6, 1911; was 69 when elected; W. H. Harrison was 68.
3. Oldest man to serve—Eisenhower—age 70 at end of second term.
4. Youngest to be elected—Kennedy—age 43.
5. Youngest to serve—Teddy Roosevelt—age 42.

Presidential Hopefuls In 1980

Republicans
Ronald Reagan
George Bush
Howard Baker
John Connally
Philip Crane
Robert Dole

Democrats
Jimmy Carter
Ted Kennedy
Jerry Brown

Independent
John Anderson

Factual Questions

1. Which of these was a member of the Watergate Committee? ________________
2. Which of these used to belong to a different party? ________________
3. Which of these are governors or former governors? ________________
4. Which are Senators? ________________
5. Which are members of the House of Representatives? ________________
6. Which of these is a former director of the CIA? ________________
7. Which of these was present at the assassination of John Kennedy? ________________
8. Which of these was a former movie star? ________________
9. Which of these have served as cabinet members? ________________
10. Which of these have dropped out of the race and stopped actively campaigning? ________________

Opinion Questions

1. Which of these candidates is the farthest to the "left"? ________________
2. Which of these is the farthest to the "right"? ________________
3. Which could you call "centrists"? ________________
4. Which candidates best represent the blacks? ________________
5. Which candidate is making the biggest issue of the national defense? ________________
6. Which of these will appeal most to your voters? ________________
7. Which appeals to the labor vote? ________________

8. Which might be considered to represent a "Populist movement"? ________________

9. Which are front runners at the present time?

____

10. Who is your choice for president? ________________

Presidents of the United States

1. Who had the shortest administration? *William H. Harrison*
2. Who had the longest administration? *Franklin D. Roosevelt*
3. Four presidents served their country in important posts after the presidency. Name any one of them and the post that he held. *J. Q. Adams, House of Rep.; A. Johnson, Senate; W. H. Taft, Chief Justice; H. Hoover, Federal Relief Agencies*

Give the political parties of each of the following presidents:

4. John Adams — *Federalist*
5. Thomas Jefferson — *Democratic-Republican*
6. Zachary Taylor — *Whig*
7. Grover Cleveland — *Democratic*
8. Abraham Lincoln — *Republican*
9. Calvin Coolidge — *Republican*
10. Harry Truman — *Democrat*
11. Woodrow Wilson — *Democrat*
12. Herbert Hoover — *Republican*
13. James Polk — *Democrat*

Name the man in office during each of the following wars:

14. War of 1812 — *Madison*
15. Mexican War — *Polk*
16. Civil War — *Lincoln*
17. Spanish American War — *McKinley*
18. World War I — *Wilson*
19. World War II — *F.D. Roosevelt*

From the following list of Presidents, name the four who did not serve as soldiers in wars for the United States.

George Washington	John Adams	William Henry Harrison
Andrew Jackson	Grover Cleveland	Dwight D. Eisenhower
Theodore Roosevelt	Ulysses S. Grant	Abraham Lincoln
James Buchanan	William McKinley	Martin Van Buren

20. *John Adams*

21. *Grover Cleveland*

22. *James Buchanan*

23. *Martin Van Buren*

Name five men who served as Vice President before becoming President:

24. ______________

25. ______________

26. ______________

27. ______________

28. ______________

(*John Adams, John Tylor, Millard Fillmore, Martin Van Buren, Thomas Jefferson, Chester Arthur, Theodore Roosevelt, Andrew Johnson, Lyndon Johnson, Calvin Coolidge, Harry Truman, Richard Nixon, Gerald Ford*)

Arrange the following Presidents in their proper sequence.

Benjamin Harrison	Andrew Jackson
Calvin Coolidge	James Madison
James Pierce	Harry Truman
Andrew Johnson	Theodore Roosevelt

29. *Madison*

30. *Jackson*

31. *Pierce*

32. *A. Johnson*

33. *B. Harrison*

34. *T. Roosevelt*

35. *Coolidge*

36. *Truman*

37–43. Place the following Presidents in the proper period of time below.

James Monroe	Rutherford B. Hayes
Chester Arthur	William Henry Harrison
James Polk	William Howard Taft
Herbert Hoover	

1789–1825	***1825–1861***	***1861–1901***	***1901–1979***
Monroe	*Harrison*	*Hayes*	*Hoover*
	Polk	*Arthur*	*Taft*

Identify the President connected with each of the following:

44. isolationism *Washington*

45. manifest destiny *Polk*

46. New Deal *F.D. Roosevelt*

47. Great Society *L. Johnson*

48. Whiskey Rebellion *Washington*

49. Louisiana Purchase *Jefferson*

50. War on the National Bank *Jackson*

51. Depression of 1929 *Hoover*

52. Missouri Compromise *Monroe*

53. an impreachment trial *A. Jackson*

54. corruption in government *Harding–Grant–Nixon*

55. The Gold Standard *McKinley*

56. Panama Canal *T. Roosevelt–Carter*

57. Spoils system *Jackson*

58. Progressive Party *T. Roosevelt*

59. New Frontier *Kennedy*

60. Annexation of Texas *Tyler*

61. Atlantic Charter *F. D. Roosevelt*

62. Marshall Plan *Truman*

63. "Speak softly and carry a big stick" *T. Roosevelt*

64. first astronaut into space *Kennedy*

65. League of Nations *Wilson*

A TASTE OF THINGS TO COME

Simulation, according to Webster, is ''pretense, feigning, imitation, acting, or looking like.'' As applied to a history class, I like to think of it as ''role playing'' or ''living through'' a period of history. It has become increasingly popular as a teaching technique in recent years. My first experience with a simulation unit was in 1961—a project known as ''The Civil War Debates.'' This project is described in detail in Chapter 6. I added a second major project in simulation in 1977. Chapter 8 deals with this unit, which covers the twenties and thirties.

Since both of these projects take place during the second semester, I designed a one day simulation exercise that I use immediately after the completion of the unit on the United States Constitution.

The handout sheet for this exercise describes five actual Supreme Court cases. In each of these cases, I present three possible decisions. One is the decision actually made by the Supreme Court. The other two are simply figments of my imagination.

The class is divided into five small groups. Each group is to represent a Supreme Court. The cases are considered one at a time. Decisions from the five "courts" are recorded on the blackboard. The object, of course, is to be the "court" that makes the most correct decisions, thereby earning the largest score.

Study the scoring system printed on the handout. Notice that a bonus is given if all five "judges" vote correctly, but they suffer a penalty if they are unanimously incorrect. This one day project creates excitement and interest and does indeed give students a taste of things to come in the second semester.

SIMULATION EXERCISE—SUPREME COURT DECISION MAKING

Reynolds v. the United States—1879

The Mormon Church was established in 1830. The people were a peaceful, hard working, thriving group. They practiced polygamy as a part of their faith (a man having more than one wife at a time).

In the 1850's most Mormons had settled in Utah. George Reynolds (already married to one woman) took another bride. He was arrested and charged with bigamy (having two wives). The Utah Court found him guilty. He appealed to the Supreme Court.

Decision: The Court ruled that:

1. Since the Constitution guarantees freedom of religion, Reynolds had the right to marry as many women as he pleased. He was, therefore, innocent.

2. Since polygamy was against the law in Utah, although the government could not interfere with religious beliefs, it could interfere with religious practices. Therefore, Reynolds was guilty.
3. Since polygamy was a deep belief of the Mormon Church, and only that one church believed in it, polygamy could be practiced only by members of the Mormon Church. Therefore, Reynolds was innocent.

West Virginia State Board of Education v. Barnette—1943

The State Legislature of Virginia passed a law requiring that all students in all schools be required to start each day with the Pledge of Allegiance to the flag. The children of the Barnette family were members of the Jehovah's Witnesses church. Their religion did not permit them to say a pledge nor take an oath. The court in West Virginia upheld the right of the state to require the pledge. The case went to the Supreme Court.

Decision: The Court ruled that:

1. Patriotism to a country was such a fundamental need that all students could and should be required to say the pledge. Therefore, the state ruling was upheld.
2. Because of the rights under the First Amendment, the law passed by the State of West Virginia was clearly unconstitutional and the pledge was to be eliminated from all West Virginia schools. The state was overthrown.
3. Compelling the flag salute and pledge denies the rights and freedoms covered in the First Amendment and therefore individual students could not be forced to say the pledge. The state ruling was overthrown.

Rochin v. California—1951

On an early July morning, policemen, trying to catch a drug ring, burst into the bedroom of Tony Rochin and demanded to know what several capsules on the table were. Before he could be stopped, Tony swallowed the pills. Police rushed him to the hospital, and over his loud protests, they had his stomach pumped. The pills were found to be morphine. He was convicted in California on possession of drugs. His case went to the Supreme Court.

Decision: The Court ruled that:

1. Because he was convicted on evidence unwillingly pumped from his stomach, he was forced to testify against himself and was therefore innocent, as his rights under the Fifth Amendment had been violated.
2. Because he was convicted on physical evidence (the regurgitated pills) rather than on a verbal confession, he had not personally testified against himself. Thus the conviction of the state court was upheld.
3. Because he deliberately destroyed evidence and obstructed justice, he was automatically declared guilty.

Francis v. Louisiana—1947

Willie Francis was found guilty of murder and condemned to die in the electric chair in the state of Louisiana. He was prepared for his death the evening before the execution—head shaved, trouser leg split, anything he wanted for his last meal, etc. The next morning he was strapped in the chair, the switch was thrown. He received an electrical shock, but he did not die! Something had gone wrong with the mechanism.

Francis appealed to the Supreme Court on the grounds that it would be cruel and inhuman punishment to make him go through this procedure again.

Decision: The Court ruled that:

1. They found that, on the basis of the Eighth Amendment, that it would indeed be cruel and inhuman punishment to attempt a second execution. His sentence was changed to life imprisonment.
2. The court ruled that since the switch had been thrown, the punishment had been carried out to the letter of the law, and therefore, Francis was free.
3. When, after a fair trial, the sentence was death, and an accident prevented the sentence from being carried out, it was not cruel for the state to try again. Francis was executed.

Katz v. the United States—1967

Charles Katz was suspected of placing illegal bets by telephone to several cities in different states (this would break a Federal law).

Government agents noted that he used a certain public telephone at the same time every day. Therefore, they put a wiretapping device on the phone. This enabled them to gather taped evidence with Katz's voice—proving that he was placing illegal bets. He was tried and found guilty.

He appealed to the Supreme Court on the basis of the Fourth Amendment—"unreasonable searches and seizures."

Decision: The Court ruled that:

1. The wiretapping was legal search for evidence, as the evidence was secured by the use of hearing—only there had been no physical contact. Therefore, the conviction was upheld.
2. Katz could rely on the Fourth Amendment protection against unreasonable search and seizure in the phone booth—that he had the right to privacy in his conversations. He was released.
3. That since there was no entry into the defendant's house or office, a search warrant was not necessary and the Fourth Amendment did not apply. The conviction was upheld.

NOTE: In each case, the number of the actual decision is underlined.

Scoring: Five people on each team—five votes for each team.
1 correct answer—1 point
2 correct answers—2 points
3 correct answers—3 points
4 correct answers—4 points
100% of group with correct answer—6 points
100% of group with wrong answer—subtract 2 points

4

Grading and Testing

GRADING SYSTEM

SHOW ME FORTY TEACHERS AND I'LL SHOW YOU FORTY different systems of grading. It rightly becomes a highly individualized process, and each teacher must determine which method best suits their needs. In presenting my own plan for grading, I offer it not as THE system of grading, but as A system for your consideration.

In covering the subject of grading, I propose to avoid such matters as school board or administration policies, school rules, and various types of report cards. Policies vary a great deal from place to place, and all teachers obviously must work within the confines of such local regulations.

I will state, however, that I prefer to use the old fashioned A B C D E letter grades. I would choose a six week grading period, rather than nine. In addition to the letter grades, I always prefer to have some way to record evaluations of students in terms of effort, attitude, and participation.

I organize my course work so that three kinds of work carry equal weight in the history grade—approximately one-third tests, one-third quizzes, one-third assignments and class work. A point system is used to establish the letter grade. Tests range in point value from 50 to 100 points. Quizzes are generally 10 or 15 questions, worth one point each. Written assignments vary in point value from 20 for a minor report, to 40 for a major map, to 75 for a major paper. (See Chapter 5, current events assignment number three.) For any of these activities—tests, quizzes, or assignments—I set up a grading scale based on the percent figures required by our school. On each test or assignment, the student receives a letter grade and the number of points earned. The scale and distribution of grades is written on the blackboard so that students can see where they stand in relation to others. On a major test, for instance, a student's grade might be 65 C. The scale on the board reads:

Points	*Letter Grades*	*Distribution*
74-80	A	3
68-73	B	7
55-67	C	10
47-54	D	1
0-46	E	2

Thus the student realizes that he had a high C and was, in fact, only a few points from a B.

Students are told that while both the points and the letter grade are recorded in my book, the grade that counts at the end of the grading period is the point value only.

At the end of the grading period, I total all points for the nine week period on a calculator and compute the final letter grade. I find that the maximum number of points for a nine week period generally ranges from 500 to 800.

After report cards are distributed, I have a short conference with each student during the free-wheeling period in class (see Chapter 2). The student is able to see exactly what his total point score was and where it fell on the grading scale. At this time we talk together about his strengths and weaknesses, which are easy to see, as I "cluster" quizzes, tests, and assignments in my grade book. I usually announce the five or six top point scores, and there is frequently lively competition for the top spots on the grading scale.

There is no such thing as a totally objective grading system, but I have found this method to be the fairest one that I can devise. Students rarely question the accuracy of their grades with me. I must confess that this system does involve quite a bit of the teacher's time, but I find it to be well worth the effort.

Grading Written Assignments

Coded Grading Written assignments in general, including the grading thereof, are covered in Chapter 5. Beyond that, I wish to discuss two grading techniques that I have found to be useful.

Since the beginning of time, teachers have struggled with the practical problems that arise when students are given frequent written assignments. Most of us agree that such assignments are an essential part of a good educational program. The limiting factor is time—teacher time. Unless you are fortunate enough to have an average class size of ten or twelve (I'm dreaming already), grading written assignments can be a staggering job. It is important that each student should clearly know that you read his work, analyze it, and evaluate it with care. It is equally important that papers be returned promptly. Therein lies the problem.

I've designed a shortcut that seems to work rather well. As an example, let us refer to a current events assignment, the first one of the year. This assignment is explained in detail in Chapter 5. For our immediate purpose, I shall summarize it briefly here.

Students are required to collect three articles each week on specified topics. Each article is to be summarized in writing and used for classroom discussion on Fridays. At the end of six weeks the entire assignment is submitted to the teacher for evaluation. I evaluate these papers on the following five criteria:

1. *Choice of Articles*—Were they items of importance and interest? Did the articles reflect a variety of news events? Were they articles of substance rather than brief notes on the news?
2. *Organization*—Were the papers fastened together? Were they assembled by the week or by the topics? Were they dated? Was there a table of contents? Was a ''scribble sheet'' provided for the teacher? Was there a cover?
3. *Neatness*—Did the assignment reflect careful handling or did it look as if it had gone through the washing machine? Was it typed or written in ink as required? Was the handwriting clear and legible?
4. *Summaries*—Did they adequately explain the articles? Did they reflect an understanding of the subject by the student? Were the summaries detailed enough to present a clear story to the reader? Were they written in the student's ''own words'' rather than copied from the source used?
5. *Effort*—In relation to the academic skills and shortcomings of the student, what kind of effort is reflected by the total paper?

The following steps are suggested for grading the student's paper:

1 Write each of the five criteria on the student's paper, using only the initial letters:

C

O

N

S

E

2. Grade the paper for each criterion, using the numerical grade equivalents shown in the box in 3 below.
3. Find the average of the five numerical grades, giving equal weight to each item. Determine the overall grade for the project by converting the average to the corresponding letter grade as in the example below:

C	4		A-5
O	4½	18 ÷ 5 = 3.6 = B	B-4
N	2		C-3
S	4		D-2
E	3½		E-1

4. One final step. Since the assignment has a value of 50 points, the B − arrived at in step three is translated into points using a 50-point grading scale. Thus we arrive at both the point and letter grade to record in the grade book.
5. When the papers are returned to the students, they must be given a clear explanation of the coded system used. The teacher can do this verbally, or by writing it on the blackboard, or by using a mimeographed handout.

Check, Check Plus, Check Minus (✓, ✓+, ✓−) There are certain routine assignments that do not call for a letter grade. They are simply learning tasks that are to be performed by all students. One such assignment that comes to mind is the vocabulary list (see Chapter 3). Since most vocabulary words are discussed in class, with a definition put together during the discussion, the teacher can rather quickly go through such papers. A check means that the assignment is completed satisfactorily. It neither raises nor lowers the student's grade. A check minus indicates that the work is acceptable, but not very well done. A check minus should be recorded along with the number of points to be subtracted from the student's grade, for example, check minus six. A check plus indicates an exceptionally good job and should provide for a few points of extra credit, for example, check plus eight.

I recommend this system for the project work in Individualized Instruction (see Chapter 7). Without this shortcut the teacher could never keep up with the mountain of work during this unit.

Extra Credit

I take a dim view of the student who approaches me frantically the day before the end of the grading period and asks to do extra work for extra credit in order to save his grade. That's a classic example of "too little, too late." In general I do not subscribe to the practice of extra credit. I explain to my students that if they wish to improve their grades, they should do so by spending more time on the assigned work. This would include better work on assigned papers, careful reading of the text, and more thorough study for tests and quizzes.

I make one exception. As explained previously, I do allow some points for vocabulary well done. I also permit the students to write identifying sentences on the important people on their lists (see Chapter 3). These will result in extra credit if they are turned in by the end of the unit. There is value in this assignment, as it helps to prepare the student for the unit test.

Quizzes

Quizzes should be given frequently: two or three times a week. This helps the student to assemble material in small doses, thus preparing the way for chapter or unit tests. I generally use fill-ins or true-false for quizzes, with a few multiple choice questions for variety. Students enjoy having an occasional "bonus" question—an extra question that adds a point if answered correctly but carries no penalty if it is missed.

I give most quizzes orally, repeating each question twice. At the end of the quiz, it is a good idea to permit students to ask the teacher to repeat any questions that still puzzle them. As soon as the papers are collected, go over the quiz again, with students supplying the answers.

I require my students to use a full sheet of notebook paper for a quiz. They are told, however, that they may write as many quizzes as they wish on one sheet of paper. As a result, quite a number of the students play little games, competing with one another to see who can fit the most quizzes on a single sheet of paper. It's only a short step further to competing among themselves for the best scores on these quiz sheets. This all adds up to a self-motivating situation that I'm delighted to see in the classroom. I add further momentum by decorating good quiz papers with all manner of stars, sayings, stamps, etc. When I return quiz papers, it interests me to know that students are not saying to one another, "What grade did you get on the quiz?" Instead they ask, "What did she put on your paper? Look what I found on mine."

Believe me, none of the students is too old to enjoy such shenanigans, nor is the teacher.

TESTING

I am stunned by my own temerity. Testing is a subject of such size and scope that a mere chapter in a book will scarcely suffice. And I propose to deal with it in a small section of a chapter!

I'm reminding myself that my goal in writing this book is to present practical procedures and programs to the new teacher, avoiding the theoretical and the philosophical. In this instance, however, I find educational theory to be tugging me in a different direction. Any discussion of testing procedures should at least review the "big three."

1. Is the test valid? Does it measure that which it is designed to measure? In this case, does it measure achievement in American history?
2. Is the test reliable? Does it consistently measure whatever it does measure?
3. Is the test as objective as possible? Is the test result free from the teacher's bias or personal judgment?

Assuming that the goal is to construct tests that consistently measure the student's achievement in American history in an objective fashion, what purpose can be served by tests? Or by grading? Why not do as some suggest and throw out the whole caboodle?

I see testing as a valuable instrument of the educational process that can serve four purposes:

1. Testing serves as an instrument for pupil evaluation. It is one way to measure his progress. It is one of several tools used by a teacher in determining the student's grade.
2. It can serve as an instrument for pupil motivation. Here we need to proceed with caution. Be sure that the "instrument" does not become a "weapon"! Tests must not be overemphasized by either the teacher or the students, and they should never inspire fear.
3. It is an instrument of reinforcement, a learning process in itself. When tests have been given, scored, and returned, the process

of going over the tests together in class can be a valuable learning experience.

4. It can be viewed as an instrument for self-evaluation by the teacher. If results on a test are unsatisfactory, either the test was poorly constructed, or something went awry in the teaching process. Individual questions, missed with great frequency, can indicate, again, either a poorly constructed question or poor teaching. A teacher can learn much about his own performance by a careful study of the test results of his students.

Having established the broad criteria for tests and the reasons for giving them, let us turn to some things to keep in mind when constructing tests.

1. Be sure to have enough items on the test to provide a fair sampling. The test should stress equally all areas of the unit to be tested.
2. Try to go beyond mere fact retention in the tests. The questions should require application and use of facts as well.
3. Include the vocabulary of the subject on every test. Again, I point out the constant goal of competency in our language in every subject (see Chapter 3, Vocabulary).
4. Be careful in your choice of words in constructing your questions. If you lose sight of the vocabulary level of your students, the test could very well turn out to be a test of reading ability or intelligence, rather than one measuring achievement in American history.
5. Avoid trick questions, and the teacher comment that often accompanies such questions, "Aha! I caught you on that one." You are testing students, not tricking them.
6. Be very sure that directions on the test are complete and clear.
7. Include a variety of questioning techniques on each test. Different students will be more adept at handling different methods of testing. A variety is fairer to all, and good experience for all students.
8. Whatever the types of questions, take pains to see to it that correct responses to questions occur in random order. Any kind of pattern in the answers should be avoided.

Essay Tests

The new teacher very quickly learns that essay tests are easy to construct and difficult to correct. Conversely, the objective questions are easy to evaluate, but require many hours of work to construct. There are advantages to both, and both should be included in major tests.

I am a staunch advocate of essay testing and wish that it were used more widely in secondary schools today. Such tests give the students good experience in interpreting and analyzing. Essay tests help to develop skills in organizing material. They serve to develop logical thinking. And above all, they provide the students with valuable experience in writing.

There are disadvantages to essay testing. It is a time consuming and difficult task to grade them objectively. The grading process can easily be thrown off balance by such factors as handwriting, spelling, grammar, and just plain bluffing. Essay tests necessarily contain few items. Therefore, an adequate sampling will not be achieved. I do feel, however, that the merits of essays outweigh the disadvantages.

When constructing essay questions, be sure that they are broad enough to require rather extensive answers. At the same time, it is important that each question be well defined and very clear. If you are giving just one essay question on a test, you may decide to provide two questions and permit the student to choose just one.

I generally make it a practice to give unit tests, rather than chapter tests. The point value of such a test is usually about 70 or 75 points. On each test I include one big essay question with a grade value of 10 points. The remaining questions are various forms of objective testing.

Here are a few examples of essay questions:

1. Andrew Jackson as president is described by some historians as "King Andrew," while others refer to him as "The Champion of Democracy." Which of these two titles best fits your view of Jackson? Give reasons for your answer.
2. Compare and contrast the empires in the New World built by Spain, France, and England. What similarities did they have? How did they differ?
3. Summarize the arguments used for and against the taxation policies of England that affected the colonies. What were England's reasons for taxing the colonists? What were the colonists' reasons for opposing them?

Objective Tests

There are clearly some advantages to objective testing. It is easier to achieve validity, reliability, and objectivity by using objective test questions rather than essays. The teacher can score objective tests more easily and quickly. The sampling in such tests can be much more extensive.

There are disadvantages as well. The construction of a good objective test is a time consuming process. Also, there is always the danger of including too much minutia in this type of testing.

I have discovered many types of objective testing techniques that are applicable to American history. I will examine 11 of these briefly and give examples of each type.

Multiple Choice This method is familiar to most of us and needs little explanation. Make it a practice to include at least four choices for each question. It is also a good idea to write the question with the longest part of the sentence in the "stem" rather than in the answers. If the four choices are too wordy, the student becomes involved in the tedious procedure of unscrambling each question before he or she can answer it. It is also wise to keep all four answers about the same length.

Directions: Each of the following statements can be completed by the words or phrases that follow it. Choose the best possible word or phrase to complete each sentence and place the letter of it in the space to the left of the number.

__B__ **1.** A function of the Supreme Court is to rule on whether or not a bill or law A. is properly written; B. is constitutional; C. is good for the majority of the people; D. can function in our government.

__C__ **2.** The President's veto can be overridden by a two-third vote of A. the Senate; B. the House of Representatives; C. both houses; D. the Supreme Court.

__C__ **3.** The executive branch of our government is headed by the A. Chief Justice; B. Congress; C. President; D. House of Representatives.

__D__ **4.** One power that Congress lacked under the Articles of Confederation was the power to A. raise an army; B. declare war; C. borrow money; D. tax.

Reverse Multiple Choice This variation of multiple choice is a particularly good technique to use when you wish to be sure that students can recognize a number of items that belong together.

Directions: Indicate the item that does not fit with the others. Three answers are correct—choose the one *wrong* answer. Put the letter in front of it in the blank space.

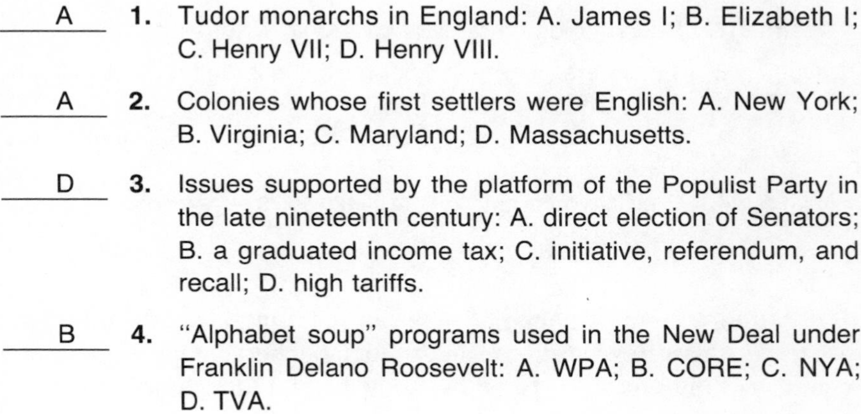

__A__ **1.** Tudor monarchs in England: A. James I; B. Elizabeth I; C. Henry VII; D. Henry VIII.

__A__ **2.** Colonies whose first settlers were English: A. New York; B. Virginia; C. Maryland; D. Massachusetts.

__D__ **3.** Issues supported by the platform of the Populist Party in the late nineteenth century: A. direct election of Senators; B. a graduated income tax; C. initiative, referendum, and recall; D. high tariffs.

__B__ **4.** "Alphabet soup" programs used in the New Deal under Franklin Delano Roosevelt: A. WPA; B. CORE; C. NYA; D. TVA.

Alternative Response Questions Any question that requires the students to choose between two answers is called an alternative response question. The true-false question is the most commonly known form of alternate response technique. True-false questions are rather easy to construct. For that reason, they are often used rather carelessly. They should be used only to measure knowledge of very specific facts. The questions should be short and contain only one idea.

Directions: Write the word True or False in the blank space in front of each statement.

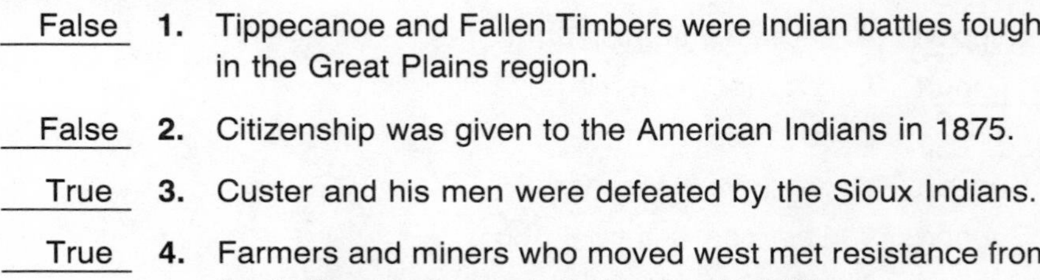

__False__ **1.** Tippecanoe and Fallen Timbers were Indian battles fought in the Great Plains region.

__False__ **2.** Citizenship was given to the American Indians in 1875.

__True__ **3.** Custer and his men were defeated by the Sioux Indians.

__True__ **4.** Farmers and miners who moved west met resistance from the Indians in the period after the Civil War.

Another type of alternative response gives as choices two terms that are opposites. The examples listed here could be used in a geography test. I consider this type of question to be most appropriate in geography or science.

Directions: In each question you will find two words underlined. Choose the correct word and write it in front of the number.

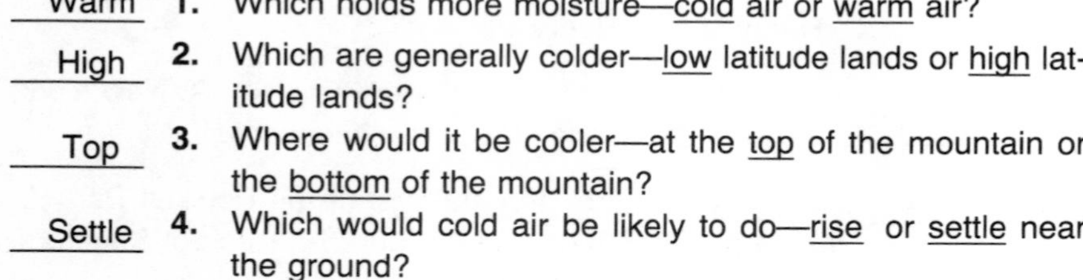

Warm **1.** Which holds more moisture—cold air or warm air?

High **2.** Which are generally colder—low latitude lands or high latitude lands?

Top **3.** Where would it be cooler—at the top of the mountain or the bottom of the mountain?

Settle **4.** Which would cold air be likely to do—rise or settle near the ground?

A third example of alternative response testing is excellent for history tests. Answering questions that call for a Support or Oppose response requires not only recall of facts, but some careful thought and analysis.

Directions: In the last half of the nineteenth century, labor union members took a stand on many issues. Indicate which of the following things were supported by union members by writing the word Support in front of the number. Write the word Oppose in front of things not supported by the unions.

Oppose **1.** unrestricted immigration

Support **2.** Molly Maguires

Oppose **3.** blacklists

Support **4.** collective bargaining

Support **5.** grievance committees

Oppose **6.** child labor

Support **7.** graduated income tax

Support **8.** Sherman Anti-trust Act

Oppose **9.** court injunctions

Oppose **10.** lockouts

Fill-ins Completion questions, or fill-ins, are quite versatile. They can be used in dealing with many kinds of material. In constructing such questions, it is important to avoid long unwieldy sentences. It is best to leave only one blank in a statement. Avoid giving clues to the correct responses by keeping the blanks uniform in size. It is a good idea to put the blanks in front of the questions and indicate where they belong in the statement by a very small blank. This makes it easier to score the test.

Directions: Fill in the blank spaces with the proper word or phrase.

Tories **1.** The name applied to the colonists who supported the king's cause during the American Revolution was ____.

Harding **2.** President ____ was the first American President to set up a disarmament conference among the world powers.

Amend-ment **3.** An addition to, or a change in, a law is called an ____.

Slander **4.** Injuring a person's reputation by saying something untruthful about him is known as ____.

Cause and Effect This is a particularly good technique for use in history tests. It is important in a study of history to recognize significant events as causative factors.

Directions: Listed here are four pairs of events. In each pair, one event helped to cause the other. In the blank space, write the letter of the event that caused the other one to happen.

A **1.** A. Spanish Armada is defeated.
B. England establishes colonies in the New World.

B **2.** A. The new Republican Party is formed.
B. The Kansas-Nebraska Act is passed.

A **3.** A. World War II breaks out.
B. The United Nations is formed.

A **4.** A. There is much speculation in the stock market.
B. The crash of '29 starts the Great Depression.

Classification This technique is frequently useful in history tests. Suppose that you have just completed a unit on social changes in America during the nineteenth century. Such a unit would introduce the names of many people to the students. In the test you might have a section with the following headings: author, painter, inventor, reformer. These headings would be accompanied by a list of ten or twelve people, and the challenge is to place each name under the proper heading.

Or you may wish to test the students' ability to associate American Presidents with important events.

Directions: In the blank space in front of the number, place the name of the person who was in office when the event occurred.

Madison	**1.**	War of 1812
Jackson	**2.**	Beginning of the Spoils System
Jefferson	**3.**	Louisiana Purchase
T. Roose-velt	**4.**	Panama Canal started
Hoover	**5.**	Depression of 1929

Sequence I thoroughly disapprove of wholesale memorization of dates in a history course. This practice is one of the things that has given the study of history a bad name. Throughout the course, very few dates should be stressed as "key" dates—dates that mark events that are so significant that they have changed the direction of the society under study. It is important, however, for the student to recognize the sequence of events, especially in a period of history where one step logically follows another. A fine example of this is the ten year period preceding the Civil War, as well as the war years themselves. A sequence question is very appropriate for this period.

Directions: The events listed here are "scrambled." They are not in the proper order. There are ten events, each with a letter in front of it. In the blank space beside number 1, place the *letter* for the event which happened first. Then locate the event that happened next and place the proper letter in the number 2 space. The event that happened third should be placed in the number 3 space. Continue in this fashion until each of the 10 letters is placed in the proper blank space.

A.	Emancipation Proclamation	**1.**	D
B.	Lincoln-Douglas Debates	**2.**	G
C.	Formation of the Confederacy	**3.**	J
D.	Compromise of 1850	**4.**	B
E.	Surrender of Lee at Appomattox	**5.**	I
F.	Secession of South Carolina	**6.**	F
G.	Kansas-Nebraska Act	**7.**	C
H.	Death of Lincoln	**8.**	A
I.	Election of Lincoln	**9.**	E
J.	Formation of Republican Party	**10.**	H

It is important for the new teacher to realize that the sample sequence shown here would not be given to students unfamiliar with this technique. Such a procedure would surely result in confusion. When students are first given sequence questions, the exercise should contain only five items. As they become more comfortable with this kind of testing, the teacher may include more items.

I offer a clue that may help teachers in grading sequence questions. I mark incorrect the *minimum* number of items which, if moved, would make the entire sequence correct. I could take two pages to explain that statement, but choose to decline. Consider it to be a challenge, a brain teaser from the author to the reader!

Matching I find matching questions to be particularly good for testing knowledge of vocabulary words or important people in history. A set of matching questions should not contain less than five items nor more than ten. Keep identifying phrases brief. Only one correct matching for each item should be possible. It is wise to include more answers than questions. In the example below, you will find five phrases and seven answers, two of which will not be used by the student.

Directions: Place the proper letter in the blank space.

__E__ **1.** Drilled for oil in Pennsylvania
__G__ **2.** Invented the telephone
__A__ **3.** Banking and steel tycoon

___F___ **4.** Laid the first transatlantic cable

___C___ **5.** An automobile inventor

A. J. P. Morgan
B. Richard Hoe
C. Ransom Olds
D. Christopher Sholes
E. Edwin Drake
F. Cyrus Field
G. Alexander Graham Bell

Maps Map questions should be a part of every geography test and a part of every history test where applicable. I do not, for instance, give map questions on the test on the United States Constitution!

Questions on maps should involve more than basic place geography. They should go further and require a knowledge of events in relation to places.

Directions: On the map below, and in the questions that follow, the numerals 1 through 8 refer to sections of the United States. On the line in front of each question, write the letter of the alternative that best answers the question.

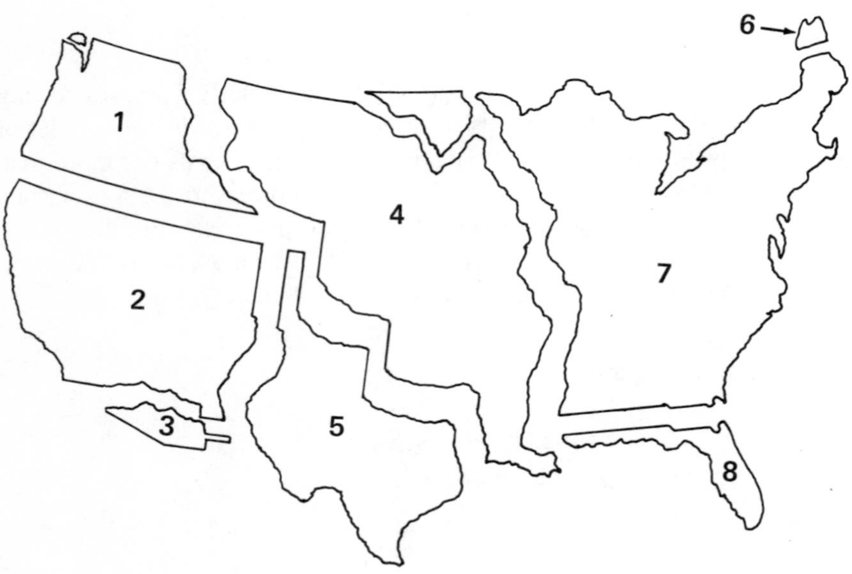

A ___ **1.** The slogan, "fifty-four forty or fight" referred to land in area
A. 1 B. 2 C. 6 D. 8

B ___ **2.** The Compromise of 1820 was necessary because of the land in
A. 2 B. 4 C. 5 D. 8

B ___ **3.** Lewis and Clark explored the lands in
A. 8 B. 1 and 4 C. 5 D. 2 and 5

B ___ **4.** Gold was discovered in
A. 4 B. 2 C. 5 D. 3

C ___ **5.** Polk was particularly interested in the land in
A. 6 B. 8 C. 1 and 5 D. 4 and 7

Review for Tests

Good procedures for review definitely should be a part of the teaching process. Students need careful guidance from the teacher in order to develop review skills. Some suggestions follow:

1. Discuss with the class the kinds of things that should be studied for a unit test—vocabulary, important people, map work, class notes, or whatever applies to the particular unit of study.
2. Call attention to any handouts, especially study sheets, that may be helpful. See Chapter 3, Handouts.
3. Encourage students to study for the test in pairs or small groups. When possible, allow some class time for this.
4. Set aside a classroom period (preferably the day before the test) for some kind of organized review for the entire class.

Review Through Games Students respond well to any kind of contest or competition used in the review process. This can be part of the class review period. I shall describe just one such review game as a sample.

An assignment is given the day before the review session—each student is to construct five short answer questions on the unit. The questions and their answers must be in writing. Any student who fails to complete this assignment must write 25 questions as a penalty. The penalty is designed to ensure that all students will be prepared and ready to participate.

On the review day the class is divided into two teams. A person from team A stands up, calls on any person he chooses from team B, and asks him a question. If the person from team B can answer the question, team B gets a point. If he cannot answer the question, the person from team A who originally asked the question may call on any volunteer from his own team (A) to answer it. In this case, team A can earn a point.

Next, the person from team B who was asked the first question (whether he answered correctly or not) chooses someone from team A to answer his question. The game goes on from there until everyone has been called on at least once. This simple review game is remarkably popular with the students and generates considerable excitement when the score is close. I encourage you to use a little imagination, time, and effort to devise some games of your own.

Extra Help Throughout the year I offer extra help before each unit test to students who might benefit from such assistance. This is a special review session held after school the night before a test. This session is designed to help only those students who have great difficulty passing tests. Students must get my permission to take part in this, as it is most effective when the group is rather small. I attempt to make this review very detailed and very thorough. There are usually about ten to twelve students who take advantage of this opportunity and are willing to put in the extra time. This kind of study in a small group does seem to be quite helpful to students who find history difficult.

Passaround Tests[1] Some teachers use the passaround test as a regular test for evaluation. I prefer to use it as a tool for review, and I have constructed a test for each unit in the course for this purpose.

To construct passaround tests, you will need a supply of unlined 5 × 8-inch cards, some transparent tape, and a number of old history textbooks that can be destroyed. Find in these books all of the maps, graphs, charts, and pictures—in short, anything visual—that deal with the unit being studied. Tape each visual to a card and construct a question that relates to the visual. The question should be typed on the card. When all of the cards are assembled, arrange them in a sequence by writing a number in the corner of each card. If you have 30 cards, the numbers will range from 1 to 30.

---

[1]Idea for this activity courtesy of Tony Niccoli, Social Studies Teacher, Brecksville Junior High School.

Students are instructed to number a sheet of paper from 1 to 30—each number on a separate line. The teacher distributes the cards face down, one to each student. On signal, each student reads the question on his card and answers it on his paper beside the corresponding number. Students are allowed only 30 seconds to answer a question. The teacher sets a timer and when the bell rings, each student must pass his card to the next person, at the same time receiving one. The method of passing the cards must be clearly understood by all students to avoid confusion during the test. See the sketch below.

Note the runner. It is considered an honor to be chosen for this post. The runner has a challenging job. During a period of 30 seconds,

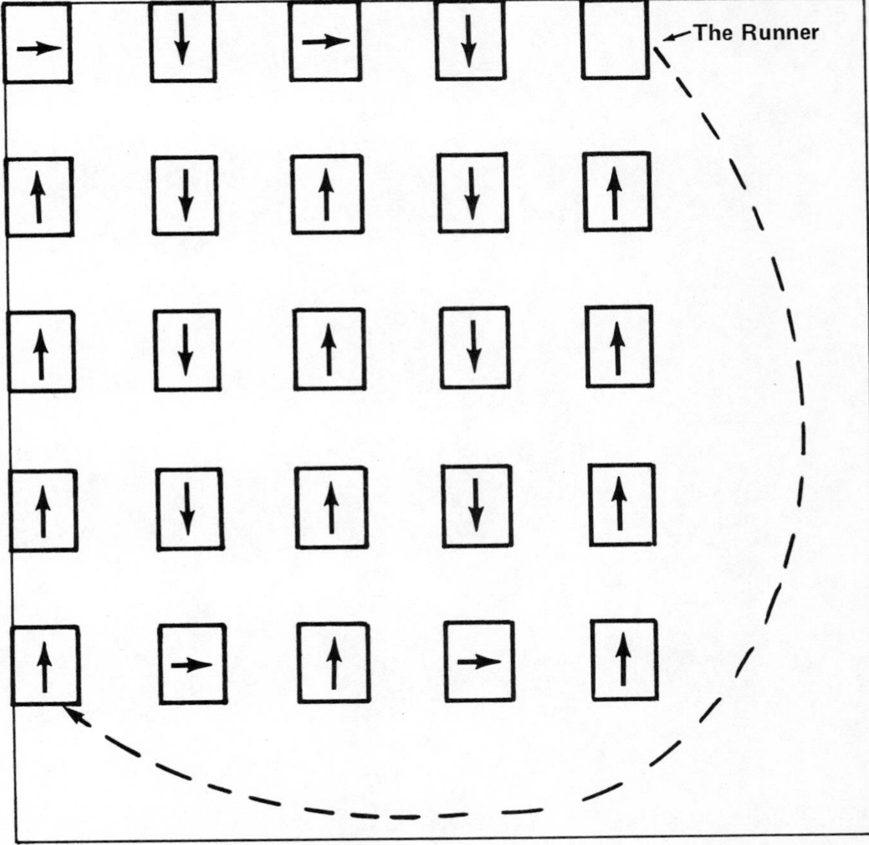

the runner must answer a question, carry the question card to the front of the room on the opposite side, and return in time for the next card.

These passaround tests are fun, and there is built-in excitement in keeping pace with the clock.

A sample of one passaround test covering the Jacksonian era and westward expansion is included between pages 104 and 105.

5

Current Events

WRITTEN ASSIGNMENTS

BEGINNING WITH THIS CHAPTER, IT IS MY INTENTION to deal with assignments and programs. Before we can get into the topic of current events, it is first necessary to turn our attention to written assignments in general. The comments and suggestions set forth in this section apply not only to this chapter, but to any written assignments that may be covered in the remainder of the book.

It is wise to put the assignment in writing and give a mimeographed copy to each student. Be sure that these directions are clear and complete. Instructions on mechanics should be specific—pen or pencil, spacing, margins, length of report, sources to be used, etc. The due date and the point value should be stated.

Written instructions are not sufficient. Follow through by going over the assignment verbally with each class and allow plenty of time for doing so. Encourage questions on the assignment from the students. Major projects and programs require specially detailed explanations. I spend a full class period explaining each of the programs discussed in Chapters 6, 7, and 8.

Share your objectives for any assignment with the students. What do you expect them to learn from this assignment? What skills will they be developing? How will this assignment help them?

Set very high standards of performance for the students on all such assignments. If you do not care about the quality of their work, they rarely will either. Let your students know that you will be very particular about spelling, grammar, sentence structure, and punctuation. You should also stress neatness, thoroughness, careful research—in short, you should expect each student to develop a habit of doing his best possible work on each assignment. This is a habit that can help him for the rest of his life.

You have an obligation to the students to be just as tough on yourself. A student who puts forth a great deal of effort on a written assignment needs to know that you will give that paper careful attention. Evaluate each paper with care. Use your red pen liberally, both to point out errors and to call attention to strong points. A particularly good learning experience results when you are prompted by the student's paper to "talk back to him," in marginal notes that raise questions, or challenge his thinking, or reinforce what he is saying. Be as prompt as possible in returning any assignment turned in by your students. If they have been motivated to turn in their very best work, they will be very eager to get it back. If you form a habit of returning papers three weeks after the due date, the assignment will have lost much of its meaning.

Don't forget that your approach to any assignment will set the tone for your classes. This brings us back to something that I stressed in Chapter 1—enthusiasm. If you cannot project enthusiasm for an assignment as you give it, it ought to be scrapped as a poor assignment. If you offer a project apologetically, just forget about the whole thing. If you offer it in a dull uninspired manner, you will receive dull uninspired work. Be confident, positive, and exciting when introducing any assignment or project.

CURRENT EVENTS IN GENERAL

Current Events—World Affairs—Weekly News—World Problems—whatever name you choose to call it, this is clearly a topic that has an important place in any history course. I consider it an absurdity to teach any kind of history without including the current problems to be solved at the national and international levels. It would be rather like serving a seven course dinner and omitting the entree!

Some teachers feel that junior high school students lack the background for understanding world affairs. They throw in the sponge and refuse to cover current events until close to the end of the year when the students have covered most of our history in sequential order. I consider that to be unacceptable.

Other teachers order standard printed weekly news magazines that are written for students and set aside a certain amount of time for discussing these papers. This I believe is acceptable, but not inspiring, unless the teacher is unusually skillful. If current events are covered routinely, always in the same fashion, they can get to be a "drag."

A creative imaginative approach in planning a coordinated program in current events for the entire year can do much to get the kids tuned-in to world affairs. The remainder of this chapter will cover the current events program that I have designed for my classroom. I do not present it as THE way to teach this subject, but as A way, AN approach. It is, and must be, subject to change, affected by the limitations imposed by time, by the abilities of the students, and by current events themselves.

As I plan my program for the year, I consider anything in the post-World War II period to be a part of current events. This concept may come as a shock to those young teachers who weren't even born by 1945! Let me attempt to justify this approach:

- How can you possibly explain the mess in the Middle East to teenagers without going back to the creation of Israel in 1948? (You may even wish to start with biblical Palestine.)
- How can you discuss the Satellite Countries, the Iron Curtain, or the Warsaw Pact without understanding how this situation came about?
- How can students talk about a current problem before the United Nations without knowing its background and function?
- How can any news coming out of East Germany or West Germany have any meaning without discussing the original separation and the continuing problems there?
- How can the students begin to understand our complicated maneuverings with the Soviet Union without some knowledge of what has gone before?

In other words, junior high school students do have a ''knowledge gap'' in terms of understanding current affairs. In order to combat that, our post World War II history should be gradually fed into the current events program as needed.

Each part of this program has definite objectives that will be explained as I cover the specific assignments. There are six assignments proposed here. Each one may be adapted to cover a three-, four-, five-, or six-week period. I usually find it advisable to allow one week (a break) between assignments.

The remainder of this chapter will be devoted to discussing each of these six assignments. In each case I will introduce the assignment with instruction sheets that describe the work to be completed just as it is described to the students. This is followed by a discussion of the objectives involved, as well as suggestions for implementing them.

Current Events—First Assignment

Student Instruction Sheet Your first current events assignment is designed to get you acquainted with the daily newspaper. You are required to bring to class each Friday three articles from the papers as follows:

No. 1

This is a picture of an early American locomotive.

A. Who invented the first American locomotive?

B. What was the name given to that engine?

No. 18

A. Which came first — the steamboat or the locomotive?

B. Which came first — Independence of Texas or California Gold Rush?

C. Which came first — purchase of Florida or the Gadsden Purchase?

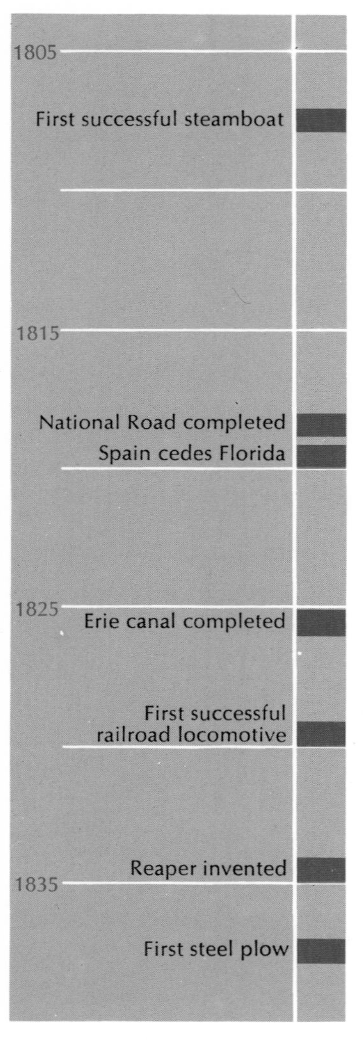

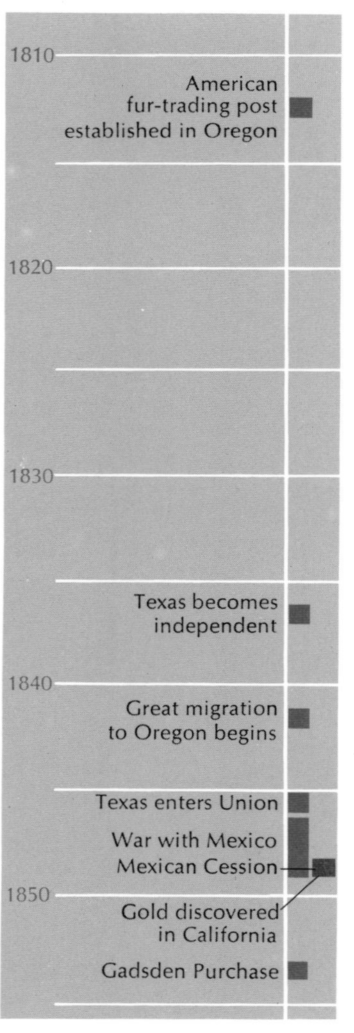

No. 12

Use the letters on the map to show:

A. letter and name for the road that was used the most in the westward movement.

B. letter and name for the road that was started during the French and Indian war.

C. letter and name of the road started by Daniel Boone.

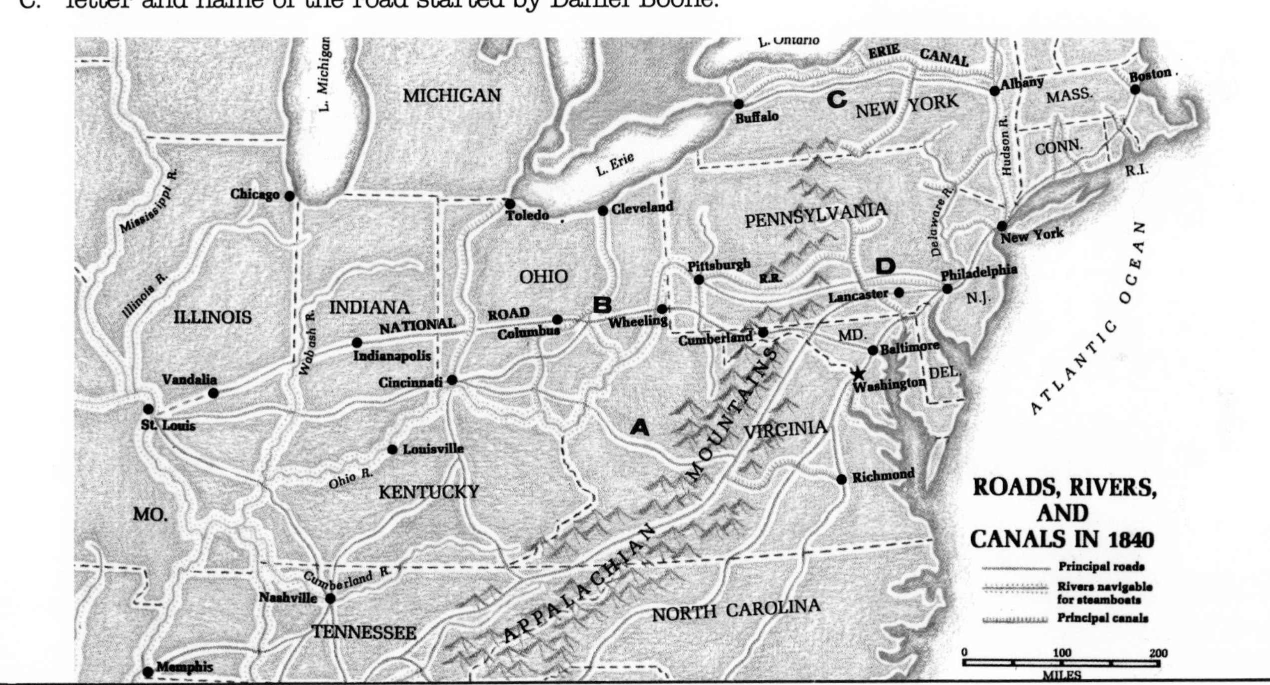

No. 16

"Liberty and Union, now and forever, one and inseparable . . . ."

A. Who is the speaker shown in this famous painting?

B. Who was his opponent in this debate in the Senate?

No. 28

A. When the Oregon question was settled in 1846, what country was on the southern border of Oregon?

B. On what latitude line did Polk hope to establish the northern border of Oregon?

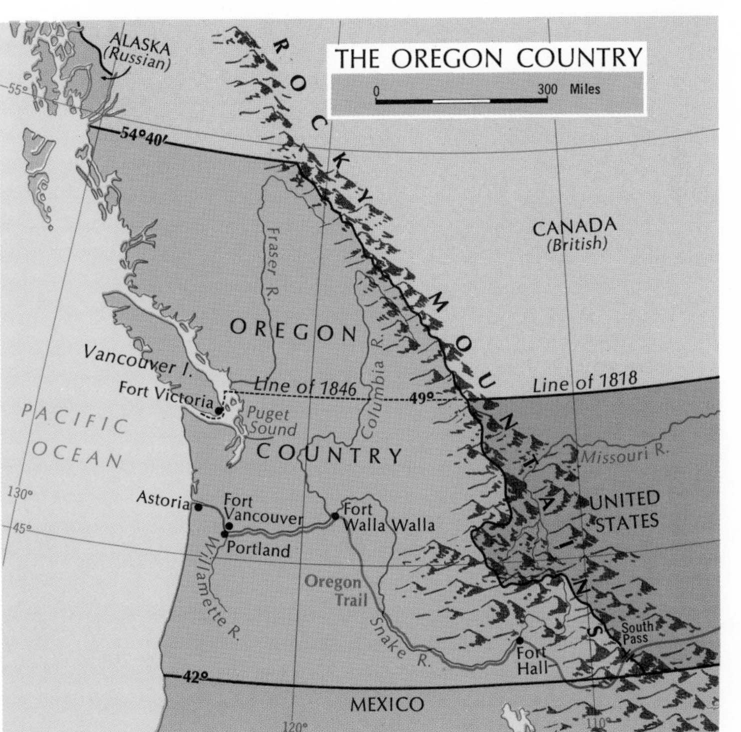

No. 21

A. Which was the 14th state admitted to the Union?

B. Which was the 18th state admitted to the Union?

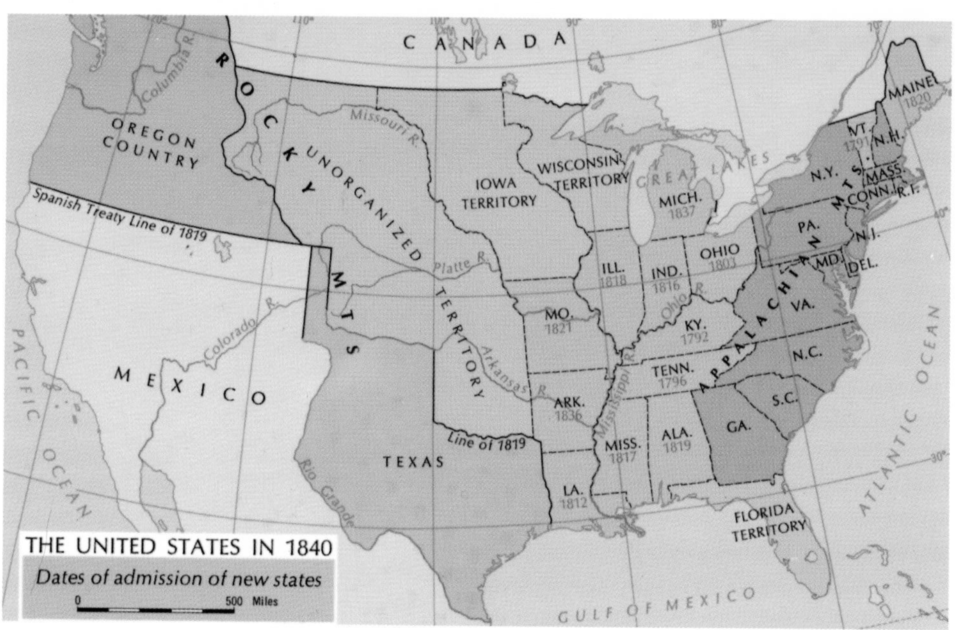

No. 29

Name three rivers, shown on this map, that were followed by any of the early western trails.

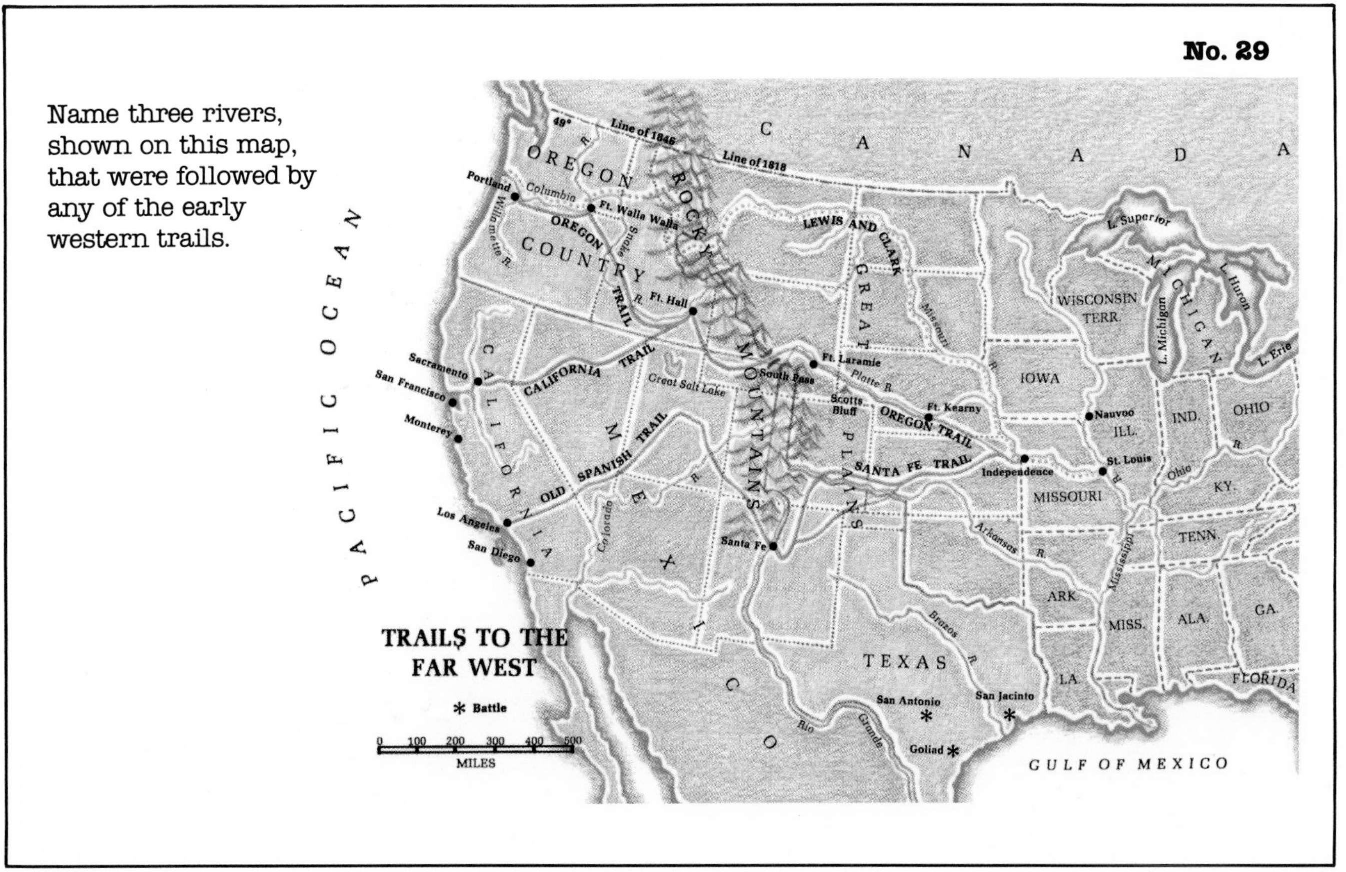

No. 30

A. From what country did we get the Oregon Country?

B. From what country did we get Louisiana?

C. From what country did we get Florida?

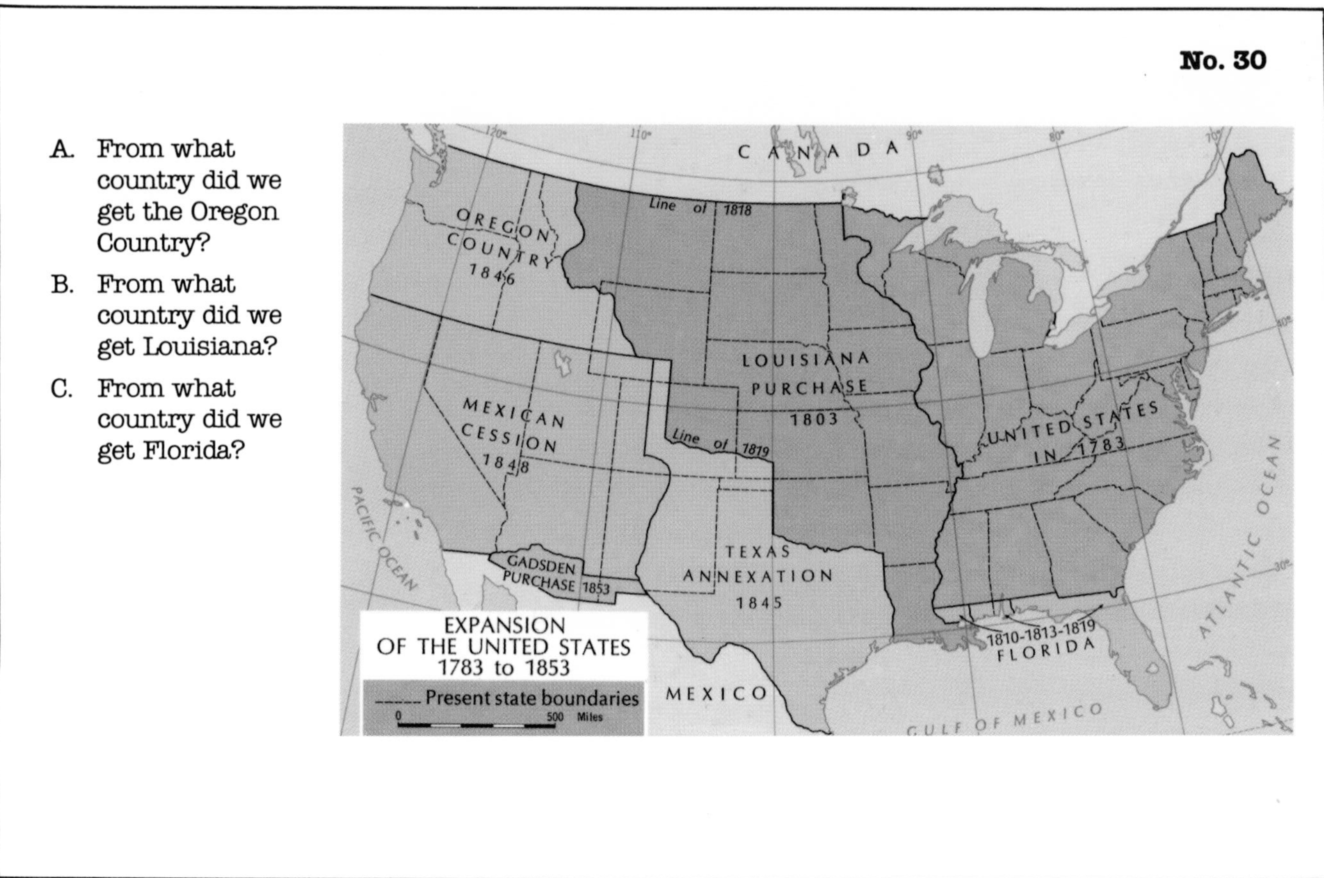

1. One article on foreign affairs. It should involve news of some other nation and, preferably, news that also relates to our country.
2. The second article is to be on domestic news—some topic that applies just to our country.
3. The third article must be on an interesting person in the news. This person need not be someone "important." It should be someone whom you found to be interesting.

Each of these articles is to be mounted on notebook paper. You are required to write a short summary on each article. In addition you should be prepared to report verbally to the class on one of your articles, whichever one you choose. In giving the verbal report, you are not permitted to read. You must talk to the class, clearly, and in an interesting fashion. You may refer to notes, however.

This assignment will be repeated for five weeks. By that time you will have collected a total of fifteen articles (each mounted and summarized). On the fifth Friday, the entire assignment is to be assembled, organized, fastened together, and turned in to the teacher for grading purposes. No material will be collected before the fifth Friday.

As we do this assignment for five weeks, the major emphasis will be on foreign affairs. Each Friday we will spend half of the period discussing some area of the world that is currently important to us. The teacher will give some historical background about this area and the problems therein. This will be followed by general discussion and questions. The second half of the period on each of these Fridays will be devoted to the verbal reports prepared by the students.

Areas scheduled for special emphasis (subject to change):

- First Friday—The Panama Canal
- Second Friday—The Middle East
- Third Friday—Russia and the United States
- Fourth Friday—China, Formosa, and the United States
- Fifth Friday—Crisis in Ireland

If you can find an article that fits with the topic of the week for your foreign affairs article, it will be helpful for our class discussion.

Due Date ______________________ Point Value ____

Let us consider the objectives for this assignment:

1. To bring the students up to date on the various trouble spots in the world. The teacher has an opportunity here to fill in any knowledge gaps.
2. To encourage the students to become interested in a daily adult newspaper beyond the funnies, the sports pages, and Ann Landers. Emphasis will probably be on front page news stories.
3. To give the students experience in making formal verbal presentations before the class. A survey cited in *The Book of Lists* stated that in a list of things that adults fear most, the number one fear was speaking before a group!
4. To develop the students' skills in reading an article and summarizing the important points in brief form.
5. To try to develop a sense of responsibility in these young people that will permit them to complete successfully a long range assignment that lasts for five weeks.
6. To allow ample opportunity for open discussion and exchange of opinions on current news.
7. And since it is the first current events assignment of the year, this exchange of news and views will hopefully facilitate the process of getting acquainted in the classroom.

I add a word of caution about this assignment. I always explain to the students that I am not interested in hearing about Betty-Boop-Boop-A-Doop, the movie star who just divorced her sixth husband. Nor am I interested in hearing about Joe Doaks who took an ax and chopped up six people. In other words, avoid the sensational and the trivial.

I do not give any tests nor quizzes on this assignment. Nor do I require the students to take notes. I explain that I do require their full attention and participation.

On the fifth Friday I go home carrying about 135 sets of current events papers, and I hole up for the weekend in order to grade them and return them by Monday. This is one of the occasions when I find a coded grading system to be very useful (see Chapter 4).

At this point both students and teacher feel that it is time to lay this assignment aside and move on to another approach.

Current Events—Second Assignment

Student Instruction Sheet The study of news for the next five weeks will be limited to "Domestic Issues" that are important at this time. You are to become an "expert" on one of the topics listed below. Choose just *one* topic; collect several articles on this topic during the next five weeks. Choose the eight best articles and write a report on your topic based on these articles plus what you have heard on radio and television. In addition, you should obtain some recent material from the school library. Your report should be about three pages in length (one side of the paper). It may be typed if you wish; if so, please double space. The report should be based only on current news and should contain what you have learned, *as well as your own opinions,* about your findings. Your eight best articles should be mounted and included with the report.

Due Date ______________________________ Point Value _________

1. *The November Elections*—Local, state, or national candidates and issues—results of elections.
2. *The Ecology*—Preservation of our environment—pollution problems.
3. *The Economy*—High cost of living, unemployment, high taxes, inflation, etc.
4. *Food*—Food shortages, rising food prices, beef, grain, bumper wheat crop, etc.
5. *Health and Medicine*—New breakthroughs in medicine, research; Public Health, cost of health care.
6. *Transportation*—Problems with big city traffic, highway safety, airlines, railroads.
7. *Local News*—Suburban news with emphasis on the Brecksville-Broadview Hts. area.
8. *Education:* Local, state, national—Educational standards, school problems, money for schools, new trends, etc.
9. *The Energy Crisis*—Oil, atomic energy, electricity, heat for the winter, coal supplies, costs.

10. *Busing* (students)—For the purpose of racial integration in schools; local and national.
11. *American Leaders in the News*—Cabinet members, governors, mayors, Congressmen, etc. (no election news here).
12. *Young People in the News*—Their problems, accomplishments, and contributions to our society.
13. *Animals*—Treatment of, overpopulation of, endangered species, protection.
14. *The United States' Security System*—The C.I.A., F.B.I., and others.
15. *Crime in the Cities and the Nation*—Types of crime and problems caused (include kidnapping and terrorism).
16. *The Military*—The Pentagon, military services, the national defense system.
17. *Big Business:* The stock market—Business trends, news, and problems.
18. *Outer Space*—Present or future programs in space—cooperation with Russia on this matter.
19. *The Consumer*—Problems, protection for the consumer—Nader, Myerson, Furness.
20. *Welfare*—Aid to dependent mothers, slum clearance, payments to the unemployed, food stamps, etc.
21. *Problems of the Aged*—Social Security, retirement problems, nursing home care, health.

The current events program for the first five weeks required one-fifth of our history class time. This allocation of time is a luxury that a teacher can scarcely afford on a year long basis. The primary consideration in developing the second assignment is to continue to expand the students' interest and knowledge in current affairs while devoting less class time to it. Hence, the student is turned loose for the five week period to follow one topic and write a paper on it. During this period of time, I set aside about 15 minutes of a class period two or three times for general class discussion on the things that they are finding on their assigned subjects.

There are several things to be gained from this assignment:

1. The student is allowed to follow a topic in which he or she has a particular interest and can share that interest with the class.
2. The student is less dependent on the teacher for this assignment than for the first one, and that is as it should be.
3. The student is forced to put together a report from several sources in his or her own words. I am appalled each year with the realization that to many young students writing a report means finding a good encyclopedia and copying! This is a habit I wish to break.
4. The student develops some awareness of the variety and complexity of domestic issues in this country.
5. The student is required to express his own views, raise his own questions, offer his own solutions. I offer a word of warning on this subject to new teachers. After all these years of teaching, I am still surprised each year to realize anew how very hesitant most eighth graders are to write about their personal opinions on issues. This is an area where most young people seem to be sadly lacking self-confidence. I must convince them each year that I want to hear from THEM, that their opinions do have merit, that thinking through a problem, taking a position, and defending that position are vital parts of the educational process.

I have found it helpful in this assignment to suggest that each student should select a first and a second choice of topics to follow. He should clip articles on both subjects for a time. Thus, if he comes up dry in material for his first choice, he has something in reserve and can simply switch topics.

In grading these reports, again you may find a coded grading system to be useful (see Chapter 4). However, in this instance, I believe that extra weight should be given to the report itself and the thinking that it reflects.

Current Events—Third Assignment

Student Instruction Sheet The current events topics for study during the next few weeks are of great importance. Please try to inform yourself as fully as possible on your assigned subject before you start to write your paper. Our school library has many materials on this assignment. Mrs. Stoddard is very familiar with these materials and is ready to give you assistance. It would be wise to get started on this assignment quite soon, rather than put it off till the last minute.

Each student is to write a paper from four to six pages in length on the assigned topic. Be careful to include all the information required below, as well as anything else that would make your topic more interesting or informative. Papers should be written in ink or typewritten. If you use the typewriter, please double space. Papers are worth 75 points—equal to a major test. A bibliography must be included with each report.

Topics:

1. *The United Nations*—Date formed, purpose, number of members, location of meetings, groups within the U.N. and their functions (the 6 major ones), problems solved in the past by the U.N., financing of this organization, officials of the U.N. and the people who have held the top post, problems currently facing the U.N., outlook for its future, your own opinions and analysis of this organization.
2. *Any Military Alliance*—Write on just *one*, for example, NATO, SEATO, OAS, ANZUS, the Warsaw Pact, or any other military alliance that interests you. In each case, tell what the initials stand for, the countries involved in the alliance, the terms or provisions of the alliance, the date when it was formed, the reasons why it was formed, the effect of the group on the United States, achievements of the alliance, problems of the alliance, your own opinions and analysis of this group and its future.
3. *Any Economic Alliance*—Write on just *one,* for example, European Common Market, British Commonwealth of Nations, Alliance for Progress, or any other economic alliance that interests you. In each case, give the countries involved, the reason for the alliance, date when it was formed, progress of the group, problems of the group, effect of the group on the United States, your own opinion and analysis.
4. *The Civil Rights Movement*—You may write on the Movement in general or any one group, for example, NAACP, CORE, Black Muslims, Black Panthers, or any other Civil Rights group that you

know of. Or, you may choose to combine two of the groups. In any approach, give some background to indicate why these groups formed, date when formed, membership, accomplishments, problems still to be solved by the group, impact on our country, your own opinion or analysis.

5. *Activist Groups—Reform*—The 1960's and 70's will probably go down in history as one of our greatest "reform periods." There are many movements in the country that are trying to get "action" and bring about basic change and reform in many different areas. Your assignment is to write a paper on these reform groups in general, or any one of the groups listed below, or any combination of groups listed below that interests you. In some cases you will find that highly organized groups exist. Consider also the loosely organized or spontaneous outbreaks that indicate a desire for reform. What are the specific aims of these movements? What has been accomplished in reform in the last 10 or 15 years? What are some of the problems faced by these groups? What problems do these groups pose for society? For the government? For the police?

   Feminist Movement
   Student demonstrations and student groups (demonstrating for change in schools or more rights for minors)
   Draft dodgers—War deserters—Pacifists—Amnesty problems
   Prison reform
   Welfare reform
   Ecology groups
   (Any others you'd like to include?)

6. *The Peace Corps* (For only one student in each class.)—Give the history of the Peace Corps, when founded, reasons for this organization, requirements for volunteers, countries affected by this group, kinds of work involved, problems of the Corps, your own opinion and analysis.

If you do not care for the topic assigned to you, you may choose another one of the topics listed *only* if you can get someone assigned to that topic to "swap" with you.

Due Date ____________________ Let's have all papers turned in on time.

Now, if you have recovered from the shock, let us proceed. This is obviously an ambitious project for eighth graders. As a matter of fact, it could properly be considered a term paper, as many students go far beyond the minimum requirements of this assignment.

My main objectives are:

1. To provide all the students with as much information as possible on all of the assigned topics. Please note how many of these topics relate to the students' own history (60's and 70's).
2. To increase the writing skills of the students.
3. To develop library skills in the field of social studies. On this assignment they will need to use the card catalogue, the *Readers' Guide,* and the Pamphlet File.
4. To help students learn how to write a proper bibliography.
5. To develop student skills in explaining, sharing, and teaching what they have learned to others.

When this assignment is made, I assign a different topic to each row in the classroom, taking pains to assign the economic alliance topic to the row with the most capable students, as I consider this to be the most difficult one.

For most of the eighth graders this assignment will be the first attempt at a major paper. Make every effort to introduce the students to sound procedures for research papers. Discuss with students the need to do considerable reading before they begin to write. Stress note taking and the subsequent assimilation of material from many sources that result in good research papers. Caution them about the ethics involved in copywork without proper quotes. Believe me, many students will continue to copy reports from the nearest and easiest source as long as teachers will permit it. Careful structure of an assignment by the teacher makes copywork difficult, if not impossible. Be sure that your written instructions provide an outline of the topics to be dealt with, and let the students know that you will hold them to following the directions on the instruction sheets.

Instruct students to acknowledge all sources of information used. I have just finished grading one hundred twenty-five of these papers—a time consuming process that leaves me feeling that I should be given a halo, or a martyr button at the very least. I was pleased and interested to find listings on bibliographies that included such comments as "my mom and dad, who explained a lot of things to me," or "a long conversation with my grandfather.'' This kind of help and support from family members results in a very positive learning experience.

The whole business of learning to ''write in your own words,'' ''acknowledge all sources,'' ''dig in a library,'' ''analyze,'' ''state your opinions and convictions,''—all of this is a vital part of the learning process. And all of it needs to be the concern of teachers in all subject areas.

I have used this assignment for several years. I always try to schedule it so that the due date falls on the last day before Christmas vacation. This permits the students to enjoy their vacation with no assignment in history and allows the teacher a lengthy period of free time for grading the papers. On this assignment I write notes and comments at some length on each paper as I grade it.

After the Christmas break, we interrupt our sequential history study to spend a week on these topics. Assigned students report on each topic; questions and discussion follow. Students are given a study sheet to use during this week. A sample of this study sheet is included here. A test is given, based on the study sheet, on the last day of the week.

Current Events—Third Assignment

Study Sheet

I. United Nations
- **A.** Number of members today
- **B.** Year formed
- **C.** Location of headquarters
- **D.** Purpose
- **E.** Chief office and the men who have held it
- **F.** Major divisions
  - **1.** General Assembly—meets how often; what nations; languages used.
  - **2.** Security Council—number of members; permanent members; veto power.
  - **3.** Trusteeship Council
  - **4.** Economic and Social Council
  - **5.** Secretariat
  - **6.** International Court of Justice—in what city.
- **G.** Problems they have solved

- H. Problems they have not been able to solve
- I. China and the United Nations

II. NATO
- A. Original members
- B. Initials stand for
- C. Purpose
- D. Specific reason for founding
- E. Date formed—renewed how often
- F. Three members added later
- G. One nation that has withdrawn
- H. Organization formed by Russia as a response to NATO
- I. Neutral European nations

III. SEATO
- A. Initials stand for
- B. Nations involved
- C. Purpose

IV. ANZUS
- A. Initials stand for
- B. Nations involved

V. OAS
- A. Initials stand for
- B. Members
- C. Purpose

VI. Other nations we have military treaties with

VII. European Common Market or EEC
- A. Initials stand for
- B. Six nations that started it
- C. Two groups that preceded this and led to its founding
- D. The nation that was kept out for a long time
- E. Organization in Europe that was founded as a response to this group
- F. Four new members

VIII. Alliance for Progress
- A. Nations involved
- B. President who started it

IX. British Commonwealth
- A. Member nations
- B. Purpose

X. Peace Corps
- A. President who started it

- **B.** Purpose
- **C.** Types of work done by members
- **D.** Length of service for volunteers
- **E.** Pay for workers
- **F.** Requirements for volunteers

XI. NAACP

- **A.** Initials stand for
- **B.** Purpose
- **C.** Founding date
- **D.** Brown vs. the Board of Education
- **E.** Montgomery bus boycott
- **F.** Civil Rights laws to date

XII. Know about CORE, Black Muslims, and Black Panthers

XIII. Other activist groups: Feminist movement; Twenty-seventh Amendment; peace groups; student groups; etc.

Current Events—Fourth Assignment

Student Instruction Sheet The topic for study during this five weeks will be the political cartoon. Each student is to collect cartoons from the newspapers and news magazines that have to do with national or world affairs. When the assignment is due, each student will turn in eight cartoons, mounted, with a brief explanation of the viewpoint of the cartoonist. These eight cartoons should be the best cartoons that you find during this five week period. It is important that they portray as great a variety of topics as possible. Also, these eight cartoons should be chosen because they represent very important topics in the news.

In addition to the above assignment, each student will complete one of the following assignments:

1. Write a paper, at least two pages in length, summarizing the news of this period as you have learned it through cartoons. Your own opinions and analysis should be included.
2. Write a paper, using references in the library, on the history of the political cartoon. When did it first appear? Who are some famous cartoonists, past and present? What are the common symbols used in cartoons that we all should recognize? What influence does the cartoon have on public opinion? Which presidents, and other public figures have been the subjects of

cartoons quite often? This paper should be at least three pages in length.

3. Construct an original political cartoon on any current issue that interests you. This assignment should be done with care—be sure that the drawings are neat and very clear. It is wise to use color—felt tip pen, paint, heavy ink—anything that will be easily readable from a distance when posted. Pencil is not permitted; neither is lined paper. Feel free to trace objects or faces if necessary. The idea behind the cartoons must be original—*not copied.*

Due Date _______________ Point Value _______________

This is an assignment that is particularly popular with the students. It is also one that I approach each year with particular pleasure. As a result, it leads to some lively discussion in the classroom.

My main objectives are:

1. To help the student develop an understanding of the function of the editorial page of a newspaper.
2. To point out the value of satire and humor as a force that can shape public opinion.
3. To familiarize the students with the symbols used in cartooning that have become standard around the world.
4. To offer to the students a creative outlet through which they can express opinions of their own on current issues.
5. Sheer fun—for the students and the teacher!

I find it difficult to restrain myself when describing this project. Each year I feel that we truly do accomplish the objectives that prompted the structure of the assignment, and it is a very satisfying feeling.

I have used this assignment every year since 1961 and have found no reason to modify it in any way. Each of the options offered serves a purpose in the classroom. Papers summarizing current news as learned through cartoons serve as a basis for classroom discussion. The library research papers are shared with all students. The original cartoons are displayed each year in the halls of our school and attract considerable attention from faculty members, students, and visitors. It is interesting to note that over the years at least 90 percent of the students have chosen to draw the original cartoon rather than to write a report.

During the weeks when this assignment is in progress, I periodically ask the students to bring to class the cartoons that they have collected, and we spend a part of the period discussing them. I raise such questions as, "Which do you think is the funniest cartoon that you have found?" "Do you have any cartoons that you cannot understand?" "Do you have any cartoons with well-known symbols on them?" "What features of the faces of various famous people are commonly exaggerated for comic effect?"

The students not only find this project to be fun, but they also find that it is not as difficult as some of the other current events assignments. Therefore, I have usually scheduled this in February. At this time, in our sequential study of the text, we have reached the Civil War period, which is a difficult unit for some students. This provides for a better balance in the work load.

During the last few years my colleagues in the junior high school history department have joined me in this project. The entire eighth grade works on it at the same time, and we all share in the displays in the hall at the completion of the unit. This year we plan to invite a professional cartoonist to visit our school for an eighth grade assembly at the completion of the unit.

Several years ago I started collecting a few of the outstanding original cartoons each year. I wish that I'd come up with that idea much sooner! You will find reproductions of some of these cartoons between pages 120 and 121.

I strongly recommend this project, especially if you can approach it with the enthusiasm that I feel for it.

Current Events—Assignment Number Five

The first four assignments already discussed should take us through the year to the middle of March or beginning of April. This brings us to the most difficult of the current events programs that I have designed. It requires a rather detailed explanation.

The assignment involves a study of various types of government and the leaders who have been in power under these systems in the twentieth century. The scheduling of this assignment is deliberately placed rather late in the year for two reasons. First, it is a rather sophisticated assignment. Students will be in a better position to succeed in fulfilling it after several months of experience in a history class. Secondly, it is concerned with systems of government that are very different from our own. I don't believe that it would be overstating the matter to point out that some of these systems are dedicated to destroying ours. I believe that the students need a very firm background in our own government and history before they turn to the study of other systems. In teaching this unit, I must confess that I turn my back on one of my own rules. In a study of the "isms," I do not hesitate to express my own views and values very strongly. (See Chapter 2—Frame of Reference.) In fact, during this study, I give a lecture on totalitarianism, pointing out the characteristics that some of the isms have in common and the things that I see as dangers to our society.

Two separate, but related, assignments are given on this project. The first one is given only to the top five students in each class. The topic for this group is "Today's Isms." This will be referred to as assignment five-A. The alternate assignment is concerned with twentieth century leaders. This one will be referred to as assignment five-B. Instructions and materials for both assignments follow.

Current Events—Assignment Number Five-A

Student Instruction Sheet—The Isms The current events assignment for this five weeks will be concerned with "Today's Isms." This is to be a library research paper. It is advisable to do considerable reading before you start writing. The report itself should be brief—two to three pages in length—and should be written in your own words. Do not attempt to be too technical nor too wordy in your report. It is important that you confine your writing to the things that you can explain and the class can understand. You will be required to report verbally to the class on this topic.

The following topics should be considered in writing your report, however, it is not necessary to write about all of them:

1. Define your ism and give its characteristics.
2. In what countries is, or was, this ism found?
3. Give strengths and weaknesses of this ism.
4. What conditions in a country would encourage this ism to take root?

5. Compare life under this ism with life in the United States.
6. What is your own opinion of this ism?

The following is a list of the isms to be discussed, along with the countries that use or have used these isms. Please note that the first two listed will be discussed as economic systems, *not* political systems.

1. Capitalism—the United States
2. Socialism—Australia, New Zealand, United Kingdom, France, W. Germany, Sweden, Norway, Israel
3. Nazism (a type of Facism)—Germany in the 1930's and 1940's
4. Fascism—Spain, Portugal, Japan, Italy (1922–1940's)
5. Communism—Russia, China, Yugoslavia, Cuba, Hungary, Poland, Czechoslovakia, E. Germany, Albania, Rumania, North Korea, Vietnam, Bulgaria

Reports must be typed or written in ink. Use only one side of the paper and be sure that the pages are securely fastened together before turning in your report. A bibliography must accompany each report.

This is a rather difficult assignment. Do not hesitate to bring problems to your teacher as you work on it. The main objective of the assignment is for you to do enough thinking and reading on "Today's Isms" to lead to a profitable classroom discussion on the topic.

Due Date ______________ Point Value ______________

An after school conference will be scheduled in about three weeks for students in all classes doing each of the isms so that the teacher may offer some special assistance on this difficult subject.

Conference Dates

Communism ______________________________

Nazism ______________________________

Fascism ______________________________

Socialism ______________________________

Capitalism ______________________________

Current Events—Assignment Number Five-B

Student Instruction Sheet—Biographies of World Leaders The current events assignment for the next five weeks will be a report on a selected world leader of the twentieth century. This will involve quite a bit of research in the library. It would be advisable to get an early start on this assignment.

While assigning each of you to do a report on a specified leader, the teacher will recognize your preferences as much as possible. However, it is important that we have information on a variety of leaders for each class. Therefore, you may not be able to have your first choice. Read with care the list of possible choices as well as the report form that you will be using.

You are to write this report on the mimeographed sheet supplied to you. Please follow the form on the sheet exactly. The space permitted for each topic indicates how much information is required. You are to confine your writing to the two pages provided for you. Add one more sheet that contains a bibliography. You will be expected to share your findings verbally with the class.

Due Date ________________ Point Value ________________

Current Events—Assignment Number Five-B

Choice Sheet—Biographies of Twentieth Century World Leaders

Communism

U.S.S.R.

1. Leonid Brezhnev
2. Aleksei Kosygin
3. Vladimir Lenin
4. Joseph Stalin
5. Nikita Khrushchev

Poland

6. Wladyslaw Gomulka
7. Edward Gierek

China

8. Mao Tse-tung
9. Chiang Kai shek
10. Chou En-lai

Cuba

11. Fidel Castro

Yugoslavia

12. Josip Broz Tito

WHICH MATCH WILL SET OFF THE BOMB?

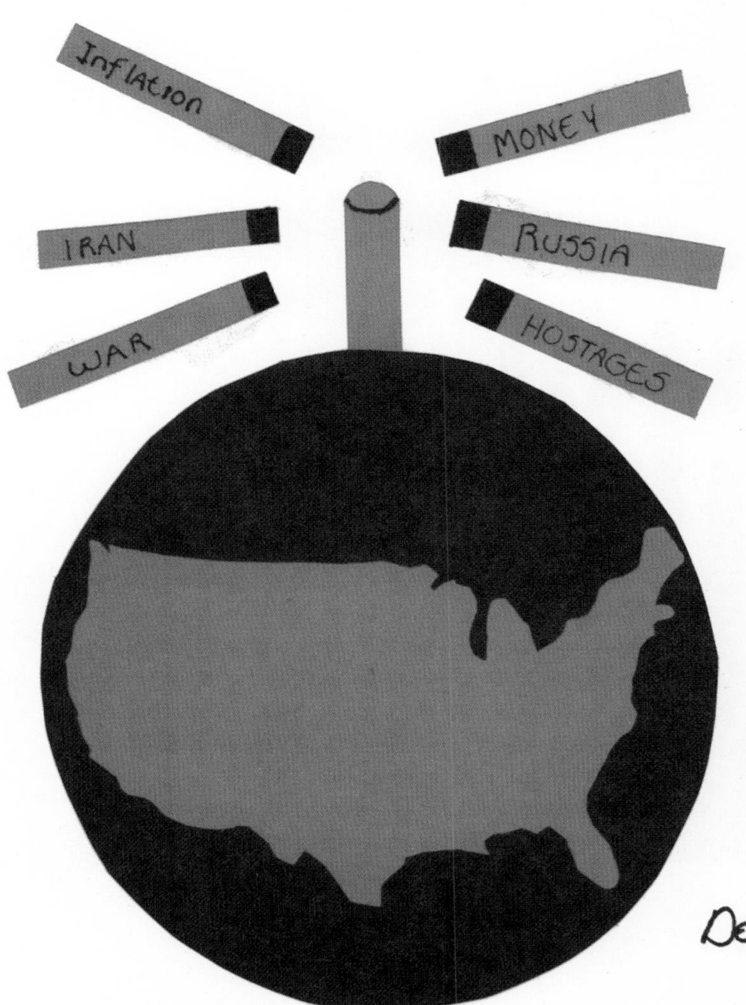

Debbie Garrett
3

NANCY KORNUTA
UPPER CLASS TAX PAYERS
MIDDLE AND LOWER CLASS TAX PAYERS
I.R.S.
206

Release...
Don't Release...
Release...
Don't Release...

THE OIL SQUEESE
UNDEVELOPED RESOURCES
ARAB OIL
COUNTRIES
JAPAN
FRANCE
SWEDEN
HOLLAND
U.S.
BRITAIN

1 2 3 4 5 6 7 8 9 10 11
Going up!
BREAD
Butter

Social Security

AMERICAN DREAM
1981
LABOR
REAGAN
BUSINESS
CIVIL RIGHTS
Wendy Peterson

East Germany

13. Walter Ulbricht

North Vietnam

14. Ho Chi Minh

Democratic Socialism

France

15. Charles DeGaulle
16. Georges Pompidou
17. Giscard d'Estaing

West Germany

18. Konrad Adenauer
19. Willy Brandt
20. Helmut Schmidt

United Kingdom

21. Clement Attlee
22. Winston Churchill
23. Edward Heath
24. Harold Wilson
25. James Callaghan

India

26. Mahatma Gandhi
27. Indira Gandhi

Israel

28. Golda Meir
29. Itzhak Rabin

Canada

30. Pierre Elliott Trudeau

Fascism—(occurred one time during this century)

Germany

31. Adolf Hitler (Nazism, a form of Fascism)

Italy

32. Benito Mussolini

Japan

33. Emperor Hirohito
34. Prime Minister Tojo

Spain

35. Francisco Franco
36. Prince Juan Carlos

Argentina

37. *Juan Perón*
38. *Eva Perón*

Democratic Capitalism

39. Any American President who you think was particularly strong in promoting the capitalist system.

Absolute Monarchy

40. Emperor Haile Selassie (Probably the last well known absolute monarch—was deposed.)

Current Events—Assignment Number Five-B

Report Form—World Leaders	
Name of person Dates of birth and death	
Name of his country Area and total population Location of country Capital city Alliances of this country	
Type of government Describe it briefly Changes in government in the twentieth century	
This person's title in the government Length of service Dates of service His political party Explain some of the beliefs of this party	
Important events while this person was in power	
This leader's impact on history—your personal analysis of him. Did this leader or his country have any effect on the United States?	
Any other interesting or unusual information about this person or his country?	

This fifth assignment was constructed to meet clear objectives:

1. To promote a study of governmental systems that differ from ours.
2. To point out the strengths and weaknesses of these systems.
3. To develop an awareness of the problems and dangers inherent in these systems.
4. To provide for the class some understanding of the leaders who have promoted various isms.
5. To develop further the library skills of the students.
6. To give the students experience in writing a report that calls for very specific information.
7. To give superior students an opportunity to "stretch" their minds on a challenging assignment and to share their findings with the rest of the class.
8. To develop an appreciation for the country in which we live and for our system of government, which has survived for 200 years despite its weaknesses and flaws.

I call your attention to the conferences provided for on assignment five-A (the isms). At each of these conferences I have five students, one from each class, who are all writing on the same ism. These conferences are important and useful. Unusually good learning often takes place as these students exchange information on their findings. I also find them raising penetrating questions for me to handle.

Note the highly structured nature of the report involved in assignment five-B. I make it clear that the lines drawn on the report form are quite inflexible. The amount of information required on each topic is clearly defined. This not only helps each student to learn to write concisely and to the point, but also provides us with valuable information.

We spend one day on each ism in the classroom. We begin with a student report on the ism, followed by reports on particular leaders who have been associated with that ism, and finally, we conclude our study with general classroom discussion.

I give a test at the end of this unit. Since this is such an advanced assignment for eighth graders, I design this test with special care.

This is a complicated and difficult assignment. It will require thorough preparation and careful guidance on your part if you choose to undertake it.

Current Events—Sixth Assignment

Student Instruction Sheet—Editorials Your last current events assignment of the year will be to write an editorial on a topic of national or international interest. This are *not* to be a research paper, but you will probably need to do some library reading in order to gather information or quotes or statistics to back up your opinions. Your opinions or viewpoints should be backed by logical reasoning and/or facts. You will not be graded on the position that you take on any issue, but on how well you present your arguments or facts—how convincing you are. There will be no "right" or "wrong" sides. You may find it helpful to read several editorials in the newspaper in order to acquaint yourself with the style of an editorial.

Your editorial should not exceed *one page* in length. It should be typed or written in ink.

Due Date ______________ Point Value ______________

Topics for Editorials

1. Should we work toward full diplomatic relations with China? If so, what should be done about Nationalist China?
2. *How* should the major powers disarm? Or—*Should* the major powers disarm?
3. Should the present two year terms for Representatives to Congress and/or Mayors be increased to four years?
4. Should the United States *require* all who qualify to vote?
5. Should the United States continue foreign aid? If so, to whom?
6. Should the United States continue its program of domestic aid—A.D.C. programs and food stamps?
7. Should the Federal government give more or less aid to education?
8. Should the Federal government give aid to private and parochial schools?
9. Should children be "bused" to different schools in order to integrate?

10. Should college students be allowed to protest? If so, to what degree?
11. Should the electoral college be abolished? If so, what should be substituted for it?
12. Should the United States require students to take tests in order to determine who should receive higher education?
13. Should the United States continue spending money on the space program?
14. Should the United States legalize gambling?
15. Should the United States pull out of the United Nations?
16. Should the United States abolish capital punishment?
17. Should the United States support Israel in the present Middle East conflict? Or some other country involved?
18. Should the feminist movement be encouraged? Outlawed?
19. Should the Amtrak program be enlarged to permit complete nationalization of our railroads?
20. Should the price of natural gas be deregulated? Partially regulated? Totally set by the government?
21. Should defense spending be cut? Increased?
22. Should the United States government take stronger action to protect our environment? If so, what?

This last assignment of the year in the current events program is certainly the simplest one in terms of structure. It is also one that is usually less time consuming for the students in terms of preparation. These factors were taken into consideration as I planned the coordinated program. By this time it is getting late in the school year. Both students and teacher are pressed to meet the demands on time and energy that come with the end of the year. It is a good time for a lighter assignment.

When I assign the various topics on the list, I try as far as possible to have a student taking each side of each topic. For example, I wish to hear from someone who believes in capital punishment and from someone who is very much against it. I want a paper from someone who favors government ownership of railroads and from someone who is opposed to this idea. This makes it possible to get some added value from the assignment. We generally have a series of informal "mini-debates," permitting the two students with opposing viewpoints to battle it out in the classroom. This is followed by general classroom discussion that is not only interesting, but often extremely spirited, as the differences in opinion become evident.

By this time of the year the students are quite comfortable with one another and most of them are no longer hesitant about speaking before the class. This is a good opportunity for the students to get acquainted with some elementary debating skills.

The writing skills involved here are also important. Note the limitation on the length of the papers. It is especially important for the student to write concisely, clearly, and in a well-organized manner.

This assignment also presents a final opportunity of the year to reinforce another important skill—the ability to make a decision, take a stand, express a viewpoint, and defend that stand vigorously and confidently.

In this assignment, it is essential that the teacher refrain as much as possible from expressing personal views. This is a very good time for the teacher to say very little and listen a lot. An opinionated teacher in this instance would have a particularly stifling effect.

SUMMARY

This chapter has presented a structured plan for teaching current events throughout the entire school year. The teaching objectives of each part of this plan have been stated and explained. By the end of the year the students will cover trouble spots around the world, domestic issues in the news, many of the post World War II organizations and movements. They will study the political cartoon throughout history, several systems of government, and twentieth century world leaders. They will have experience in reading and writing editorials.

In the process of gathering and sharing information on all of these topics, they will develop skills in library research, speaking, writing, and analytical thinking. Hopefully, all of this can be accomplished without disrupting the orderly sequential study of American history that is taking place during the year.

If you choose to follow this program, or develop one similar to it, there is another factor for you to keep in mind. By the time you finish World War II in your study of the text, your work for the year is virtually finished. You will find that you have covered most of the post World War II period in the current events program. This may be quite important to you if you are short of time at the end of the year.

A planned, coordinated current events program is not our sole responsibility in this area. As social studies teachers, we should all be very quick to utilize any significant news story for classroom use. A five minute discussion in class from time to time can be most useful. Such discussions should take place as current news or student interest dictates.

Be alert throughout the year to recognize opportunities to tie past events to recent ones. Such comparisons can lead to some thoughtful class discussions. Consider these suggestions:

- It is an easy leap from the Boston Massacre to the riots at Kent State.
- In a study of the unpopular War of 1812, Vietnam comes immediately to mind.
- While covering the United States Constitution in terms of its development and its structure, be watching for current news at the national government level.
- When you discuss the Dred Scott decision of 1857, this might lead to a discussion of another Supreme Court case that came almost 100 years later, Brown vs. the Board of Education.
- A study of Teddy Roosevelt, his "Big Stick," and the Panama Canal naturally leads us into a very current problem.
- If you do not invite a comparison of the assassinations of Lincoln and Kennedy, I assure you that your students will.

In conclusion, those of us who work with students at the secondary level need to be very much aware of the fact that these young people must be able to handle adult responsibilities in their communities and in their country within a comparatively short span of years. Many of them will have no training beyond high school. We owe it to all of them to give them the best possible foundation.

6

Civil War Debates

I CAN THINK OF NO PROFESSION, OTHER THAN TEACHING, that can offer once every year such a special feeling of a new beginning, a fresh start, another chance to do it all better. There is excitement in that first day of school each September—the pleasure of seeing colleagues after the summer's absence, the anticipation of new teaching assignments, and above all, an eagerness to meet and greet the new students. It will be a sad day for me when the opening day of school takes place without me!

This past September, on opening day, I watched my last class of the day file into the room. It was a large class, and at first glance, a lively one. I made a mental note at the time that this bunch might take a bit of special handling, an assumption that has proved to be valid. (They refer to themselves as my rowdy class.) As the students took their seats, one boy spoke out in a stage whisper, obviously meant to be heard, "History, Y-u-u-ck!"

This is the kind of comment that can really hurt a history teacher. Furthermore, I didn't want this kid to set the tone for the opening day of school. I turned to the student and, in a light tone said, "Hey, you're talking about my favorite subject! What's your name?"

"Joe," he growled.

"All right, Joe, tell us what you mean by 'history, y-u-u-ck.' "

Joe wasn't about to back down one little bit. "It's so dull and boring and all those dates and notes and stuff."

"It looks like I'll have to change your mind," I said. I decided that I might as well really live dangerously. "I'll give you odds, Joe, five to one, that you'll change your mind by the end of the year. How about it? Are you willing to risk a buck?"

"Why not?"

"All I ask of you at the end of the year is an honest answer," I replied. "One dollar might get you five."

This incident may come back to haunt me at the end of the year. I have no idea whether or not Joe's attitude has changed. I've been careful not to raise the question. But I shall follow through in June to collect, or pay off, as the case may be.

There's a point to this story that I would like to pursue. Many, many students approach the study of history with the kind of attitude demonstrated by Joe on the first day of school. What alarms me even more is the fact that I see an increasing number of students each year who are bored with school in general. It's a real challenge to turn these kids around and teach them to approach their studies with interest and pleasure. The best weapon we have for meeting this challenge is programming—exciting, creative, imaginative programming. We need programming that will intrigue the students, and involve them actively in the learning process. But, at the same time, we must be careful to provide and promote the basic educational skills and knowledge that are too often overlooked in the "progressive classroom."

Chapters 6, 7, and 8 are designed to offer you a glimpse of the "best of both worlds." I will have further comments to make about the place of such special programs in the total educational program in Chapter 9.

The Civil War debates, which are to be covered in the remainder of this chapter, can be used as an example of a means of taking the "y-u-u-ck" out of history.

BACKGROUND

The year was 1961. It was the beginning of the Civil War Centennial. One semester's work was behind us, and we were approaching the study of the Civil War. The students in a particularly good class got into a lively discussion on the Civil War that turned into a hot argument. The excitement was generated because a number of students were taking the viewpoint of the South. I sat back and let the discussion run its course, thoroughly enjoying every minute of it. In the heat of the argument, several students started talking about having a formal debate on the war and turned to me with their suggestions. I like to encourage any worthwhile project initiated by the students, so I quickly agreed. However, I wanted this "debate" to be an activity involving all of the students, not just two teams. I suggested that the class should become the United States Senate. This senate would debate the issue that had started the argument in class—whether or not the South should have been allowed to secede. We agreed that the issue would be presented as a bill before the senate in the year 1858.

I still remember the beginning of the opening speech by a "Southern senator." "Fourscore and two years ago our forefathers brought forth on this continent a new nation . . ." I found myself wondering what in the world he was doing with the Gettysburg Address, when he suddenly zoomed in with his punch line ". . . and we have never been able to get along together! The time has come to divide this nation into two new countries which can learn to live side by side as peaceful neighbors."

I'm also remembering, from that first debate, the senator from Virginia who, with typical Southern charm, asked the senator from Michigan if he would rise to answer a few questions. Both stood up to face each other, and this conversation followed:

VIRGINIA: Do you believe that people in this great democracy should have the right to settle issues by voting?

MICHIGAN: Of course I do. That is the American way.

VIRGINIA: (Holding up a map of the state of Virginia as it looked in 1858) Some of the people in our state have asked that they be allowed to separate from the great state of Virginia and form a new one to be called West Virginia. They have voted on this issue in the western part of the state and are asking for separation because they disapprove of slavery. What do you think should be done about this matter?

MICHIGAN: I think that they have every right to form their own state. If they don't like slavery, they shouldn't have to stay with you.

VIRGINIA: (Holds up map of Virginia which he has prepared to separate easily into two parts, representing Virginia and West Virginia.) Then you think they have a right to separate from us? (Pulls map apart to show two states.)

MICHIGAN: Certainly, you have no right to hold them.

I sat there amazed at this eighth grader, baiting a trap so perfectly. Sure enough, he sprang it!

VIRGINIA: (Suddenly unrolls a map of the United States that had been prepared to separate at the Mason-Dixon line. He pulled it apart, then continued.) Then why do you Northern states oppose our wish to be separated from you Yankees?

I determined on the spot to make this a permanent part of my program. Thus, a tradition was born. I have developed a simulation exercise that lasts for one school week. We have used this program every year since 1961, except for one year when I was ill.

I find it difficult to put into words my feelings for this project. It is such fun for the students. Somehow they find it possible to relate to the problems of that period in history and they slip into their respective roles very easily. They are willing and eager to put forth extra effort and time in order to be well prepared for the two debate days. They are intrigued with the procedures and rules involved in this exercise and listen very attentively as I explain them.

Each year I find myself to be a bit apprehensive as I open the first day's debate. The bill itself is presented, and I call for discussion by saying, "The floor is open for debate. Who would like to be recognized to speak toward this bill?"

Each year I think, "What if no one responds? What if this doesn't get off the ground?" In 17 years I have never found it necessary to call on someone. The debate simply starts and quickly picks up steam and catches all of us up in the mounting excitement. It's such a feeling of total involvement for all of us that it seems like a bit of magic.

But I cannot dwell on the magic. If I truly wish to share this project with the readers, it is now time to turn to a description of this five-day simulation that must necessarily be given in painstaking detail.

FIVE DAY SCHEDULE

First Day

1. Explanation of the unit by the teacher.
2. Detailed description of debate procedures.
3. Each student given a state to represent.
4. Assignment for the day: each student is to write a bill to propose to the class.

Second Day

1. Choosing the two best bills to debate, one with a Northern viewpoint, the other proposed by the South.
2. Committees chosen to write the bills in detail.
3. Assignment for the day: all students begin research on the bills that were chosen.

Third Day

1. Committees spend the period writing the bills in detail.
2. Other students begin writing their speeches about the bills.
3. Assignment for the day: each student writes a two minute speech for or against the bill to be debated on the fourth day.

Fourth Day

1. One of the bills is debated.
2. Roll call vote is taken on the bill.
3. Assignment for the day: each student writes a two minute speech for or against the bill to be debated on the fifth day.

Fifth Day

1. The second bill is debated.
2. Roll call vote on the bill.
3. If time permits, students' reactions to the debates are discussed.

ASSIGNMENT OF STATES

Each student in the class is to be a senator from a certain state. Note that in each classroom there will be only one senator from each state, rather than the usual two. Students are given choices as far as possible. Some students, however, may not get their preferred states, nor, in rare cases, their preferred regions. It is essential to maintain balance between North and South in the interests of fairness. The following states existed in 1858:

South	*North*	*Border States*
Alabama	California	Delaware
Arkansas	Connecticut	Kentucky
Florida	Illinois	Maryland
Georgia	Indiana	Missouri
Louisiana	Iowa	
Mississippi	Maine	
North Carolina	Massachusetts	
South Carolina	Michigan	
Tennessee	Minnesota	
Texas	New Hampshire	
Virginia	New Jersey	
	New York	
	Ohio	
	Pennsylvania	
	Rhode Island	
	Vermont	
	Wisconsin	

Obviously, all eleven Southern states must be assigned. The border states play a very important role in this simulation. These are the four states where the most ambivalence was to be found in the decade before the Civil War. Therefore, senators from these four states will not have a built-in loyalty to either the North or the South. As I assign these four states, I caution the students who choose them that they must enter the debates uncommitted. They are expected to cast their votes in the senate solely on the basis of what they hear during the debates. I also make it clear to all of the students that border state senators are not to be bribed, threatened, or harassed! In a class of twenty-six, there will be eleven Southern senators, eleven Northern senators, and four border state senators. In such a situation, the outcome of the proposed legislation may very well be determined by those very important border states.

As the simulation exercise progresses through the week, most of the speech and action of each student is dictated by his or her feelings about the state and region to which he or she has been assigned.

THE BILLS

On the first day of the unit, each student is assigned the task of writing a bill. This bill, or proposed law, should, by its content, demonstrate the sectionalism of the times (1858). A senator from Illinois clearly would represent the Northern viewpoint, while the senator from South Carolina would write a very strong bill that would reflect the rebellious position taken by the state that had proposed nullification as early as Jackson's time.

Each student is expected to confine himself in fulfilling this assignment to writing the "bare bones" of a bill. In other words, he must provide simply an idea for a bill that he might have proposed in 1858 as good legislation for his country as he viewed it through the eyes of a senator with deep loyalties to his state and his region. Here are a few of the many bills that have been proposed by students:

Northern

1. A plan shall be made for the gradual abolition of slavery.

2. Any slave escaping into Northern territory shall be freed.

3. Plantations shall be inspected every three months by Government inspectors to assure fair and humane treatment of slaves.
4. Any new states entering the Union shall have no slavery. Slavery will be confined to the areas where it presently exists.

Southern

1. The Dred Scott decision shall be written into law. Slavery cannot be forbidden anywhere in the United States.
2. A constitutional amendment shall be passed allowing all tariff laws to be under the control of the states, rather than the national government.
3. Any person convicted of helping slaves to escape shall be hanged.
4. The United States shall be divided into two independent nations.

On the second day of the unit the teacher writes all the bills proposed by the class members on the board. All students vote, first to select the best Northern bill, then to select the best Southern bill. The student is cautioned here, in casting his vote, not to vote on whether or not he favors the bill. Instead, he must vote, in each case, for the bill that he would consider to be the most exciting to debate, regardless of sectional interests.

Thus the class selects two bills to debate, the best Northern bill and the best Southern bill. One of these is scheduled for debate on the fourth day, and the other for the fifth day. For homework on the second day, the students are asked to begin research to gather ''ammunition'' for or against the chosen bills.

On the third day, two committees are chosen—one for each bill. The task of these committees, in each case, is to write up the finished bill with every detail, including all provisions, the means for implementing each provision, as well as the penalties for infractions of the provisions, should they be passed into law. This is the time for putting the ''meat'' on the bare bones of each bill. While these committees work, all other students begin to write their speeches. The committees report to the entire class during this period, as soon as their work is complete. Assignment for the third day for everyone is to construct a speech in writing and be prepared to deliver it orally during the senate debate the next day. Homework on the fourth day, again, is to prepare a speech for the fifth day's debate. The following bill is a sample of the work accomplished by one of the committees.

Sample Bill*

The honorable senator from the state of South Carolina submits to this Senate for consideration a bill known as the Garvin-Sheppard Bill. The provisions are as follows:

1. The country now known as the United States of America shall be divided into two nations, each one to be a free and independent republic.
2. This division shall take place on January 1, 1860.
3. The line dividing these two nations shall be the Mason-Dixon line east of the Mississippi River, and the 36-30 line west of the Mississippi River.
4. All military installations in Southern territory shall belong to the new Confederate States of America.
5. All weapons and arms now stored in armories shall be divided equally between the two new nations.
6. The new United States and the Confederate States of America shall sign a military treaty for mutual protection against any foreign aggressor.
7. Both nations shall recognize the right of the new Confederate States of America to trade freely with other nations without restriction and to set their own prices on raw cotton.
8. Both nations shall agree to full and open use of the Mississippi River.

HINTS ABOUT SPEECHES

I remind the students that each one of them is playing a role, and that emotions ran very high during this period of history. Consequently, speeches should be dramatic, often reflecting anger and frustration. Southerners should feel that they have their backs to the wall defending a way of life that the rest of the world no longer accepts. This should be matched by the ardent passion of Northern abolitionists.

---

*This is the complete text of the bill prepared by Emily Garvin and Joan Sheppard.

In any case, students should put their knowledge of history to good use. There should be references to the Kansas-Nebraska Act, Fugitive Slave Law, *Uncle Tom's Cabin*, John Brown, Lincoln-Douglas debates, and other appropriate events.

Quotes should be used liberally—Clay, Calhoun, Webster, Hayne, Jackson, Lincoln, the Declaration of Independence, the Constitution, etc.

I have suggested that some of them might want to invent quotes. I am amused when some youngster starts out, "I was talking to my good friend Abe Lincoln the other day and he said . . ." Or, "I will never forget what that great Southerner, John Calhoun, whispered to me on his deathbed . . ." The name of the game is "ham" and there is plenty of it in the classroom during these debates. Included here is a sample of a good speech written by an eighth-grade student.

Sample Speech

Our country, the United States, or more accurately, "the Partially United Sections," is falling apart. Ever since the first settlers at Jamestown in 1607 and the first Negro slaves in 1619, this country has been divided. We won the Revolution, the War of 1812, and the Mexican War *together—but*, at the same time we have grown further apart.

Now everyone is yelling about states' rights. Right now all of Europe is watching us, ready to come over here and conquer us the minute we break up. This is a period of time where everyone wants to be a world power. We need to be the *United* States—no more states' rights, but long live the country as a *whole!*

The first time South Carolina tried to secede, Andrew Jackson, threatening force, stopped it right away. Now South Carolina is asking for legal secession—no way!

You also want to make a military treaty with us—Ha! And you want to set your own cotton prices—that's a joke! Do you really think that we would agree to give you one-half of the United States arms? And you want us to share the Mississippi with you. Dang it! Why don't you ask for the kitchen sink, too? What if the North says, "No!" Will it be war? No, you are too weak. Will it mean secession—no! Without our support you would have to come back in a few years.

If you try to secede, the only reason we will stop you is for your good, our good, and the good of the *whole nation*.

In closing, I remind you of the words of the great senator who once held the seat which I now hold. ''Liberty and union, now and forever, one and inseparable.''

Signed.

Tom Rittman

TOM RITTMAN, Senator from Massachusetts

SETTING THE STAGE

The teacher serves as the Vice President of the United States, and in that role, presides over the senate sessions. This requires considerable skill and, frequently, quick thinking. I do not recommend delegating this role to a student.

The room itself must assume a new role. No longer is it a classroom. It becomes the senate chamber in the Capitol in the year 1858.

Student identities are set aside completely for the two days of debate. No names are used. Each student is addressed as ''the Senator from Mississippi,'' ''the Senator from Indiana,'' etc. Each student is required to prepare a cardboard sign bearing the name of his state. It must be constructed so that it can stand upright on the student's desk. The name of the state must be visible from both the front and the rear of the room. Some of these signs are made quite elaborately.

While there is no attempt to make this a costume day, students are permitted to use any props or costumes that will contribute to the atmosphere. There are usually a few Southern colonels, complete with white hair and goatees. One such colonel arrived this year with a mint julep in hand! There is often a tall Texan wearing a ten gallon hat and boots. We also see Confederate flags, state symbols, and assorted canes, straw hats, and other such bits of originality.

A senate page is provided for each session of the senate. This role is played by a student from study hall. The function of the page is to serve the senators by carrying notes from one senate desk to another. This allows a senator to communicate with a colleague in order to set up strategy, obtain an answer to a question, or establish a means of getting the floor. (Imagine the joy of the students when they find that, for once, they may legally pass notes in class!)

The chairman of the committee that drew up the bill to be debated is expected to introduce the bill to the senate. Every provision must be clearly stated and explained. Another member of the committee is assigned to make the first speech—one that should strongly support the bill and give detailed reasons for that support.

DEBATE RULES AND PROCEDURES

The rules for our debates are an ungodly mixture of *Robert's Rules of Order*, actual senate procedures, and tidbits from my vivid imagination! I am less concerned with authenticity in this case than I am with effectiveness. I take pains to make the two days of actual debate as exciting and full of fun as possible. At the same time, it is important that the ground rules and techniques be carefully explained and thoroughly understood in advance if the debates are to be successful. Rules and procedures follow:

1. The chairperson calls the meeting to order.
2. He or she recognizes the sponsor of the bill. The bill is introduced to the senate.
3. For the sake of clarity, the chairperson summarizes the provisions of the bill.
4. A seconding speech is made by another member of the committee that wrote the bill.
5. From this point on, there is a two minute limit on debate. At the beginning of each speech a timer is set. When the timer rings, if the speaker is still talking, he or she is cut off in mid-sentence.
6. The floor is now open for any speaker who can obtain recognition from the chair. The chair is bound by a few rules in this regard. It is bound by the rules to recognize first any person who has not yet had the floor. He or she may recognize a person for the second time only if there is no one wishing recognition for the first time. He may not recognize any speaker for the third time under any circumstances without first securing the general consent of the senators. The chair also is expected to give equal time as far as possible to Northern and Southern senators. A bit of mathematics is in order. If there are thirty

senators, and the senate session (class period) is forty-five minutes and debate limit is two minutes, time becomes a problem. This in itself, however, adds excitement to the session.

7. A senator who wishes to speak more than once has three options for obtaining the floor. He or she might be lucky enough to be recognized by the chairperson. Or the senator could send a note (using a senate page) to a friendly senator asking him or her to obtain the floor and yield part of the two minutes to the note sender. The third possibility involves waving while a senator from the opposition is speaking. That senator might welcome the challenge of taking on an opponent and ''yield'' to that opponent ''for a question.''

8. This brings us to the subject of yielding. When a speaker has completed his or her speech, and if there is time remaining on the clock, the student may:

   a. Yield the floor and sit down. This will permit the chairperson to proceed to another speaker.

   b. Yield the floor to a friendly senator. In this case that senator may speak only until the fraction of time remaining on the clock is gone.

   c. Yield to an opposing senator ''for a question.'' This procedure gives the floor to the opponent only long enough to pose an argumentative question. The remaining time immediately goes back to the senator who had the floor originally, unless he or she wishes to engage in a one-on-one debate with the challenger.

9. Hand signals are involved in these procedures. The senator raises a hand to attract the attention of the chair, waves a hand vigorously when challenging an opponent to ''yield for a question,'' and raises a finger to signal the page to pick up a note for delivery.

10. A senator may interrupt proceedings at any time for a ''point of order''—to object to any procedure he or she thinks is improper. A senator might call out, ''Point of order—the chairman has recognized three Southern senators in a row. Northern senators want equal time.'' Or the chair may be challenged with, ''Point of order—the honorable senator from Massachusetts has already been recognized twice. I object.''

11. Senators may call for a caucus at any time—a request that may be granted or denied at the discretion of the chairperson. A senator speaks out, "I call for a caucus of Mississippi, Alabama, Virginia, and Texas," or, "I call for a caucus of all of the border states." The chairperson replies, "Request granted—30 second caucus in front right corner of the room."
12. Debate continues until the chairperson decides that it must end. It is wise to allow ten to fifteen minutes for the roll call vote and a short discussion on the strengths and weaknesses of the day's experience.
13. As the session nears an end, many students are usually waving frantically for recognition, and by that time very few of them succeed in obtaining the floor. As in show business tradition, it's always best to "leave 'em hungry." Just before the close of the debate, I allow a one minute time slot so that proponents of the bill may quickly make last minute comments. They are instructed by the chair to make good use of this time by speaking quickly and yielding the time to colleagues. I've seen as many as ten senators make use of this one minute time slot. This is followed, naturally, by a one minute summary period for the opponents of the bill.

THE ROLL CALL VOTE

At the close of debate, the page is stationed at the blackboard to record the vote. The chairperson calls the roll of the states. It is wise to alternate Northern and Southern states in this roll call and name the four border states last. This, of course, adds to the suspense. As the name of each state is called, the senator is required to rise beside his or her desk, name the state, and cast his or her vote. The chairperson repeats the state and the vote cast as the page records it (formal and proper to the very last!).

GRADES

Since this project does absorb the full time and attention of students and teacher alike for one school week, evaluation is a factor that must be considered.

I put a 50 point value on this total assignment. Three things must be turned in to the teacher in writing—the student's bill (due on the second day) and the two required speeches (one on the fourth day, the other on the fifth). In addition, the student should be evaluated on his or her participation and oratorical style during the two days of debate.

After many years of refining and improving this project, I now find myself able to run the timer, wield the gavel, and take notes on each speaker, assigning letter grades as the debate proceeds. I combine these notes with the written work and arrive at a single grade for the project.

PITFALLS

This project is not for all teachers. The teacher who is rather serious and formal, for example, might not be comfortable with it. I feel obliged to point out that the teacher, as well as the students, must be able to assume a role. It is helpful if the teacher sincerely enjoys "play acting." Anyone who undertakes this project must also be very enthusiastic about it and be able to infect the students with that enthusiasm. The teacher should also be one who is proficient in the art of explaining things in detail. Look back at the debate rules and procedures listed for this unit. It is essential that the students grasp all of this detail before the two days of actual debate. Of all the projects and programs described, this one can most easily fall with a dull thud, if it is not handled with care.

Another possible problem should be anticipated by the teacher. This project could easily become a contest between two teams where the loyalty to the team becomes so fixed that the issues get lost and the voting is totally predictable. Students need to realize that a good senator is able to look beyond the party line and beyond his own parochial interests to the issues involved in any legislation. I explain to the students that, in spite of the deep division in our country in 1858, Southern senators did occasionally vote with Northerners on issues, and vice versa. I urge the students to have enough courage to vote according to conviction, rather than blindly following the crowd.

I call to your attention one other potential problem. Is this project desirable in an inner city school? Might it possibly serve to inflame old antagonisms in an integrated school? Or would it, instead, foster better understanding through the role playing approach to this difficult period in our history? Since my experience has been limited to a suburban school system, I have no answers to this—only questions.

ALTERNATIVE ASSIGNMENTS IN ROLE PLAYING

A one week simulation assignment of this kind could be applied to various other events in history. How about a mock session of the Second Continental Congress? The students would need to decide what to do about good old King George. Would students vote in such a session to write and sign a Declaration of Independence?

A simulated meeting of the Constitutional Convention is another possibility. The many quarrels within this group—between conservatives and radicals, Northerners and Southerners, large states and small states—all would lend themselves to debate.

These two historical events, mentioned above, come too early in the year in our study to suit my purposes. I feel that special programs of this kind should be used only after firm groundwork has been laid in the vocabulary of history, basic historical facts, study habits, and classroom procedures. Some teachers, however, may not agree with that premise.

How about a simulated meeting of the United Nations to debate and vote on a current world problem?

In Chapter 8, you will find a detailed description of a major project using role playing. This, too, could be adapted to other periods of history. Whatever type of incident in our history suits your fancy for this type of program, I do recommend that you try one such project. Plan it with care, add a lot of imagination and a real shot of enthusiasm, and it will surely be a success.

OBJECTIVES

I decided to break all the rules and discuss objectives toward the end of this chapter, rather than at the beginning. It seemed important, in this case, to provide the reader with a description of the project first.

The sectionalism that finally resulted in a tragic Civil War was a thread through our history from the very beginning. In the classroom, throughout the first semester's study, we are aware of this sectionalism and the many factors that nourished it. In spite of this, however, the students have difficulty comprehending the scope of this war, the bitter feelings involved, and the magnitude of the problems to be solved. It is a good time to set the book aside. My primary aim is to involve the students in the events of this period, rather than confine them to the written words of the text. I want them, if possible, to feel what it must have been like to live during the pre-Civil War period, facing the problems of the times.

There are several other reasons for using the role playing approach to this period:

1. It certainly is an active learning process. Almost every student eagerly participates in the debates.
2. It gives the students a better understanding of our legislative process. Among other things, the students discover firsthand how difficult it is to get a bill through Congress. They also discover that a bill cannot be carelessly put together. If it is, it will face certain slaughter in the Congress.
3. It serves as a means of motivation. In preparing speeches and arguments, the students really dig into the books in order to be armed with as many facts as possible.
4. It is a good change of pace that comes at the right time, early in the second semester. It does generate excitement and fun in the classroom for all. My principal usually visits one of my classes during the debates. His comment to me this year was, "I believe that you enjoy this even more than your students do." He may be right.

In any event, I must admit to having a special feeling for this project, probably because I have used it successfully for so many years.

February 8, 1962

Dear Madame Chairman,

The Southern States would like to thank you for making this session of Congress possible. This letter comes mostly from Georgia and the state of Alabama. It is my contention that this debate was done very well by both the South and the North. Even though we only won one bill, I think the two minutes that you gave each Senator from either the South or the North, was ample time for a person to say what he wanted to say with good words. The South is greatly indebted to you for letting us and our adversaries make our wish come true. I think everyone had a real good time doing it and learned something from this formal session of the United States Congress that we had on the eighth day of February.

This session to the South was worth more than all the history of the Civil War. Most teachers would not permit us to do this sort of thing in our History class, but we are fortunate to have one who will permit this type lesson. The South may not have won the Division of the Union, but I think they learned a few things.

I was proud along with others to be a part of the United States Congress for those two days. The South gives their thanks to you.

Yours truly,

Gary Rose
Senator of Georgia
(approved by the
Senator of Alabama)

P.S. I'm enclosing this money to remember the South by.

CIVIL WAR CENTENNIAL COMMISSION
Washington 25, D.C.
13 February 1962

Mrs. Severance
Brecksville Jr. High School
Brecksville, Ohio

Dear Mrs. Severance:

Eugene Michlenko, one of your pupils, has written us about the mock-Senate session held by his 8th grade American history class this month. He gave the details, so nicely expressed, and heaped upon you considerable praise for encouraging the students thus to dip realistically into the American past.

Such a program for school children seems tremendously useful. And we are pleased that the project met with so much success.

With every good wish,

Sincerely yours,

Scott Hart
SCOTT HART
Historian

7

A Unit in Individualized Instruction

WHAT IS INDIVIDUALIZED INSTRUCTION?

THE NAME OF THE GAME IS CHOICE. THE TEACHER outlines the work to be done, offering as many options as possible to the student. He then sets the time limit—in this case four weeks—and permits the student to chart his own course during this unit. There is required reading in the text (four chapters), but the student sets his own pace for reading. There is a short test on each chapter, but the student decides when to take each test. In order to broaden the options, the teacher prepares two tests for each chapter. If the student does not pass the first test, he is required to take the second one. If he passes the first test and is not satisfied with his score, he may choose to take the second one. If he elects to try the second test, that will be the score recorded in the grade book, even if it is lower than the score on the first test.

In addition to the reading and testing, the student is required to choose a topic for specialized study during this unit. Again he faces a choice as there are six possible topics. And here we begin to compound the choices. The student is presented with a list of learning activities relating to his topic. These activities offer as much variety as possible—reports, maps, graphs, sketches, dialogues, interviews, creative writing, songs and poems, charts, tables, transparencies, and film strips. He must choose the kinds of activities he wishes to pursue, as well as the number of activities he feels that he can undertake. As he makes these choices, he realizes that his unit grade will depend upon both the quality and quantity of his work.

WHY USE INDIVIDUALIZED INSTRUCTION?

I can make no claims that students learn better by this method, since I have not attempted to make any controlled tests. I offer two pieces of evidence, however, to support the value of individualized instruction. First, the great majority of my students have improved their grades during this unit. Secondly, student responses on evaluation sheets have been very favorable. I first tried this unit in 1975 with ninety history students. On anonymous evaluation sheets, 89 students indicated that they liked this unit and thought it should be repeated every year. Only one student gave a negative response.

In my judgment, there are several other reasons for using this approach to teaching. It surely offers a good change of pace. After several months of hard work on the basics of history, it is a welcome change.

It also offers the student an opportunity to develop self-direction and self-discipline. During the three years that I have used this unit, I have been surprised to see how well the eighth graders measure up in this respect. Only a few students needed prodding to complete their work, and there was remarkably little last minute pressure by procrastinating students.

I found that there was a dividend to this unit that I had not expected. I spent most of my classroom time during the unit having conferences with individual students, guiding and advising them. I was surprised and pleased to realize how much better I got to know each one of my students. The value of such a bonus can scarcely be overemphasized.

The final objective that I would submit is the fact that this type of program offers to both student and teacher a great opportunity to be creative. The teacher must be creative to design a good program. The students, in many cases, initiate projects of their own to add to the unit. Students should certainly be encouraged to express this creativity.

WHEN SHOULD INDIVIDUALIZED INSTRUCTION BE USED?

I have heard of teachers who have planned an entire history course using individualized instruction. I do not favor such an approach. To begin with, it is my opinion that, on a year long basis, this program would eventually bore both students and teachers. In addition, I question how effective the learning process would be if the students were not first firmly grounded by several months of conventional classroom work. It takes time to establish classroom discipline and routine, rapport between students and teacher, basic history vocabulary, and proper study skills. I would never use this approach during the first semester.

The unit described in this chapter is designed for the period of time that follows the Civil War and covers American history from 1865–1900. This period is admirably suited for individualized instruction because the themes are so clear. Consider the six topics offered for specialized study:

agriculture, railroads, the American Indian, big business, labor unions, and immigration. This unit falls in the second semester after a firm base has been established in the classroom. It also generally falls in February or March, months that can sometimes start dragging. This form of study has proven to be a refreshing change for my students, and the four week period allowed for it seems to be just right.

WHO CAN BENEFIT FROM INDIVIDUALIZED INSTRUCTION?

In terms of age, I would suggest that seventh through twelfth grade students can benefit from this form of study. I feel that students at the elementary level need a more structured classroom atmosphere.

In terms of ability, I would not suggest this program for slow learners. This kind of unit requires many materials, and it would be difficult to find enough books and visual aids that would be suitable for slow learners. Even if that obstacle were to be overcome, many of these students would lack the necessary self-discipline.

This is a good program for the average student. Since he has so many options, he can more easily achieve the satisfaction of success by choosing his own learning activities.

It is also a good approach for the superior student. There is no limit to what he can accomplish when free to set his own pace.

It occurs to me that one point needs clarification. In the broad sense, "individualized instruction" should always be offered by all teachers to all students. The limitations set forth above regarding participation in individualized instruction refer only to the use of structured independent study units.

In our school, the entire eighth grade uses this individualized instruction unit. Because so many materials are needed for this project, placing heavy demands on the library, we stagger our schedules. One history teacher uses this program for the first four weeks of the second semester, another teacher follows the second four weeks, and a third teacher waits for the third four-week period.

Now that we have covered who, what, when, and why, it is time to turn to the program itself. The next section of this chapter is a copy of the mimeographed booklet that is given to each student at the beginning of this unit. This booklet describes the program in detail.

AMERICAN HISTORY

A Unit Plan Utilizing Individualized
Instruction Within the Classroom

Planned and written by Mrs. Myra Severance
Social Studies teacher Brecksville Junior High School

Text used: One Nation Indivisible, *Charles E. Merrill Publishing Co., Columbus, Ohio, 1971*

TABLE OF CONTENTS

American History—a unit plan utilizing individualized instruction within the classroom

Unit Title—The Growth of America—1865–1900

Text: pages 330–366

Chapters 16. *The Awakening Industrial Giant*
America's Resources
Rise of Major Industries
Inventions
Corporations and Trusts
17. *The Vanishing Frontier*
Development of American Railroad
Cattle Ranching
Western Mining
The American Indian
18. *The Farmer and the Land*
Farming in the West
Money Problems
The Rise of Third Party Movements
19. *Immigration and the Advance of Labor*
Immigration
The Labor Movement

To the student and the parent:

A slightly different approach to American history will be used for the next four weeks. This booklet contains an outline of the work to be covered. Each student is to complete this work at his own pace. While working on this unit, the student will find that he has many choices of learning activities to pursue, as well as a selection of a subject for specialized study. At all times his progress and activities will be closely supervised by the teacher, whose role will be to advise, assist, and guide, rather than to direct. Certain minimum standards will be required of all students during this four weeks, and the students will find these clearly defined. Each student may choose to go beyond these minimums as far as he wishes in order to:

1. follow his interests
2. improve his grade
3. develop his study skills
4. contribute to the entire class

It is hoped that the students will find this approach to be interesting, flexible, and challenging. Reactions from both parents and students at the end of the Unit will be welcomed.

Schedule—Four weeks

1. This Unit will be covered in 20 school days.
2. Each Monday there will be a lecture by the teacher (four days).
3. Each Friday will be set aside for discussion in small groups (four days). On Fridays the class will be divided into five small groups. Each group will be assigned a broad question for discussion within the group. Towards the end of the period, a spokesman for the group will report findings to the entire class. Questions for discussion can be found on pages 167–170.
4. Tuesdays, Wednesdays, Thursdays, students will be free to undertake other optional learning activities on a special subject. These activities are listed on pages 156–167.

Lectures

First Monday—"The Robber Barons" and "The Automobile Age."
Suggested Reading for the first week—Chapter 16.

Second Monday—"Transportation in the West."
Suggested Reading for the second week—Chapter 17.

Third Monday—"Money" and "The Rise of Third Party Movements."
Suggested Reading for the third week—Chapter 18.

Fourth Monday—"American Immigration—1607–1975" and "The Labor Movement—1865–1975."
Suggested Reading for the fourth week—Chapter 19.

Minimum Standards for All Students

1. Attend the Monday lectures and take careful notes.
2. Take an active part in the discussion groups on Fridays.
3. Read the four assigned chapters very carefully.
4. Pass a short test on each chapter.
5. Choose one subject for specialized study and complete at least four of the learning activities listed for that subject.
6. Pass a test on the chosen specialized study.

Topics for Specialized Study

1. The American Indian
2. Big Business—Corporations and Trusts
3. Agriculture
4. Railroads
5. Labor Unions
6. Immigration

Testing and Grading

1. A possible 220 points are involved in this unit. Of these, 110 points will be in test grades as follows:
   a. Each chapter test is 20 points. Whenever a student is ready to take one of the chapter tests, he notifies the teacher. He must make a score of at least 70% on chapter tests. If he fails to do so, or if he is not satisfied with his test result, he discusses his work with the teacher, does some more study on the chapter, and takes another test. The second test score is recorded regardless of the result.
   b. The test on the Specialized Study subject is 30 points. Only one test will be given on the Specialized Study.
   c. All tests must be taken before the fourth Friday of the Unit.
2. The remaining 110 points will be the activity grade and will represent the number of learning activities performed by the student to the satisfaction of the teacher. Completion of the minimum standards listed above would result in a grade of "C" or point range of 82–92 points. Completion of the minimum standards plus two additional learning activities would result in a grade of "B" or point range of 93–100 points. Completion of minimum standards plus four additional learning activities would result in a grade of "A" or point range of 101–110 points.
3. The total points from the four weeks unit will be averaged into the nine weeks' grade.

RECORD SHEET FOR ENTIRE UNIT

Activity No.	Description Of Activity	Teacher's Init.	Date	Activity No.	Description Of Activity	Teacher's Init.	Date
1.				19.			
2.				20.			
3.				21.			
4.				22.			
5.				23.			
6.				24.			
7.				25.			
8.				**TEST SCORES**			
				Chapter	First Score		Second Score
9.				16.			
10.				17.			
11.				18.			
12.				19.			
13.				Specialized Study Test			
14.							
15.					Points	Letter Grade	
16.				Total Test Scores			
17.				Activity Grade			
18.				Total Unit Grade			

Specialized Study—Learning Activities

Big Business—Corporations and Trusts

1. Define the following terms:

   industry
   raw materials
   monopoly
   dividend
   stock
   trust
   proxy
   commerce
   philanthropist
   corporation
   natural resources
   vertical combination
   generator
   fractional distillation
   board of directors
   interlocking directorate

2. Identify the following people by writing one sentence about each one:

   Andrew Carnegie
   Edwin Drake
   John Deere
   Thomas Edison
   Henry Ford
   Henry Bessemer
   Richard Hoe
   Samuel Morse
   F. J. Sprague
   Ransom Olds
   Cyrus McCormick
   J. P. Morgan
   Otto Merganthaler
   Cyrus Field
   Christopher Sholes
   The Duryea brothers
   The Wright brothers
   Alexander Graham Bell
   John D. Rockefeller

3. For the bulletin board: make a chart that diagrams the structure of a corporation.
4. For the bulletin board: make a chart on the inventions from 1860–1900 with the following headings: invention, inventor, year, importance.
5. For the bulletin board: show the location of the important resources of our country on an outline map of the United States.
6. For the bulletin board: make a chart on major United States cities today (limit 12–15) with the following headings: city, current population, the two most important industries, reason for growth.

7. For the bulletin board: make a two column chart listing:
   a. The advantages of big city life.
   b. The problems caused by the rapid growth of cities.

8. For the artist: choose eight inventions of this period that you consider to be important. Draw sketches of the inventions or scenes showing their use.

9. Dialogue: three students—a reporter, a big businessman, and a laborer. Reporter is to interview the other two people to get their views on a proposed income tax (about 1875). Prepare well and make arrangements to present this to the class.

10. Interview: interview any person you know who is in corporate management about the free enterprise system of the United States. Construct your questions in advance and discuss them with the teacher before the interview.

11. In writing: tell the story of the Sherman Anti-trust Act (1890) and the Clayton Anti-trust Act (1914). Give provisions, purpose, and importance.

12. In writing: tell the story of the development of *one* of the following: Standard Oil or United States Steel.

13. In writing: describe the good and bad effects of the rise of "Big Business."

14. In writing: for the student who welcomes a challenge! See what you can find out about the sources of capital for our industrial growth from 1860–1900.

15. In writing: do a biography, at least two pages in length, of one of the "Robber Barons."

16. Filmstrip: view *one* of the following filmstrips and write a two page report about it.
   a. "The Emerging Giant—The United States in 1900" Part one only.
   b. "The Industrial Revolution in America" Part two only.

17. Transparencies: choose one of the following transparency sets and study it on the classroom overhead projector. Write a two page report on your findings.
   a. "Growth of the United States Economy"
   b. "United States Growth of Industry and Cities"

18. Filmstrip: "The Gilded Age"—view this strip and write a two page report on it.
19. Filmstrip: "Shaping an Urban Society"—view this strip and write a two page report.

Railroads

1. Explain the following terms and people:

right of way	air brakes
Pullman car	Promontory Point
Leland Stanford	Union Pacific R.R.
George Pullman	Cornelius Vanderbilt
standard gauge	Central Pacific R.R.
Credit Mobilier	George Westinghouse
James Hill	Transcontinental R.R.

2. For the bulletin board: make two maps of the United States, one showing the railroads in 1870 and another showing them today.
3. For the bulletin board: on an outline map of the United States, show the routes of the following: the Butterfield Overland Express, the Pony Express, and the First Transcontinental Railroad.
4. For the bulletin board: make a chart or graph showing total miles of railroad track in the United States every 20 years from 1840 to 1970.
5. For the artist: draw a simple sketch of a modern diesel locomotive and a locomotive typical of the 1880's.
6. For the artist: draw a poster to attract workers for the railroad in the 1860's. "Men Wanted—Apply to the Union Pacific Railroad."
7. For the artist: draw a series of sketches showing the following: railroad beds and their construction, types of track, signals and equipment used on railroads.
8. For the artist: draw sketches of trademark symbols of various famous railroads.
9. For the artist: sketch different types of railroad bridges.
10. For the artist: through sketches and a report describe the system of signals, whistles, and signs used in railroading.

11. Dialogue: two students—a Northern and a Southern Senator debate on the floor of the Congress (before the Civil War) on the question of what route should be followed by the first transcontinental railroad.

12. Interview: interview any person you know who works for a railroad about his job. Construct your questions in advance and discuss them with the teacher before the interview.

13. In writing: explain the effect of the first transcontinental railroad on each of the following: farming, cattle ranching, mining, immigration, and the westward movement.

14. In writing: describe the accomplishments and problems of the Butterfield Overland Express and the Pony Express.

15. In writing: describe the following inventions and give their importance to railroading: Pullman car, airbrakes, standard gauge track.

16. In writing: tell the story of the organization of the first big railroad—the New York Central.

17. In writing: tell the story of the Interstate Commerce Act and the Hepburn Act of 1906. Give provisions, purpose, and importance today.

18. In writing: poems and songs are often written about important developments in our history. How many can you name on railroading? Make a list and tell a little bit about each one.

19. In writing: write a biography of any real or fictional person involved in railroading.

20. In writing: a report on the construction procedures of the early railroads: labor force, hourly pay, length of day, speed of laying track, etc.

21. In writing: a report describing different kinds of engines and railroad cars. You might include some famous trains.

22. Filmstrip: view *one* of the following filmstrips and write a one page report about it.

   a. "The Industrial Revolution In America" Part two only.
   b. "A Nation Rides The Rails—1860–1900"

23. Transparency: "The West 1860–1912" Study this on the classroom overhead projector and summarize your findings in writing.
24. Filmstrip: "The Golden Spike." View this strip and write a two page report.
25. Filmstrip: "The Iron Horse." View this strip and write a two page report.

Agriculture

1. Define the following terms:

contour plowing	sod house
open range	tenant farmer
long drive	Grange
migrant workers	dry farming
one crop system	Chisholm Trail
scientific farming	roundup
reclamation	sharecropper
cow town	

2. For the bulletin board: construct a chart or a graph showing the amount of land used in the United States for each of the following: farming, forests, Indians, parks, cities, railroads, and highways.
3. For the bulletin board: construct a chart or a graph showing the top ten states in the United States in farming. Use farm income or acreage in production as your units of measure.
4. For the bulletin board: prepare a chart or a table showing the changes in farm population during the nineteenth and twentieth centuries.
5. For the bulletin board: draw a map showing early cattle trails and "cow towns."
6. Dialogue: two people—a farmer of the Great Plains in the 1880's discusses with his wife (or with a friend) whether or not they ought to return to the East. Prepare carefully and make arrangements to present this to the class.
7. Interview: interview a farmer, or someone who is in a business connected with farming, on the problems of the American farmer today. Construct your questions in ad-

vance and discuss them with the teacher before the interview.

8. For the artist: choose *one* of the following:
   a. Make sketches of equipment used by cowboys.
   b. Draw sketches of different kinds of cattle found in the West.
   c. Make sketches of various brands used to identify cattle in the West.
9. In writing: discuss the following legislation on farming: Homestead Act, Morrill Act, Hatch Act, Agricultural Adjustment Act, and the Soil Bank Act.
10. In writing: discuss the machines that were invented that helped the farmer and tell of their importance.
11. In writing: tell about the founding and development of any Land-Grant college in the United States.
12. In writing: describe the geography of the Great Plains as found by the farmers a century ago. Consider the following: precipitation, natural vegetation, soil, growing season, topography, resources.
13. In writing: write two or three pages in an imaginary diary of a boy or girl who lived in a sod house on the Great Plains in 1880.
14. In writing: write a two page report on the daily life of a cowboy in our West in the year 1875. Be sure to include the hardships he faced as well as the rewards.
15. In writing: describe several breeds of cattle and dairy cows, giving characteristics of each.
16. In writing: poems and songs are often written about developments in our history. How many "prairie" songs can you name? Tell a little about each one and include some favorite quotations.
17. Filmstrip: from the set, "Yesterday's West," view the filmstrip, "Cattlemen and Homesteaders." Write a one page report about this strip.
18. Transparency: "Growth of the United States Economy"—sheet two only. Study this on the classroom overhead projector and summarize your findings in writing.

19. Filmstrip: "The End of the Wild West." View this strip and write a two page report.
20. Filmstrip: "Rural America." View this strip and write a two page report.

Labor Unions

1. Explain the following terms and people:

injunction	collective bargaining
yellow dog contract	feather bedding
picket	Samuel Gompers
strike breaker	lockout
Uriah Stevens	strike
A.F. of L.	closed shop
fringe benefits	grievance committee
blacklist	Knights of Labor

2. For the bulletin board: make a chart with two columns listing:
   a. Reasons for having right-to-work laws
   b. Reasons for having a closed shop
3. For the bulletin board: make a chart with two columns listing:
   a. Methods used by unions in labor disputes
   b. Methods used by employers in labor disputes

   Include nineteenth century tactics on this chart.
4. For the bulletin board: construct a graph showing the growth of labor union membership in the United States.
5. For the artist: draw a poster to attract workers to join the American Federation of Labor in 1890.
6. Dialogue: two students—the year is 1886. Two working men are having an argument about whether or not they should join the new American Federation of Labor. Prepare carefully and make arrangements to present it to the class.
7. Interview: interview a worker who belongs to a labor union about the advantages and disadvantages of union membership. Construct your questions in advance and discuss them with the teacher before the interview.
8. In writing: name and describe briefly the major labor unions in the United States today.

9. In writing: give the provisions, purpose, and importance of the Wagner Act, the Taft Hartley Act, and the Landrum-Griffin Act.
10. In writing: tell the story of the Department of Labor including date of formation, purpose, main branches, and present leader.
11. In writing: explain the following legislation: minimum wage laws, child labor laws, workmen's compensation, unemployment compensation.
12. In writing: write up a contract between a union and management for a specific factor in the year 1880. Include at least eight provisions and be sure that they are logical for that period in history.
13. Filmstrip: "The Growth of the Labor Movement," Part One and Part Two. Write a one page report about this strip.
14. Transparency: "Growth of the United States Economy," sheet one only. Study this set on the classroom overhead projector and summarize your findings in writing.
15. Filmstrip: "Strike." View this strip and write a two page report on it.

The American Indian

1. Explain the following terms and people:

Comanche	Crazy Horse
Shoshone	Geronimo
Dawes-Severalty Act	Sioux
Oklahoma Territory	reservation
Sitting Bull	Great Plains
Blackfoot	Red Cloud
Apaches	George Custer
Cochise	

2. For the bulletin board: show the location of important Indian tribes in the early nineteenth century on an outline map of the United States.
3. For the bulletin board: construct a chart on "Indian Wars" in United States history including date, tribes, location, and results.

4. For the bulletin board: show the location of Indian reservations today on an outline map of the United States.
5. For the bulletin board: construct a chart of Indian tribes, including original location, present location, population then and now.
6. For the artist: make a series of sketches showing tools, equipment, and weapons of the Indians.
7. For the artist: make a series of sketches showing various types of shelter used by the Indians.
8. Dialogue: two students—two Indian chiefs are about to attend a large tribal council in the year 1880. The two chiefs are to conduct an argument as to whether or not the Indian should go to war with the white man in the West. Prepare well, and make arrangements to present this to the class.
9. In writing: explain the importance of the buffalo to the Western American Indian. Give details on the use of various parts of the animal's body by the Indians.
10. In writing: describe the situation of the Indians of today. How many are there? How many on reservations? What problems do they have? What kind of work do they do? What educational opportunities do they have?
11. In writing: discuss Indian culture. Can you find any old Indian songs or poems or sayings or superstitions? How about religion?
12. In writing: describe the typical costume and dress used by one major Indian tribe, *or*, for the artist, show this in a sketch.
13. In writing: write a report on the hunting methods used by the Indians including dressing of the animals caught.
14. In writing: write a biography of any famous Indian chief.
15. In writing: write a report on the life styles of Indians in different areas of the United States during the seventeenth century.
16. Filmstrip: "The American Indian: A Dispossessed People." Write a one page report about this filmstrip.

17. Transparency: "Effect of Western Settlement Upon the Indians." Write a one page report.

18. Transparency: "Indians' Clothing." Write a two page report.

19. Filmstrip: "The Iron Horse." View this strip and write a two page report on it.

Immigration

1. Explain the following terms and people:

alien	Alexander Graham Bell
immigrate	Sam Gompers
emigrate	Enrico Fermi
naturalization	James Hill
quota system	Victor Herbert
"Old Immigration"	"Open Shore"
tenements	Albert Einstein
"New Immigration"	Irving Berlin
"Gentlemen's Agreement"	Jacob Riis
Andrew Carnegie	

2. For the bulletin board: on an outline map of the United States show the areas where particular nationality groups of immigrants were likely to settle.

3. For the bulletin board: construct a bar graph showing the total number of immigrants that we have had from at least ten different major countries.

4. For the bulletin board: construct a bar graph showing the total number of immigrants during ten separate peak years in our history.

5. For the bulletin board: construct a chart with the following headings:
   - **a.** Problems caused by immigrants
   - **b.** Contributions of immigrants to the United States
   - **c.** Reasons for immigration to the United States

6. For the bulletin board: construct a chart with the following headings: city, nationality groups of immigrants found there, types of jobs available; other reasons for immigrant settlement. Cover at least ten cities.

7. For the artist: draw a sketch of the Statue of Liberty. Include with this a report on this famous statue.
8. For the artist: draw sketches of typical poor immigrants entering the United States in the early 1900's.
9. Dialogue: two students—the year is 1945 (World War II just ended). Two Senators debate the immigration policies that should be set up through legislation. Prepare carefully and make arrangements to present this to the class.
10. Dialogue: two students—the year is 1922. An Italian peasant and his wife discuss whether or not they should leave their homeland and immigrate into the United States. Prepare carefully and make arrangements to present this to the class.
11. Interview: interview a person who has immigrated to the United States (either an alien or a naturalized citizen). Discuss the problems and rewards of moving into our country. Construct your questions in advance and discuss them with the teacher before your interview.
12. In writing: write a report on Ellis Island as a center for immigration. Describe the life there, the routine of entry, rules, regulations, etc.
13. In writing: discuss the following legislation:
    a. Chinese Exclusion Act
    b. Immigration Quota Act
    c. McCarren—Walter Act
14. In writing: compare Indians and Black Americans with other immigrants. How were they similar? How were they different? What problems did they have in common?
15. In writing: write several pages in the diary of a boy or girl who immigrated to the United States in the 1920's.
16. In writing: how many terms, customs, and foods that are commonly used in America can be identified with immigrants from certain nations. Include the following on each term: its beginning, country of origin, and importance. You might start with the following: kindergarten, Santa Claus, log cabin, Mardi Gras, Easter eggs, ranch, spaghetti, chop suey. You should cover at least twenty items.

17. Transparency: "Immigration: Settlers from Norway." Obtain from the classroom teacher and study it in class. Write a two page report on this set of transparencies.
18. Filmstrip: "America Comes of Age"—Filmstrip 2—"The Immigrants." View this strip, taking careful notes. Write a two page report on this filmstrip.
19. Filmstrip: "The Other American Minorities." Choose *one* of the following filmstrips from this series. View it, take good notes, and write a two page report.
    a. "The Mexican American"
    b. "The Puerto Rican/the Cuban"
    c. "The Oriental American"

Discussion Sheet

First Friday, Chapter 16

1. The government exercises control over "Big Business" and large personal fortunes in several ways—corporate taxes, anti-trust laws, income tax laws, etc. What do you think might happen to our economy if these controls were removed? Do you feel that government control on business should be tighter? More relaxed?
2. In many countries today, the major industries are owned and operated by the government rather than by private companies. What do you see as the advantages and disadvantages of such a system?
3. In recent years we have come to realize that many industries are destroying our environment. What suggestions do you have for solving this problem? What is the responsibility of industry in this respect? What role should government play? Private citizens? Schools?
4. In the last two years, we have faced a major power crisis. Many people feel that the "big oil companies" have manufactured the oil crisis and have taken advantage of the crisis to make huge profits. What do you think the government should do about energy?
5. The United States today is known to be the world's leading industrial power. Discuss all of the reasons why this is true.

Of these reasons, which single factor do you consider to be the most important? Do you think that any other nation will pass us in industrial power? If so, which one and why?

Second Friday, Chapter 17

1. During the railroad building era, the government of the United States gave millions of acres of the "public domain" to the railroads. Was this "giveaway program" justified? Could private companies have built the railroads without government help? Should they have done so?
2. The official policy of the United States government was to push the tribes westward as the nation grew. Eventually most Indians were put on reservations. What is your opinion of this policy? What other types of plans might have been used that could have allowed the white man to develop the country and still be fair to the Indians?
3. Railroad companies today claim that they lose money on passenger travel. Their rates are controlled by the Interstate Commerce Commission, and the I.C.C. states that railroads must maintain passenger service in certain areas. Passengers complain that the service offered is so poor that it discourages passenger travel. Do you see any solution to this problem? In view of crowded highways, pollution, the move to suburbia, and the energy crisis, do you think railroad travel should be increased? If so, how?
4. The farmer, the cattleman, and the sheepherder were in conflict for many years as the West developed. Describe the rights that each of these three were trying to protect. Which of the three had the "best case"? Which of the three had to change the most?
5. Most of us think of the growth of the West as a glamorous and exciting chapter in American history. This image has led to the development of the movie western. Discuss all the ways in which the mining industry helped to create this glamorous image of our West.

Third Friday, Chapter 18

1. Is the statement true that "A prosperous country must have prosperous farmers"? Give reasons for your answers. Be

sure and consider the economic problems of today's farmers.

2. The United States has 25 percent of the world's usable land to feed 6 percent of the world's people. This is the only country in the world that regularly produces more food than it can use. Discuss the following statements in terms of our surplus:
   a. The Federal Government spends millions of dollars each year to store surplus food.
   b. The Federal Government spends millions of dollars each year to pay farmers *not* to grow food on their land, and at the same time, spends millions of dollars on dams and irrigation projects to open up new land for farming in the dry areas of the West.
   c. Our surplus crops are getting smaller every year.
3. There are over three billion people on earth. It is estimated that two billion people go to bed hungry every night. Should the United States make a bigger effort to do something about this? If so, what?
4. Review the Platform of the Populist Party. How many of the things that they proposed would help the farmer in America? In what states were the greatest centers of Populist Party support? Why?
5. How are debtors affected by rising prices? By declining prices? How are creditors affected by both? (A real tough question—have a go at it!)

Fourth Friday, Chapter 19

1. Provisions have been made to prevent corporations from growing too large and thereby getting a "monopoly." Should the government likewise pass legislation designed to keep unions from growing too powerful? Could the AFL-CIO be considered a monopoly?
2. In recent years there has been discussion (and in many cases, action) about forming unions for teachers, firemen, police, federal and state employees, and other "vital" jobs. What would be the advantages and disadvantages of such unions? Do you favor them?
3. Because of the serious inflation of the last couple of years,

union workers in many industries are either striking or threatening to strike. In view of our serious economic problems, what is your opinion of this?

4. Do you favor restrictions on immigration today? Why or why not? What would be the problems created if we had completely unrestricted immigration? What kind of immigration policy do you think we should have today?
5. A Swiss citizen spoke contemptuously of Americans compared to the Swiss as follows: "The Swiss are a people." This was spoken with great pride. Then he went on to say, "Americans are not a people—they are just a nation." He felt that our "Melting Pot" had weakened us. What do you see as the advantages and disadvantages of being just one kind of people, as the Swiss are?

Contract Sheet

Number of Activities	***Letter Grade***	***Points***
2	D	70
3	C−	76
4	C	82
5	C+	87
6	B	93
7	B+	97
8	A	101
9 and up	A+	depends on the number completed

Contract

I hereby sign a contract to complete __________ Learning Activities for a letter grade of __________. It is my understanding that there is no penalty if I do not succeed in making my contract. I also understand that it is permissible for me to complete more activities than my contract calls for. I hereby state that the number of activities that I have contracted to complete represents my best estimate of the amount of work that I can accomplish in four weeks.

____
Student's Signature

____
Teacher's Initials

Independent Study Project

Some general instructions that might be helpful.

1. Testing may be done only on Tuesdays, Wednesdays, and Thursdays.
2. If you need to see the teacher on Tuesday, Wednesday, or Thursday, take a number from the desk as soon as you come in the room or as soon as one is available.
3. You do *not* need a number to get a library pass—they are available at all times at the teacher's desk. Nor do you need a number to turn in a test that you have finished. You do need a number for all other purposes.
4. Be very careful not to mix up the books on the cart (from the library) with those on the green table (texts). In either case, please return the book to the table or cart from which you got it.
5. As far as possible try to avoid using the library during the lunch periods, as they are quite busy during those times.
6. In general, it is a good policy to discuss with Mrs. Stoddard any difficulties you are having finding materials. All other questions should be directed to Mrs. Severance.
7. This reminder is probably not necessary, but should be mentioned—your "free days" on Tuesday, Wednesday, and Thursday—must not be wasted. You have a challenging job ahead of you. You are expected to maintain an atmosphere that is quiet and businesslike, similar to that of a library. Obviously, behavior that disturbs other students or disrupts the group will not be tolerated.
8. Remember that there can be much value in working together with another student—that is why we are setting up conference areas. You may help each other to study for tests, or to work out projects, or to find and share material.
9. *IMPORTANT*—PLEASE REMEMBER THIS INSTRUCTION. Be sure that the following information is included with every paper that you turn in: Your name, your class period, the topic of your Specialized Study (Indians, Railroads, Agriculture, etc.) and the *number* of the activity that you are turning in.

RESPONSIBILITIES OF THE STUDENTS

The first thing that the student must do after reading this booklet is to make a number of carefully considered choices. What specialized topic does he wish to pursue? How many activities should he undertake? What kinds of activities interest him? What kind of a grade is he trying to reach? While making these choices, he has to plan in detail his schedule for the four weeks. Careful organization will help him to achieve his goals. After he has come to grips with all of these things, it is time to fill out the contract shown on page 170.

In addition to these personal responsibilities, he has several obligations to the class. The teacher should make these clear at the outset of the program. During the ''free wheeling'' days (Tuesday, Wednesday, and Thursday), it is important to maintain a study atmosphere in the classroom. If students and teacher do not work together to achieve such an atmosphere, these days could easily deteriorate into social periods.

Students should also be alert for opportunities to work with other students. They may study in pairs or small groups for chapter tests. They may help one another to find materials for their projects. The dialogue suggested for each area of study requires student interaction. Students can help one another at the overhead projector as they study transparencies. In addition, I have found that students often initate new projects that are not in the booklet (first getting the teacher's approval). These, too, should be shared with other students.

Finally, the student needs to realize that he must keep in close touch with the teacher throughout this unit. Frequent conferences on a one to one basis are essential to the success of this program.

THE ROLE OF THE TEACHER

Prepare this unit months in advance. And prepare in detail, as there is much to be done. If you study the student booklet, for example, you will find that you must construct fourteen tests for this unit! You should also consider the fact that your librarian will need several months' notice so that she can collect materials and plan her schedule. Last minute, haphazard planning on the part of the teacher could destroy this unit.

When the student booklets are distributed, it is most important that the teacher allow plenty of time for giving detailed instructions to the students. I have found that I must set aside an entire class period for this purpose. Introduce this unit in a manner that will generate excitement. Your enthusiasm about the project will help to motivate your classes.

Set very high standards for the project work, and let your students know that you expect their best efforts throughout the unit. If a student turns in a project that reflects minimal effort, return it for a rewrite job.

Be prepared to act as a personal advisor to each student; frequent conferences are essential. Watch carefully for stragglers. Each year I've found about three or four students who lack the ability to be self-starting. Such students may need a bit of prodding.

Keep right on top of the grading chores—both test and project work should be evaluated each day and returned to the students promptly. I assure you that this will help to keep the students interested.

Make maximum use of bulletin boards. It is important to post each day all work that is well done. Your students will take great pride in a room full of their best efforts. Also, there is much to be learned from these shared displays.

As you plan and execute this kind of program, be aware of the amount of "busy work" involved. I refer to such thing as maps and graphs that have been assigned, which students can sometimes simply copy from a book. A number of such projects are in my plan. These assignments have value for some of the slower students as a way to get them started on this program. However, as you have conferences with students, try to help each one to plan a program that will properly challenge him. Superior students should definitely be discouraged from opting for the easier assignments.

In order to keep things running smoothly, I have set up a number system similar to the routine in bakeries or specialty food shops. When a student wishes to see me, he takes a card with a number on it, then continues his work until his number is called. This eliminates the need to stand in line. It also gives the student a feeling of importance. Let's face it, a certain amount of "ham" in any teacher makes learning more fun.

Finally, I offer a word of caution. Do not view this as a four week vacation for the teacher simply because the students are working independently. That would be a fatal mistake. If you choose to use this program, or design one of your own that is similar, be prepared to work very hard. If you conduct this program properly, you will expend much more time and effort than you would with a traditional approach.

ROOM USE

Effective and imaginative use of the classroom and its facilities can contribute substantially to the success of this unit. The very fact that a major change of the classroom furniture may be required adds a sense of drama that impresses the students. The sketch of the room shown on page 175 deserves some study.

Note the teacher's desk in the rear of the room. It is placed right next to the file cabinets so that the teacher has easy access to any of the fourteen tests needed for this unit. The extra chair at the teacher's desk is to be used by any student who needs a conference.

Six desks have been set aside for testing purposes and are placed so that students taking the tests have their backs to the rest of the group. The testing area offers a measure of quiet and seclusion.

The overhead projector is placed near the screen and is available for student use at all times.

A large conference table at the rear of the room is used by groups of four or more students who may wish to work together. In addition, there are three sets of desks where students may work in pairs.

The remaining student desks are placed in three rows. These are used by students working independently on projects or study.

In the front of the room are a book cart and a small table. The cart is for library books and the table holds my entire collection of history texts for both the junior and senior high school levels. All of these books are available to all students, but they may not be removed from the classroom.

This arrangement of the room furnishings tends to reinforce the rules. Students in the conference area, in pairs or in a larger group at the back table, are allowed to talk. Students are also encouraged to work in small groups with the transparencies at the overhead projector, and again, conversation is necessary and desirable.

Those who are in the independent work area or the testing area are required to maintain silence.

During the three years that I have used this project, students have adjusted to the rules and procedures very quickly. Their approach to this unit and the work to be completed has been quite satisfactory.

If you choose to use this unit, or construct one that is similar, I would urge you to make every effort to design a good plan for room use. It is definitely a factor in a successful program.

ROOM USE

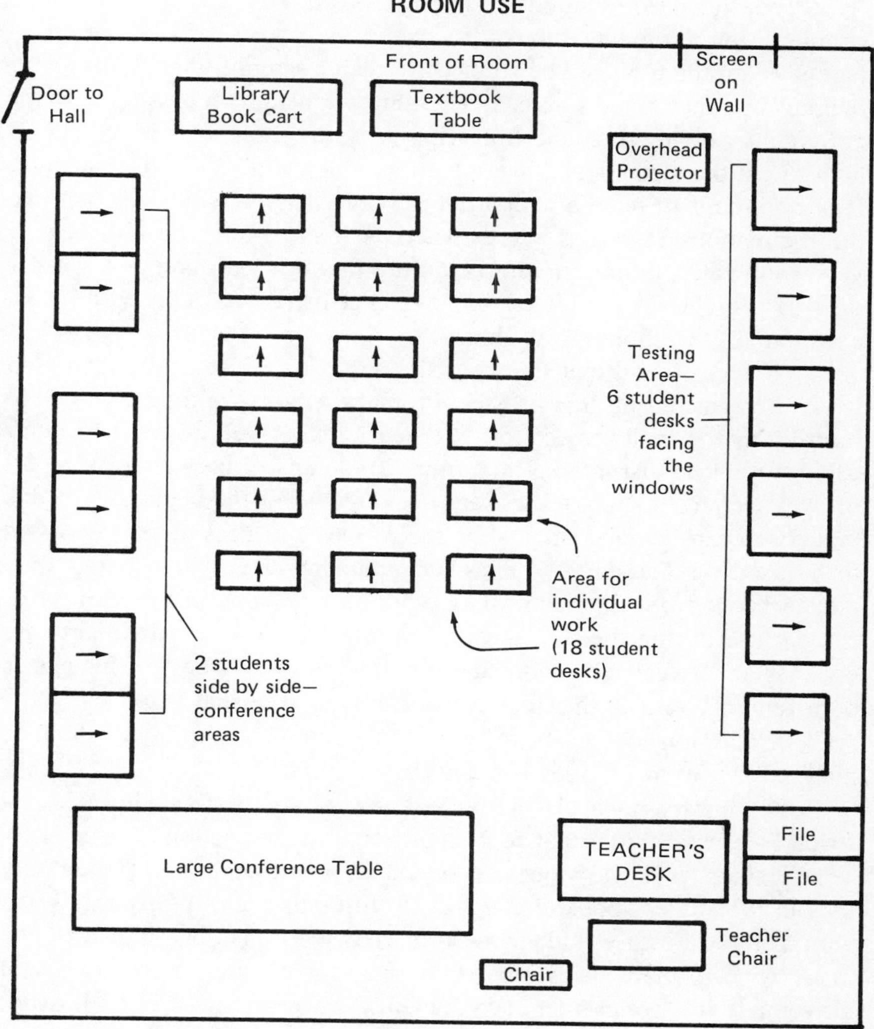
Front of Room
Screen on Wall
Door to Hall
Library Book Cart
Textbook Table
Overhead Projector
Testing Area— 6 student desks facing the windows
Area for individual work (18 student desks)
2 students side by side— conference areas
Large Conference Table
TEACHER'S DESK
File
File
Teacher Chair
Chair

MATERIALS

Suggested materials and equipment are based on a program with 125 students during a four week period.

You will need hundreds of library books. You will need at least a couple dozen various textbooks, a dozen film strips, and a dozen transparencies on the topics to be studied. In the classroom, there must be an overhead projector and a screen. The library must provide equipment for individual viewing of sound filmstrips. It is advisable to seek secretarial help to cut the stencils and assemble the booklets given to the students. It is important to have a supportive school principal who will approve the requisitions for all of these materials. Above all, you will need a very cooperative librarian who is willing to work with you as a partner on this project. This unit could never get off the ground without an exceptionally well-equipped library.

We have found that library usage and activity is usually increased by 20 percent during this project. Proper advance planning is essential in order that special projects of other teachers, as well as normal library use, will not be disrupted at this time. Two carts of books, covering all of the specialized study topics, are made ready for the beginning of this unit. Each cart contains about 120 books. One cart goes to the classroom to be used on Tuesday, Wednesday, and Thursday. These books may not be taken from the room. The other cart remains in the library for student use during the day and for overnight loan. These two carts are exchanged between classroom and library on a weekly basis. This places both sets of books in the library on Friday for weekend loan.

In addition to the above, a special section of pertinent reference materials of 30 to 35 titles is set up in the library.

The library must also provide a special area for viewing of filmstrips. We have found that four small screen combination filmstrip cassette players, with earphones, is adequate for this project. The activity lists in the student booklet suggest 18 different sound filmstrips on the various topics. Many students wish to view more than one filmstrip, and many wish to view strips more than once for a better understanding. I have made it a policy that each student must use at least one filmstrip. This is the one place where I interfere with the student's right to choose during this unit.

Our librarian is on constant alert for new materials, both print and non-print that might add to this unit. She is aware of the circulation of materials so that she can determine where further duplication or substitution of materials is indicated. As a teacher, you will find that the efforts of the librarian on this project are as necessary as yours are.

The program described in this chapter offers a real challenge to the students. We owe it to them to secure the best possible materials.

GRADING

You will find grading and testing for this unit on page three of the student booklet. A brief summary here might be helpful.

There is a total of 220 points possible on this unit. Tests account for 110 points (four 20-point chapter tests and one 30-point specialized study test). The remaining 110 points are for the project assignments, and a single grade will be given for the project work.

I find it best not to give letter grades on each assignment submitted to me. This is a very good place to use a check, or check plus, or check minus (see Chapter 4, Testing and Grading). When the time comes to compute the activity grade, you might use the following scale: (Please note that you will also find this scale in the student booklet on the contract sheet, shown on page 170.)

Number of activities	*Letter grade*	*Points*
2	D	70
3	C−	76
4	C	82
5	C+	87
6	B	93
7	B+	97
8	A	101
9 and up	A+	depends on the number completed

When computing a student's activity grade, start by using the scale shown here and add two points for every plus received on activity grades. Subtract two points for every minus shown. For example, suppose that a student had completed six projects. The six grades were: check, check plus, check plus, check plus plus, check, and check. According to the scale the base score is 93. Add to this eight points for the four plus marks. The total activity grade would be 101.

Consider this example: A student has completed fifteen activities. The fifteen grades were:

check	check	check plus
check minus	check plus	check
check	check	check plus plus
check	check plus	check
check	check plus	check

This student has clearly "gone over the top." Start with the base score for an "A"—101 points. Add two points for every plus, in this case twelve points. Subtract two points for the minus. Finally add two points for every activity beyond the eight required for an "A"—in this case, fourteen points. The final activity score would be 125, an exceptionally good score.

This has proven to be an efficient and workable grading system for this unit. It might be helpful to some of the readers.

Whatever system of grading you choose to use, I'd suggest that you compile a distribution sheet of grades for all classes involved in the unit. This sheet should include test scores, activity grades, and the total unit grades. Be aware of records set over the years that beg to be broken. Such records provide excellent motivation for future classes. For example, the highest test score I've seen in my classes is 109 out of 110 possible points. The largest number of activities completed is 24 (a remarkable achievement). The highest number of total points stands at 243 out of a possible 220. Each year ambitious students attack these existing records vigorously. I make a point of giving sample distribution sheets to students at the beginning of the unit. It helps them as they set their goals for this project.

CHALLENGE—A SPIN-OFF

This is a new program for my classes—so new, in fact, that I probably cannot evaluate it with any degree of validity. I designed it for the gifted student and chose to call it CHALLENGE. I offer it here as one example of a way to enrich an existing program. No matter how successful a project or program may be, it is good to be constantly alert to the possibility of revisions, changes, or improvements.

This particular ''spin-off'' came about because of two factors. First, my current eighth grade classes are blessed with an unusually large number of students who are talented and very bright. I have found the maturity, perception, and sensitivity of some of these kids to be downright exciting, and it made me wish to channel some of that excitement into a valuable learning experience for them. In addition, I must confess that I was just plain curious to find out how much they could do.

Another factor that helped to lead me into this new program was the fact that I am serving on a faculty committee that was organized to set up programs for gifted students in our school district. I'm a maverick on that committee—silently—but a maverick, nonetheless. On the committee I'm still listening, but, in terms of this book, the time has come for me to speak out. I'm not at all sure that we need special programs for the gifted students. Most of the truly good students are going to learn in school, no matter what—sometimes in spite of us. If we have extra time, extra energy, and extra funds, there are, in my view, several other kinds of students whose priorities should come first. How about the chronic failure, the underachiever, the potential dropout, the poorly motivated? And how about that famous ''Johnny who can't read''?

I find myself shrinking from the idea of a self-contained program for gifted students. I do not like the elitist overtones of such a situation. I'm keenly aware of the reality of peer pressure at the teenage level. The outstanding student at this level must chart his course very carefully in order to protect his right to be ''different'' in terms of academic excellence, and at the same time, preserve his identity as ''one of the boys.'' Let us not make it any harder for him to chart such a course.

I also find myself favoring enrichment rather than acceleration for the gifted student. (In taking this position, I am well aware of the fact that I am bucking current trends.) Why should we rush gifted eighth graders through American history, world history, American government, and world problems when there are countless avenues to be explored in a regular eighth grade American history course? If the teacher is creative enough to help them discover such avenues, the gifted students will not be bored and will gain much from remaining with their peers.

As I look back, I find that the last several paragraphs concentrate on things that I'm against. The last sentence in the paragraph above leads me into what I'm for. And it comes right back to the individual teacher in his own classroom using every weapon and tool available in order to reach not only the gifted, but all of the students in his classroom. Again, I call for careful programming, assignments that are well thought out, and flexible enough to fit the needs of all. I offer a few concrete examples:

1. Chapter 5—the second current events assignment. Note the wide variety of topics offered. They allow for a wide range of abilities, as *well* as a range of interests.
2. Chapter 5—the third current events assignment. A report on the United Nations or the Peace Corps is a relatively easy assignment. Economic and military alliances are challenging topics for eighth graders and suitable for the outstanding students.
3. Chapter 5—the fifth current events assignment. A report on any of the ''Isms'' is a bit much for the average eighth grader, but is certainly geared for the gifted student. Reports on the twentieth century leaders are appropriate for the other students, and all gain from the exchange of information that should follow.
4. Chapter 6—the Civil War Debates—fun, exciting, and good learning for students of all abilities.
5. Chapter 7—study the learning activities offered in the individualized instruction unit and note the range of skills called for.

All of this background for CHALLENGE should meet the needs of the reader. It is now time to get into the program itself. CHALLENGE was carefully described in pamphlet form for the students. I include it here.

CHALLENGE
A corollary to the Individualized Instruction Project. This program is designed for the gifted history student.

Myra Hayes Severance
Social Studies Teacher
Brecksville Junior High School

Each of you is offered an opportunity to take part in a pilot program that has been designed for the gifted history student. This program will demand from you extra effort, a great deal of time, and much energy. Please do not undertake it unless you are willing to meet this kind of a challenge.

Each of you will use the instruction book that was given to all of the other students as a base for your work. Like the other students, you will need to choose one of the six major themes for your study. Along with your classmates, you will be relatively free to set the pace and the direction of your study. Here the similarities end and the differences begin.

Instead of completing various separate activities, you will be asked to write a single major paper within your chosen subject field, focusing on one emphasis that you would like to pursue. Everything that you do for the next four weeks in history will be a part of that paper.

You will not be required to take any tests during this unit. Your entire grade, 220 points, will be given on the one major paper that you submit to your teacher at the end of the four weeks. It will amount to one-half of your total nine week's grade.

You should be reminded that the name of the game for this four weeks is "choice." Be assured that this choice will not be taken away from you. You may choose to take part in this pilot program, or you may choose to complete the project in the same fashion as the other members of your class. You will need to make your choice, however, by ________Date________.

By all means, discuss this first with your parents. Nobody knows you better than they do, and they should be a part of this decision. You and your parents might decide that this project is not appropriate for you.

If you do decide to undertake the CHALLENGE, your parents can be very helpful to you, if they help you in the proper way. They may assist you in choosing a topic for your paper. They may discuss with you your progress and problems as you proceed on the project. They may help you to find some of your material, or set up contacts for interviews. However, please do not expect them to do your work. The research and the writing must be your very own.

If you do choose to try this more challenging approach to the project, you will have an individual conference with Mrs. Severance on ________Date________ to discuss the direction and scope of your paper. You will also be scheduled for an individual conference with the librarian, Mrs. Stoddard, on ______Date______. You will need to work very closely with both of these people throughout the four weeks. Both of them stand ready to assist you.

You will find listed here some suggested topics for your paper. You may choose to use any one of these, or to make a selection of your own. If you choose a title or topic of your own, it must be approved by both Mrs. Severance and Mrs. Stoddard.

Indians
- Indian Reservations throughout our history
- The United States' policy toward the American Indian
- A study of an Indian Tribe from earliest history to the present

Immigration
- The United States as a melting pot
- Immigration in the Midwest (emphasis on Ohio/Cleveland)
- Gateways to America (New York City and San Francisco)
- A comparison of Asian and European immigration

Big Business
- In defense of the free enterprise system
- The Golden Age of industry
- Inventions and the rise of big business
- Monopolies and the free enterprise system

Agriculture
- The Populists as champions of rural America
- The farm as big business
- The American farm and a hungry world

Railroads
- The railroad and the westward movement
- Government land giveaways and the railroad
- Problems of American railroads today

Labor Unions
- Labor and the American standard of living
- Labor unions and public employees
- Balance of power—big business, big government, big labor

After reading all of this, talking to your parents, making your decision, and choosing a topic, you are ready to consider some suggestions for procedures that will make your work easier:

1. Do a great deal of reading before you start to write.
2. As you read, take notes on any material that might be useful to you. Be sure that you include in your notes the sources used for each part of your research.
3. No matter what your topic, start your paper with some background information. How about labor unions before 1865? What do you know of the very early history of the American Indian? What are the roots of the American system of business and industry? What changes had taken place in American farming before 1865? And so forth.
4. As you begin to feel better informed from your reading, it is time to construct an outline of your paper that will show the topics to be covered and the probable sequence of material. Discuss this outline with Mrs. Severance before you proceed further.
5. Next comes the hardest part—start writing.
6. Make use of the materials in your project instruction booklet. No matter what the topic of your paper, you should include maps, graphs, charts, tables—any kind of graphic material that will lend interest and information to your paper. An interview might be appropriate, or you may wish to include some sketches.
7. Be very sure that the source of all work that is not original (your very own) is given proper credit in your paper. You may not copy from a book unless you use quotation marks and a footnote.
8. It is important that you have frequent conferences with Mrs. Severance as you progress. For example, if you choose to use an interview, be sure that she gets to see your questions in advance. If you construct an original graph, ask her to check your first draft before you proceed to the finished copy. Likewise, it is a good idea to maintain very close contact with Mrs. Stoddard as you search for more information.
9. When you finally get past the first rough draft of your paper, there are a few rules to follow:
   a. Papers should be typed if possible. They should be dou-

ble spaced, and the left-hand margin should be wide enough to permit the pages to be fastened into a folder. If papers are handwritten, please write neatly and double space.

b. You must include a Bibliography. Follow the form that you have been taught to use in your English classes; a copy is included with this material. You are expected to number the entries on your Bibliography (see sample Bibliography). These numbers will be useful to you when you record your footnotes.

c. All quotations should be enclosed with quotation marks. When using these marks, be sure that other punctuation marks such as commas, question marks, or periods, are placed inside the quotation marks.

d. Each quotation in your paper must have a footnote. Footnotes are numbered consecutively. Place the footnote number as shown in the example below, one-half space above the typed line.

"The 1920's was the period of the Charleston."[1]

Place the same number at the bottom of the page along with the *number* of the book on the Bibliography list that contains the quotation and the page on which you found the quotation. [1]Number 3—page 287. This footnote tells the reader that it is the first footnote in your paper, that it came from the third reference on your Bibliography, (*Fads, Follies, and Delusions of the American People*), and that it was found on page 287.

e. Here is another sample:

> "Teen-agers have shown a recent trend toward an appreciation of classical music."[2]

---

[2]Number 13—Page 66.

This footnote tells the reader that it is the second footnote in your paper, that it came from the thirteenth reference on your Bibliography (*Musical America*), and that it was on page 66. A final word about the use of footnotes. Be sure that you acknowledge any graphs, charts, maps, or tables that are copied from any source.

You will have many questions as you write this paper. Do not hesitate to ask such questions and persist until you have the understanding that you need. Good luck to all of you!

MUSIC BIBLIOGRAPHY (SAMPLE)

Books

1. Bernstein, Leonard. *Young People's Concerts*. New York: Simon and Schuster, 1970.
2. Ewen, David. *Famous Modern Conductors*. New York: Dodd, Mead and Company, 1967.
3. Sann, Paul. *Fads, Follies and Delusions of the American People*. New York: Bonanza Books, 1967.
4. Stambler, Irwin and Landon, Grelun. *Golden Guitars*. New York: Four Winds Press, 1971.
5. Van der Horst, Brian. *Rock Music*. New York: Franklin Watts, Inc., 1973.

Encyclopedias

6. "Music." *Compton's Encyclopedia Yearbook*, 1975, 309–311.
7. "Music." *Encyclopedia International*, 1974, XII, 373–381.
8. "Music." *World Book Encyclopedia*, 1972, XIII, 784–800b.

Magazines

9. Klein, Hans. "Low-cost Synthesizers: Switched-on Home Music Fun." *Popular Mechanics*, January, 1974, 126–129.
10. "Music Makers To Make," *Better Homes and Gardens*, January, 1974, 54–55.
11. Paul, Anthony M. "Music Is Child's Play for Professor Suzuki," *Reader's Digest*, November, 1973, 269–275.

Pamphlets

12. *Bandwagon*. Indiana: No Publisher given, 1975.
13. *Musical America*. New York: Music Publications, Ltd., September, 1961.
14. *Popular Music as a Career*. Chicago: Institute for Research, no date given.
15. Sloan, Charles H. *Talented Campers Make Michigan Woodland Ring*. Washington, D.C.: National Geographic School Bulletin, November 29, 1971, 178–181.

RESULTS OF CHALLENGE—(FIRST YEAR)

Eighteen students were invited to take part in this new program; fourteen accepted, nine girls and five boys.

The papers that resulted from this CHALLENGE project exceeded by expectations in every way. It was most enlightening for me to discover the capabilities of the gifted eighth grade students. Grades on the papers ranged from A to A+; they were so well done that any other choice was unthinkable. Papers ranged in length from 20 to 139 pages. Students mastered skills involved in researching, note-taking, footnoting, interviewing, and graphing. They analyzed the material they had compiled; they drew conclusions; they raised questions; they formed convictions of their own and defended them. Most of them had frequent conferences with me, and I found those to be a delight. They also conferred frequently with the librarian, Mrs. Stoddard. Most important of all—they took great pride in the results of their efforts.

I am keenly aware of the fact that the success of such a difficult project depends heavily on the support and encouragement of family members in the home. I know that parents helped these students in many ways, and in the right ways. Students told me of discussions with family members, parent assistance in finding materials, contacts made for interviews, correction of grammar and spelling, and assistance with typing. I took pains to encourage this type of interaction within families. The students clearly had help from the teacher, the school librarian, and their families. Such a combination surely must result in a good educational experience.

I include here brief excerpts from some of the CHALLENGE papers—excerpts that demonstrate some of the critical thinking reflected in these papers.

It was a good project. I find myself eager to try it again.

America, the Melting Pot by Carolyn Matheson

> . . . In my opinion, immigration was the greatest thing that ever happened to the United States.
>
> It is the blending of the world's cultures that has made us unique.
>
> However, some people feel that this has weakened us. They claim that we have no culture of our own—that we only have little bits and pieces of everyone else's and very little that is original.

I disagree. I think that the mixture itself is *the* American culture. After all, few of us are all German or all Italian—instead, we are Americans, with a mixture of nationalities, and, therefore, a mixture of traditions and cultures. For example, I am Scottish, Irish, and Welsh. I have a kilt in my family tartan, wear green on St. Patrick's Day, and our family eats a British Christmas dinner. But we also have a German Christmas tree, love Italian spaghetti, and my favorite Saturday lunch is a sandwich made from bologna and Lebanese pocket bread. On top of that, we celebrate truly American holidays such as Thanksgiving and the Fourth of July. See what I mean about the American culture?

Perhaps the best way of explaining America and her culture of cultures is America's motto: *E Pluribus Unum*—meaning "From many, one."

The Sioux Indians by Debbie Sprow

. . . I have come to conclude that the way of life for the Indian in America was not exactly the greatest. For I believe the Indians have been unjustly treated. I feel the Indians have been denied the right—that which has been in our Declaration of Independence since the birth of our nation—the right to pursue happiness. The Indians were pushed onto reservations and they were forbidden to perform their sacred Sun Dance. They were guarded and watched closely; it was much like a concentration camp. No one was permitted to leave, that is until they were civilized, or rather, Americanized.

What is the standard American? Is not American, like America, a label of the Europeans? Just like the standards of the American were evidently set by immigrants from Europe? Who gave the first European immigrants the right to decide what was American and what wasn't? What about those who came second, third, and fourth? Even the first Europeans weren't first; the Indians were here long before them. Shouldn't the Indians have Americanized the European?

Even today everyone is trying to be like everyone else. If the clothes style changes, everyone wants a new wardrobe. People are letting somebody else make up their minds. What is the matter with being oneself? What about old family tradition? But people don't want to be different. Is being accepted the most important thing? At this time it probably is, for we take too much stock in labels. Prejudice, and dividing people into races is hardly fair. The race with the majority of people will always come out on top.

What does America stand for? Should I be proud to be an American? Don't get me wrong; this is a great country, but I feel we have made some mistakes in the past, and we should own up, and make up for them for the sake of our future.

The Indians were once a proud people. They tried to hang on to their old ways, but we would not let them; it wasn't considered proper. They were thought of as wild savages that must be trained.

I feel the Indian was badly mistreated. First they were cheated out of everything they owned. Then the white man, through his ignorance, had to change the Indian. Even though he continued to change the Indian through force, until there was nothing left to change, the Indian was still not truly accepted.

I know it's too late to change any of that, but maybe it's not too late to learn from our mistakes and try to do something about labeling and prejudice. Make life worth living the way you yourself want to live, and not the way somebody else thinks it ought to be.

Comparison of Asian and European Immigration by Bob Coy

. . . A fraction of Asian immigrants have come to the United States compared to the vast numbers that have migrated from Europe. The laws passed because of the hatred of Orientals by many Americans greatly decreased the number of Asian immigrants who came to the United States.

Most Orientals settled on the west coast and a sizable number also settled in New York. The areas in which these Orientals settled were called "Chinatowns" or "Little Tokyos." Europeans were spread over the entire country, but there were large clusters in big cities and major industrial areas. They made up a major part of the labor force in the big cities. Both Europeans and Orientals were located in farm areas, with Orientals being a major factor in the advance of agriculture in the Pacific coast states. The Europeans were a major factor in agriculture in the area of the Middle West.

Reasons for coming to the United States varied. Europeans came to the United States for economic opportunities, religious persecution in their homeland, political views in their homeland, and to make money so they could eventually have enough to go back to their homelands feeling successful. Asians came to the United States because of the California gold rush, for job opportunities, to build the railroads, and for economic advancement. For the most part the immigrants who came from both Asia and Europe did better themselves in life, some to a greater extent than others.

I feel that the immigrants who have come to the United States have greatly benefitted their new land. In many ways they have made great contributions to the United States. They have provided a needed labor force for industrial development, customs, culture, and skills that contributed to the melting pot to form the great United States of America.

SUMMARY

This chapter offers a well developed unit in individualized instruction. This particular program has been used successfully for three years. The best feature of this approach is the wide variety of choices open to the students. Hopefully, each student will find a topic that is appealing, as well as many different kinds of learning experiences that are interesting and exciting.

This kind of a program can be carried out successfully with different age groups and most ability levels. The type of history unit to be used should be chosen with care. It needs to be a period of history that clearly presents a variety of themes.

A successful unit in individualized instruction calls for an abundance and variety of educational materials. The school library will be involved quite heavily.

Both the creation and the execution of this type of a program present a challenge to the teacher. But the rewards can be great—the change of pace, the interest and efforts of the students, and the results in terms of higher grades. All of these can be most gratifying to a teacher.

8

The Twenties and Thirties—Simulation

THIS CHAPTER IS NOT FOR THE FAINTHEARTED! THE unit described here requires many hours of preparation, meticulous attention to countless small details, and a heavy workload for the teacher for 21 school days.

This unit is, however, for student and teacher alike, fun, exciting, and satisfying. A new dimension is added to the learning process through the deep involvement that results from a simulation experience.

This book has already covered two examples of simulation—a one day exercise (see Chapter 3, A Taste of Things to Come) and a one week project (see Chapter 6, Civil War Debates). The approach to learning in this new unit is similar to that described in Chapters 3 and 6. The major difference is the length of time—21 days of concentrated involvement with the "Roaring Twenties" and the "Depressed Thirties."

This is the only project described in this book that is not my own original work. I discovered a booklet published by a firm called Interact[1] that I found to be excellent material. I have used the basic structure of their unit, along with the necessary forms and materials suggested by them. To this material I have added several activities of my own, designed to lend further drama and excitement to the total project. As I describe the various procedures used in this unit, I shall use a symbol (I) to identify things that I have borrowed from Interact and a symbol (S) to designate my own contributions. I use the symbols (I and S) to indicate that the basic material belongs to Interact, but that changes or additions have been provided by Severance. If this unit appeals to you, and you are interested in setting up a similar project, I would urge you to obtain a copy of *Panic* to supplement whatever you find here.

Explanation of this unit to the students must be done with special care. The overall plan is necessarily complex in order to cover all facets of this period of history. If the project is confusing to the students, it will lose its effectiveness at the very beginning. I use a handout as a base for the first day's introduction to the unit. It is included here for your use. Directions and explanations throughout the unit should be given carefully and thoroughly, orally and in writing.

I had fun preparing this unit—I hope you have fun doing it. Now, to the details!

---

[1]*PANIC*. Copyright 1968, INTERACT Co., published by INTERACT, Box 262, Lakeside, CA. 92040

STUDENT HANDOUT

Simulation Unit—Twenties and Thirties Introduction

1. ***Meaning of simulation:***
   Role Playing
   Games
   Team Contests
   Competition
   Examples—The Supreme Court Cases and the Civil War Debates
2. ***Purposes of this unit:***
   a. To make it possible for students to feel what it was like to live in the 1920's and 1930's.
   b. To put fun and excitement into the learning process.
3. ***Personal success*** in this project will depend on three things:
   a. Dictation—by the teacher
   b. Chance—pure luck (or misfortune)
   c. Skill—knowledge
   strategy
   choices
   After all, these three factors do affect us in real life. This was especially true during the 1920's and 1930's.
4. ***Total success*** of the entire project will depend on the following:
   a. Students' ability to follow directions carefully so that all progresses smoothly
   b. Ability of students to exercise self-discipline in a rather informal classroom situation
   c. Ability of students to be good losers or good winners—sportsmanship—some students will have tremendous good fortune—others will have rotten luck.
5. ***Reading-study-materials***—There will be no assigned reading for the four weeks. It is important for each student to become very well informed on this period in history, and it is expected that each one will do so at his own speed.
6. ***Text reading***—pages 476–501.
   All other books on the book cart should be explored for

material on this time period. Other materials will be available in the library for students' use.

7. ***Identities***

Each student will be given an identity for the four weeks that will include the following:

- **a.** An occupational group
- **b.** A section of the country
- **c.** An economic group (and a beginning bank account)
- **d.** A political party

Each of the above factors will affect decisions that students make.

IDENTITIES (I)

On the opening day of the unit each student is given an identity that will determine the role played by the student throughout the unit—a laborer, businessman, banker, woman, farmer, or activist. Also, everyone is assigned to a region of the country—West, Southwest, Plains, Midwest, East, or South. The student's economic status is chosen—upper class, middle class, or lower class. Everyone is given a short test that determines their politics: Republican, Democrat, or Independent. All of this information is put on each student's name tag, which is worn throughout the unit. Name tags should be made from three different colored cards. I use blue for the upper class, yellow for middle class, and white for the poor people. All other identifying information is written on the card. Included here is a sample name tag.

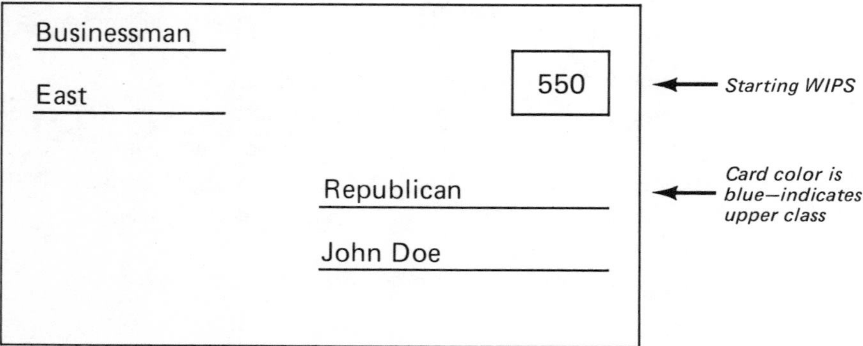

Directly below you will find a copy of the test that will determine each student's political party. When students have completed the political attitudes survey, count the number of "A" answers and the number of "B" answers. A majority of A's indicates that the student should be a Democrat. A majority of B answers identifies a Republican. If the A's and B's are split equally, the student is an Independent.

POLITICAL ATTITUDES SURVEY (I) Do not write on this paper

No answer is right. No answer is wrong. Number 1 to 10 on a separate sheet of paper and print A or B after each number.

1. I believe that the most important task of man is
- **A.** to improve his environment.
- **B.** to improve himself.

2. I believe competition among citizens for business and professional success should be
- **A.** regulated by the government so that all citizens will have an equal opportunity.
- **B.** as free of all regulation as possible so that business can prosper.

3. I believe an individual who does not succeed and is lazy is that way because
- **A.** his environment made him that way.
- **B.** his character is rather weak.

4. I believe the main purpose of a college education is to prepare man to
- **A.** improve his society.
- **B.** compete successfully with others.

5. I believe
- **A.** laws should be changed if environmental conditions change.
- **B.** environment should be changed to meet the basic laws.

6. I believe a man is
- **A.** what his environment makes him.
- **B.** what he makes of himself.

7. I believe that the vote should be given to
- **A.** all citizens.
- **B.** only citizens who can demonstrate that they understand the political issues.

8. I believe the Federal Constitution should be
   A. interpreted loosely (giving the government considerable power).
   B. interpreted strictly (limiting the power of the government).

9. I believe the President should be
   A. a vigorous leader who actively promotes programs of his own design.
   B. primarily a servant of the public will.

10. I believe the Supreme Court should base its decision on
   A. a study and understanding of the problems of today.
   B. the stated provisions of the Constitution.

WIPS (I)

WIPS stands for Wealth in Points. They will serve as the unit of exchange and the means of "keeping score" throughout the unit. Part of the challenge of this unit will be to see how many WIPS each student can accumulate. At the beginning of the unit, each student will be given a designated number of WIPS with which to start his account. These WIPS are assigned to him when his identity is being established and the appropriate number will be printed on his name tag. These beginning WIPS totals will vary from 50 to 600, more or less based on chance, but somewhat reflecting the economic group and the occupational group to which the student is assigned. The student may build his WIPS account in many ways, or, in fact, may lose WIPS, or go totally "broke." Students' WIPS may be affected by any of the following things:

stock transactions
banking
pressure cards
group scavenger hunts
general statements
interviews
problem solving
alphabet soup
legislation
quizzes and tests

Not only will these affect the WIPS account, but there will also be a few little surprises along the way.

Make it clear to students at the outset that WIPS are simply numbers, or scores, kept in various records. All financial transactions throughout the unit will be carried out by shifting these numbers, called WIPS, from one account to another. This will be explained more clearly in the section on the stock market and banking.

WIPS and Grades

This is one place where Interact and Severance part company. The authors of *PANIC* suggest that WIPS should determine the student's unit grade, and they give a rationale for this approach in their booklet. I suggest that you read their booklet and give the matter some thought.

I feel strongly that WIPS should not determine the unit grade. I believe that WIPS and grades must be kept separately, because WIPS are so frequently affected by chance, by circumstances that cannot be controlled by the students. All assignments and tests are graded during the unit, and a record is kept of these grades that is entirely separate from the WIPS account. All grades affect the student's WIPS, but WIPS do not affect the student's grade.

For the sake of efficiency, all grades should be in units of twelve points (12, 24, 48, etc.). Any assignment or tests graded by the teacher should show both the WIPS and the point grade recorded in the teacher's grade book. The following tables should be helpful:

GRADES AND WIPS FOR ALL ASSIGNMENTS (S)

12 POINT ASSIGNMENTS

Letter Grades	*Grade Points*	*WIPS*
A+	12	60
A	11½	55
A−	11	50
B+	10½	45
B	10	40
B−	9½	35
C+	9	30

GRADES AND WIPS FOR ALL ASSIGNMENTS (S)

12 POINT ASSIGNMENTS

Letter Grades	*Grade Points*	*WIPS*
C	8½	25
C−	8	20
D+	7½	15
D	7	10
D−	6½	5
E	6 or below	

24 POINT ASSIGNMENTS

Letter Grades	*Grade Points*	*WIPS*
A+	24	120
A	23	110
A−	22	100
B+	21	90
B	20	80
B−	19	70
C+	18	60
C	17	50
C−	16	40
D+	15	30
D	14	20
D−	13	10
E	12 or less	

48 POINT ASSIGNMENTS		
Letter Grades	***Grade Points***	***WIPS***
A+	48	240
A	46	220
A−	44	200
B+	42	180
B	40	160
B−	38	140
C+	36	120
C	34	100
C−	32	80
D+	30	60
D	28	40
D−	26	20
E	25 or less	

Example— A student has been assigned to write a paper worth 48 possible points on his grade. His paper is given a B+. According to the chart, the following is written on his paper:

B+42 180 WIPS

Example— A student takes a short test worth 24 possible points. His paper might read:

C+18 60 WIPS

STOCKS (I and S)

This has to be a very important part of a simulation project of the 1920s and 1930s. A stock market is established. There should be only a few stocks available for the sake of simplicity. I add a good touch here, naming the corporations for teachers in our school. Last year's stocks on our market were Vargo Car Company (our principal), Pajk Florida Land Company (a favorite math teacher), and Johnston Agricultural Equipment (a popular geography teacher who farms in the summertime). The stockbroker is the history teacher.

I plan in detail what is going to happen to each of the three stocks long before the unit begins. My husband, in his best "Walter Cronkite" voice and delivery, is used as the "daily business news announcer." Together we prepare a tape containing the daily news broadcasts for the entire unit. Each day, toward the end of the class period, the broadcast for the day is played. It is supposedly a radio newscast at that time in history. At the end of the daily broadcast, the stock market is opened each day for ten or fifteen minutes.

Before we proceed with the mechanics of buying and selling stock, it is necessary to introduce the WIPS balance sheet.

On the first day, each student is given a WIPS balance sheet that serves as his personal financial record. I caution the students to bring these sheets to class each day, and to avoid losing them at all costs. This sheet is the student's lifeline throughout the unit. He records on this sheet all WIPS gained or lost, spent or saved.

Study the sample on page 202. This is a businessman who starts the unit with 550 WIPS. Whenever he spends WIPS or loses WIPS, this is recorded in the minus column. When he earns WIPS or gains them, this is recorded in the plus column. It becomes an exercise in elementary bookkeeping, and students must keep accounts up to date at all times.

This WIPS account serves not only as a record but as a checking account as well. Each student must decide how much of his wealth should remain in this account. Students must know that this account earns no interest, nor does it pay any dividends. It just sits there. It might seem at first glance that this would be a totally safe place in which to keep one's wealth. Such is not the case—this account is put in jeopardy through the use of pressure cards (to be explained later).

WIPS CHECK	
Name of Bank Bilek Brecksville Bank	
	April 15 19 78
Pay to the Order of Severance Brokerage	WIPS 100
One hundred and ———————— no/100 ———————— Wealth in Points	
10 shares Whittaker Washers Purpose	John Doe Signature

Use green paper

The following steps are taken by a student when buying stock:

1. He writes a WIPS check.
2. He fills out the stock certificate.
3. He takes these papers to the stockbroker for signature. The WIPS check serves as the stockbroker's record, and the stock certificate is the student's receipt.
4. He records the transaction on his WIPS balance sheet.

Study the sample on the next page.

In the prepared business news tape, somewhere there must be a message announcing the stock market crash. Last year I "sprung" this surprise right in the middle of a sound filmstrip. I snapped off the filmstrip and snapped on my tape to hear the calm voice of the business announcer saying, "We interrupt this program to bring you an important announcement . . ." The students scrambled for pens and papers in order to take notes on this surprise report and sat there stunned at the news of a total crash.

In one class a student, who had invested his entire wealth in the stock market, got out of his seat, walked up to the front of the room, threw open a window and climbed up on the ledge as if to jump out of the window. Fortunately, my room is on the ground floor.

WIPS BALANCE SHEET – DAILY RECORD (I)

Name John Doe | Occupation Businessman | Tag Color Blue

Date	Item	+	–	Balance	Date	Item	+	–	Balance
4/10/78	Beginning WIPS	550		550					
4/11/78	Bank Deposit		100	450					
4/11/78	10 shares Vargo Car at 10 WIPS per share		100	350					
4/12/78	Quiz (12 points)	55		405					
4/13/78	Stock Dividend (5 WIPS per share)	50		455					
4/14/78	Income Tax		80	375					
4/15/78	Pressure Card	300		675					
4/16/78	Sold 10 shares of Vargo at 15 WIPS per share	150		825					

STOCK CERTIFICATE			
Buyer John Doe			
Seller			
	Herrick Aviation	Kan Cosmetics	Whittaker Washers
Date			4/15/81
No. of Shares			10
Price per Share			10
Total due			100
No. of shares still owned			40
WIPS to record on balance sheet			−100
Signature of Broker			

Use pink paper

I will long remember student response to a request of mine on the day of last year's crash. I explained to each class that it would minimize the surprise effect if the news got out to subsequent classes that the market had crashed. I was flabbergasted to find out that 120 thirteen-year-old kids had totally kept that secret all day long. The last class of the day was just as surprised as the first one was. I considered this kind of cooperation to be a reflection of their keen interest in the total project.

BANKING

There are three major options open to each student in terms of spending his WIPS. One is the WIPS balance sheet account. The second is the stock market. It is now time to deal with the third option, the savings bank.

I find it to be impossible for the teacher to handle both the stock market and the bank. Therefore, I choose one very good student from each class to serve as the banker for that class. These bankers need to stay after school one evening for a training session. At this time, a math teacher trains them in the use of a calculator and reviews their math skills in computing percentages. I follow up with an explanation of the daily financial procedures and the forms and records that will be used.

Deposits and withdrawals can be made daily, immediately after the business news of the day. The following steps are taken by a student:

1. He fills out a banking slip
2. He takes it to the banker
3. The banker signs the bank slip and returns it to the student after recording the transaction on his Banking Record Sheet

Study the samples of the banking slip and the banking record sheet.

I "pay" these bankers 30 WIPS a day, raise them to 50 WIPS after several days, and cut them to 10 WIPS daily after the crash. They certainly earn their WIPS. Since each day of the project represents one year, these bankers must compute interest on all of their accounts daily. Incidentally, don't share that tidbit of the time represented by one day with the students; it would make it too easy to anticipate the crash.

On the first day of the unit, each student chooses one of six banks offered. Each bank is given the name of a teacher in the school (see the banking record sheet for examples). Students are not allowed to change banks. There will come a time, of course, when the business reporter announces the closing of the banks. After a day or so they will reopen, but only one bank will be able to credit its depositors with no losses in their accounts. Other banks will be totally bankrupt or pay to each depositor a certain percentage of his account.

I include here the script for the most recent business report tape. It contains information about both stocks and banks. It is certainly worth the effort to put these daily business reports on tape. It adds suspense and excitement to the unit.

BANK RECORD SLIP			
Name	John Doe		
Date	4/15/81		
Deposit		Withdrawal	
Amount	100.00	Amount	
Account Total	100.00	Account Total	
Record on WIPS Sheet	–100.00	Record on WIPS Sheet	
Teller	G. M.	Teller	
Name of Bank	Chidsey Commercial Savings		

Use yellow paper

Script for Stock Market Tape—Simulation, 1920s and 1930s—1978 (S)

This is your annual business report from radio station WBJH—January 1, 1921.

The outlook for the coming year is good. The stock market is strong—trading is heavy. Banks are stable and paying 1% interest on all deposits. Businesses are booming and many new ventures are available for interested investors. Here are some stocks to watch:

For a sound investment with slow, but rather safe growth, give some thought to Whittaker Washers. This company has been in business for over 50 years and has a good record. Originally this company manufactured washboards and metal tubs. They have recently introduced a newly developed electric washing machine.

A new stock came on the market last week—it looks promising—the Kan Cosmetic Corporation. Since women have recently accepted the use

BANKING RECORD SHEET (I)

Name and Bank	Dep	With	Int	Bal	Dep	With	Int	Bal	Dep	With	Int	Bal	Dep	With	Int	Bal
John Doe	100			100												
			2.00	102												
Chidsey Commercial	75		2.04	179.04												
Savings		50	3.58	132.62												
Jane Smith																
Stoddard Savings																
and Loan																
Bob Jones																
Dooley Domestic																
Savings																
Bridget Brown																
Mitchell Merchants																
Association																

of such products as lipstick, powder and rouge, there is quite a large market for these products. As women become more emancipated, this stock should grow in value.

For the more daring investor, consider the Herrick Aviation Co. This enterprising company believes that the airplane is here to stay. They specialize in making biplanes and hope to find a market for selling planes to the general public. This, of course, is a luxury item—a bit risky, but paying high dividends at the present time.

WBJH announces that, starting tomorrow, there will be a daily broadcast giving the banking news, stock prices, and stock dividends. Tune in each day at this time.

No. 1

Here is the business news for the day from WBJH. Banks continue to pay 1% interest on deposits.

Kan Cosmetics is at 10
Whittaker Washers, 15
Herrick Aviation is at 15.
Stocks in general are rising. Trading is light.

No. 2

Now for the stock market news from WBJH. Stocks rose sharply today in a day of heavy trading.

Kan Cosmetics is at 20—up 10—and issued a dividend of 50 cents a share.
Whittaker Washers is at 17—up 2—and issued a dividend of $1.50 a share.
Herrick Aviation is 16—up 1—and issued a dividend of 25¢ a share.

No. 3

We bring you the business news from WBJH. Interest rates on savings deposits went up today to 2%. New York's Chase Manhattan Bank announced the raise this morning. By nightfall, banks all across the nation had agreed to the 2% rate. The stock market continues its rapid rise.

Kan Cosmetics is at 23—up 3
Whittaker Washers is at 19—up 2
Herrick Aviation is at 16—holding steady.

No. 4

From WBJH—the business news. Banks continue to pay 2% interest.

Kan Cosmetics is at 28—up 5—and issued a dividend of 10 cents a share

Whittaker Washers is at 21—up 2—and issued a dividend of 50 cents a share
Herrick Aviation at 18—up 2—and issued a dividend of 25 cents a share.

No. 5

Radio station WBJH brings you the daily business report. Bank interest rates hold steady at 2%.

Kan Cosmetics is at 33—up 5
Whittaker Washers at 22—up 1
Herrick Aviation at 18—holding steady.

No. 6

Here is the business news for the day from WBJH Radio. Banks across the nation raised their interest rates today. Interest rates on all savings accounts will now be 3%. Here are today's stocks.

Kan Cosmetics is at 30—down 3
Whittaker Washers at 24—up 2
Herrick Aviation at 20—up 2.

No. 7

Now for the stock market news from WBJH. Bank interest rates hold steady at 3%.

Kan Cosmetics is at 22—down 8—issued a dividend of 10 cents a share
Whittaker Washers at 26—up 2—issued a dividend of 50 cents a share
Herrick Aviation at 21—up 1—issued a dividend of 50 cents a share.

No. 8

Business report—WBJH—Two big items in the news today. First, the banks raised interest rates again today—the current rate is 4%. Second, the news just reached us that the Kan Cosmetic Corporation has declared bankruptcy. Their stock is now worthless. The president of the company left the country today, carrying over 50 million dollars of the company's funds. The board of directors met in emergency session this afternoon and concluded that they had no choice other than to declare bankruptcy. Rumor has it that the company president is safely settled in Brazil and cannot be touched by our government, as we have no extradition treaty with that country.

Whittaker Washers is at 24—down 2
Herrick Aviation at 20—down 1.

No. 9

We bring you the business news from WBJH. Banking interest rates hold steady at 4%.

Whittaker Washers is at 26—dividend issued at 25 cents a share
Herrick Aviation is at 23—up 3—dividend issued at 50 cents a share.

No. 10

Here is today's business news from WBJH. Banking interest rates continue at 4%.

Whittaker Washers is at 33—up 7
Herrick Aviation jumped to 33—up 10.
There was a sharp rise in the market today—trading was heavy.

No. 11

We interrupt this program to bring you a special news bulletin from WBJH. The stock market has crashed! We repeat—the stock market has crashed. Stocks tumbled rapidly on a day of unprecedented heavy selling. Sell orders came in so fast that the brokers could not keep up with them. The scene on Wall Street is madness itself. Several important financiers have jumped out of 12th story windows. Fortunes have been wiped out overnight. Stock holders all over the nation have lost all their savings. Most stocks are totally worthless. One of the few remaining stocks with any value is Herrick Aviation, which is now at 10.

No. 12

We interrupt this program for a special news report. Franklin Delano Roosevelt closed all the banks in the country this morning and declared a "Bank Holiday." All of the banks in the country will be carefully examined. Those declared to be financially sound will be opened again in a few days. The President urged all citizens to remain calm. He will speak to the nation this evening in one of his famous radio "Fireside Chats."

No report for the 13th day

No. 14

We interrupt this program for a special financial announcement. Most banks throughout the country will open again tomorrow. Some banks will be in a position to give depositors full value on their accounts—others will pay only a certain percent to each depositor. In a few unfortunate cases, some banks must declare total bankruptcy. Watch your local news for more details.

No. 15

Here is the business news of the day from station WBJH. After a very careful examination the banks will reopen today. Unfortunately, many depositors will be taking a loss on their savings. Here is the report on the financial standing of the local banks:

McCombs Merchant Association will pay 25 cents on the dollar
Turk Trust Co. will pay 60 cents on the dollar
Folkman Finance Corporation will pay 40 cents on the dollar
Cox Commercial Savings is in excellent condition. Depositors in that bank will take no losses
Bilek Brecksville Bank will pay 80 cents on the dollar
Esarey Establishment of Finance was found to be unsound. It will not open its doors and has declared bankruptcy.
On the stock market—Herrick Aviation is at 8—down 2.

No. 16

Radio Station WBJH brings you the daily business report. The economy remains sluggish. Bank interest rates have dropped to 3%.

Herrick Aviation is at 7—down 1.

No. 17

Business report—WBJH. Unemployment across the nation has risen. Trading on the stock market is light.

Bank interest rates dropped today to 2%
Herrick Aviation is at 6—down 1.

No. 18

Here is the business news for the day from station WBJH. The top business news of the day concerns the failure of one of our local banks. Every effort was made to save this bank. Deposits have declined and several risky loans made by the top management have made it necessary for the Turk Trust Company to declare bankruptcy.

Bank interest rates hold steady at 2%.
Herrick Aviation is at 7—up 1.

Business Report—No. 19—final report

From WBJH, an important business report. The spread of war in Europe is beginning to affect the American business scene. Bank rates across the nation rose to 3% today. Stocks are showing slight gains. Many factories are turning to production of war materials. As a result, the economy is growing.

The biggest news story of the day comes from Washington, D.C. President Roosevelt announced in a newscast this morning that the Federal Government has placed orders for defense equipment of all kinds. He explained that, in view of the present crisis in Europe, it is essential that this country should be ready to protect itself against any possible aggressor.

The largest single order, in an amount reported to be over two billion dollars, went to the Herrick Aviation Company. This resulted in a sharp rise in Herrick stock. It tripled in value today. It is now selling at 21—up 14.

This announcer would like at this time to make an announcement of a personal nature. This is my final business broadcast. I have decided that it is time for me to retire. It is my intention to travel around the world with my young and beautiful wife.

It has been my pleasure to serve the listening public for these many years. I wish all of you good fortune in your future business ventures.

SCAVENGER HUNT (S)

This is an excellent opening to the unit. I'm proposing, of course, a scavenger hunt using books, and the object of the search is to find information.

This is another activity that is dependent upon cooperation from the school librarian. For this exercise I request a cart of assorted books that deal with the 1920s and 1930s. This cart also should contain one complete set of encyclopedias.

Students are divided into groups according to their occupations. This provides us with six teams. Each team is given six to eight books, along with a couple of history texts, as well as their own textbooks. Identical handout sheets are distributed, one to a group. Each sheet contains 30 questions. The object is to find the answers to these questions and record them as quickly as possible.

A timer is set when the hunt begins. At the end of each five minute time slot, each group must immediately pass its books clockwise to the next group. This gives all groups an equal opportunity to use the various sources.

There is a schedule for this entire unit at the end of this chapter. If you consult this schedule, you will find that I use these scavenger hunts for three days. This does not result in an overexposure to this technique. I find that the students have so much to learn about the financial aspects of the unit that only fifteen minutes of each of these three days can be devoted to the hunts. These hunts are exciting, noisy, and downright hectic. However, they serve several good purposes:

1. They serve as a good "ice-breaker."
2. They provide an opportunity for the members of the group to learn to work well together.
3. They give the students a bit of the flavor, the feeling of the twenties and thirties.
4. The total class time needed for scavenger hunts can be very flexible, thereby allowing extra time for business transactions, a crucial need early in the unit.

My scavenger hunt questions are included here to serve as a sample. You will probably need to construct your own questions in order to be certain that the answers can be found in the books available to your students.

Each day members of the winning team each receive a price of 75 WIPS. Second place team members are awarded 50 WIPS, third place, 25. Allow 10 WIPS to each member of losing teams—for trying!

Simulation Project—Scavenger Hunt—The 20's and 30's

1. The state where Herbert Hoover was born.
   Iowa
2. Home town of President Harding.
   Marion, Ohio
3. The color of Henry Ford's Model T cars.
   Black
4. Number of speakeasies in New York City during Prohibition.
   32,000
5. Who said, "I never met a man I didn't like"?
   Will Rogers
6. Nickname of New York City's Fiorello La Guardia.
   Little Flower
7. Number of jigsaw puzzles distributed in the United States in 1934.
   3,500,000 (allow from three to four million)

8. Man who ran against Roosevelt in 1936.
   Alf Landon
9. Cabinet position held by Hoover before his presidency.
   Secretary of Commerce
10. Ratio of ships allowed to England, the U.S., and Japan according to 1921 disarmament treaty.
    5-5-3
11. What was Charles Kettering known for?
    Self Starter in the Automobile
12. Boxer who beat Jack Dempsey in 1927.
    Gene Tunney
13. Name of the man who ran against Hoover in 1928.
    Al Smith
14. Who was the "Brown Bomber"?
    Joe Louis
15. Who was the "Little Brown Saint"?
    Mahatma Gandhi
16. What was the total national population of the U.S. in 1920?
    106,466,000 (allow from 105–108 million)
17. The percent of American people engaged in buying and selling of stock in 1929.
    One percent
18. The name of the scandal involving Albert Fall (cabinet member under Hoover).
    Teapot Dome
19. Number of members in the Ku Klux Klan in 1923.
    5 Million (allow 4–6 million)
20. The "Great Lover" of the silent screen.
    Rudolph Valentino
21. Who said, "We have nothing to fear but fear itself"?
    F. D. Roosevelt
22. The famous book written about migrant workers.
    Grapes of Wrath
23. Number of people killed while building the George Washington Bridge.
    Twelve

24. The year of Woodrow Wilson's death.
1924

25. The city where the dirigible Hindenburg burned.
Lakehurst, New Jersey

26. The annual income of the Rockefellers in the 1930's.
30-35 Million

27. Amount of the National debt in 1932.
19,487,002,000 (allow from 15–25 billion)

28. The most famous child star in the 1930's.
Shirley Temple

29. The length of the "Bank Holiday" in 1933.
Four Days

30. Amount of the Federal debt in 1974.
468,256,000,000 (allow 400–600 billion)

31. Date for the opening of the Empire State Building.
May 1, 1931

32. Name of the dam built on the Colorado River in 1936.
Hoover

33. Number of Woolworth stores in the country in 1930.
1800 (allow 1750–1900)

34. Nickname given to the famous trial over Darwin's theory of evolution.
Monkey Trial

35. The year of the first "talkie"—*The Jazz Singer.*
1927

36. Who was Aimee Semple McPherson?
An Evangelist

37. Meaning of the A.A.A. of the New Deal.
Agricultural Adjustment Act

38. Meaning of the C.C.C. of the New Deal.
Civilian Conservation Corps

39. Author of *The Good Earth.*
Pearl S. Buck

40. Price of a Model T Ford in 1925.
$300 (allow $250 to $350)

41. Lawyer who defended Scopes in his trial.
Clarence Darrow

42. Date for the first use of traffic lights.
1920

43. The year that airmail started.
1918

44. Fads of the 1920's—a tile game.
Mah-Jongg

45. Fads of the 1920's—records set in heights.
Flag Pole Sitting

46. Fads of the 20's—type of dance contest.
Marathon Dancing

47. Fads of the 20's—the most famous type of dancing.
Charleston or Black Bottom

48. Name of F. D. Roosevelt's program in office.
New Deal

49. Babe Ruth's age when he retired from baseball.
Forty

50. What was the "100 days"?
The first 100 days of F. D. Roosevelt's New Deal

51. Number of electoral votes received by F. D. Roosevelt in 1932.
472

52. The most famous golfer of the thirties.
Bobby Jones

53. The first man to fly over the North Pole.
Richard Byrd

54. The amendment that gave the vote to women.
Nineteenth Amendment

55. Number of tons of paper used in the New York City parade honoring Lindbergh.
1800 (accept 1700–1900)

56. The name given to F. D. Roosevelt's radio broadcasts.
Fireside Chats

57. Famous woman pilot who vanished.
Amelia Earhart

58. Name of the genius—German Jew who immigrated to the United States in 1933.
Albert Einstein

59. Which amendment is called the "Lame Duck" Amendment?
Twentieth Amendment

60. The number of movie tickets sold per week in the United States in 1930.
100,000,000 (accept 85–110 million)

61. Name of the treaty signed by 60 nations in 1928 renouncing war.
Kellogg Briand or Pact of Paris

62. The Vice President under Harding.
Coolidge

63. The stock market crashed on what day of the week?
Thursday, Oct. 24–Tuesday, Oct. 29

64. The city where the famous world's fair of 1933 took place.
Chicago

65. The city where "Wrong Way Corrigan" landed his plane.
Dublin, Ireland

66. The man who kidnapped the Lindbergh baby.
Bruno Hauptmann

67. Ever since 1937, what is the date for the Presidential inauguration?
January 20th

68. Who started the "Good Neighbor Policy" toward Latin America?
F. D. Roosevelt

69. Who was the first chairman of the Securities and Exchange Commission in 1934?
Joseph Kennedy

70. What was the name given to the political party of Vladimir Lenin?
Bolshevik

71. What was the nickname of Clara Bow?
The "IT" girl

72. What type of fruit was sold on the street corners during the depression?
Apples

73. Who was the director of the F.B.I. during the thirties?
J. Edgar Hoover

74. What was the number of consecutive ball games played by Lou Gehrig?
2,130 (accept 2000–2200)

75. What was the total number of league home runs hit by Babe Ruth?
714

76. What was F. D. Roosevelt's hobby?
Stamp Collecting

77. What was the most popular "get rich quick" scheme of the 1930's?
Chain Letters

78. What was the most disliked and the most disobeyed law in our history?
Prohibition or the Volstead Act

79. Who said, "I do not choose to run"?
Calvin Coolidge

80. Name the famous ventriloquist's dummy of the 1930's.
Charlie McCarthy

81. Who was the American woman for whom the King of England gave up his throne?
Wallis Simpson

82. Who was president when the T.V.A. was created?
F. D. Roosevelt

83. Name the popular comedian of the thirties who was killed in a plane crash.
Will Rogers

84. Who was "Scarface"?
Al Capone

85. Who wanted "A return to normalcy"?
Harding

86. Who was the leader of the coal miners in the 1930's?
John L. Lewis

87. Who was "Public Enemy Number One"?
John Dillinger

88. Who was "The Galloping Ghost of the Gridiron"?
Red Grange

89. What is the length of the Grand Coulee Dam?
4000 ft.

90. Who said, "The business of America is business"?
Coolidge

GENERAL STATEMENTS (I)

This is an exercise in expository writing, and it is an excellent addition to the unit. Each student is given a general statement as a topic sentence or central idea. In each case the statement relates to the occupational group represented by the student. Thus, the farmers will find themselves writing about farm problems of the twenties and thirties, while the bankers will have an assignment concerning financial matters, etc.

Whatever the general statement may be, the task is to write a short paper that will logically and clearly support the statement. The teacher should make every effort to maintain high standards while grading these papers. Consider the following criteria:

1. Is the writing style concise and direct?
2. Does the information offered truly support the general statement?
3. Has the student provided sufficient specific details to adequately cover the subject?
4. Has the student taken pains with the mechanics involved in writing a good paper—spelling, punctuation, sentence structure, and penmanship?
5. Does the vocabulary used in the paper represent an understanding of terms relevant to the twenties and thirties?
6. Is the work neatly done?

In spite of the role playing and the fun and games involved in this unit, there are a number of worthwhile, serious assignments along the way, and this is one of them.

This paper is assigned on the seventh day of the unit. Most of the class period is set aside so that students may work on this paper, using the resources on the library cart. The papers are due two days later. On that day, various students give oral reports on their papers. Discussion follows. (See schedule at the end of this chapter.) I allow a possible 24 points for this assignment. WIPS are awarded as well. The general statements used in this assignment follow.

Businessmen
Industry and technology were changing America a great deal during the ten years after World War I.

Bankers
Many Americans became very excited about the many opportunities to "get rich quick" during the 1920's.

Farmers
Even before the Great Depression of 1929–1941, farmers faced great hardships during the 1920's.

Laborers
For several reasons the "Golden Twenties" were not "Golden" for most American laborers and their families.

Activists
Activists commented on many changes in the way people lived in the period after World War I—changes in morals, life styles, fashions, values, etc.

Women
The 1920's brought about a revolution in the thinking and actions of American women.

For Anyone—in exchange for one of the preceding topics—with permission from the teacher.
Economists explain several causes for the Great Depression of 1929–1941.

PRESSURE CARDS (I and S)

The period under study in this unit was certainly a unique period in our history. Many people had very little control over their lives, especially in financial matters. They were subjected to numerous surprises, many of them unpleasant. Consider for a moment the wild speculation on the stock market that took place in the twenties—the stock market crash—the Great Depression—the bank "holiday"—unexpected "pink slips"—the dust bowl—migrant workers—soup kitchens—bread lines—and finally, the gathering of war clouds in the thirties. And in the midst of all these problems, some people were making fortunes.

A major objective in this simulation unit is to provide a situation that will allow the student, through the involvement of role playing, to experience both the successes and the severe hardships that were a part of the twenties and thirties. Pressure cards were designed to do just that. A set of cards is prepared, each one containing good news or bad news. Each student determines his fate by drawing one of the cards. Some students will find themselves wiped out financially. Others may have their fortunes doubled or tripled.

Here is another place where Interact and Severance proceed differently. Interact applies the pressure card to the student's total wealth. I apply it only to the balance shown on the WIPS balance sheet. In other words, the student's stock and savings account are not affected by the draw of the pressure card. I make this choice because it does heighten the excitement. Students are informed of the pressure card draw two days in advance. Each student must make a difficult choice. Should he transfer WIPS from stock and banking to his WIPS balance sheet and hope for a lucky draw? Or, should he play it safe and invest everything in stocks and banks until the draw has passed?

I use pressure cards twice during the unit—once during the twenties and again during the thirties. I include two sets of pressure card statements:

Pressure Cards—First Set (The 1920's)

Bankers

1. You have friends on Wall Street who have been giving you tips on a regular basis. You have invested heavily in Texas oil stock. You make a fortune. Gain 300 percent. (I)

2. You get caught up in the terrific business boom of the twenties. As businesses expand at a record rate and interest rates soar, you make loans at a record rate. Unfortunately, you have made too many risky loans, your bank is forced to close its doors. Lose 80 percent. (S)
3. Your brother owns a large construction company. You arrange the financing for his company to build office buildings, apartments, and skyscrapers as the country changes from a rural-farming society to an urban-industrial society. Gain 150 percent. (I)
4. You arrange and manage the union of 35 local utility companies into one giant holding company that controls the majority of Ohio's gas and electricity. Gain 100 percent. (I)
5. You are given the opportunity of investing your personal funds in a big business opportunity that seems to be a sure thing. Short of funds, you embezzle money from the bank for which you work. You expect to repay the money from profits on your investment before the shortage is discovered. Unfortunately, the investment turns out to be a bad one. You are caught and sent to jail. Lose 90 percent. (S)

Businessmen

1. Better research has resulted in your marketing a radio receiver noted for its clarity of tone—a much needed improvement. Gain 75 percent. (I)
2. You are a big "wheeler-dealer" who has been arranging oil leases for the oil companies with the national government. You are caught in the Teapot Dome Scandal and sent to jail. Lose 85 percent. (I)
3. You are a restaurant owner in Chicago. Out of a very deep conviction, you have worked very hard for the passage of the prohibition amendment and you happily close down the bar in your restaurant. An illegal speakeasy opens right next door to you and manages to stay open by paying off corrupt policemen. The speakeasy attracts so many of your customers that you are forced to close your restaurant and go into another business. Lose 40 percent. (S)
4. Because your salesmen have been moving cars with record sales each month, your auto dealership is thriving. Gain 100 percent. (I)

5. You own a small clothing store in Cicero, Illinois. An organized crime syndicate demands payment of "protection money" from all of the merchants in your area. You refuse to pay—as a result, your plate glass shop windows are smashed and much of your merchandise destroyed. You recognize the warning and start making regular payments to the mob. Lose 25 percent. (S)

Farmers

1. You take a gamble that this year will be a particularly good year for corn. You double your usual acreage of this crop. Your efforts are successful. Gain 15 percent. (S)
2. After living for several years at a near poverty level on your farm, you have a stroke of good luck. Oil is discovered on your Texas farm. You lease the mineral rights to a big oil company and your royalties provide a steady income. Gain 75 percent. (S)
3. You are discouraged and bitter because your family is not sharing in the general prosperity of the twenties. All of your expenses are constantly rising, especially for machinery. At the same time, agricultural prices, and your income, are dropping. Lose 40 percent. (I)
4. You and your neighbors have pressured your congressman to try to get legislation passed that will help the farmer. A number of congressmen from farming states form a "farm bloc" in the Congress and manage to get several laws passed that will help the farmers. But all that legislation is vetoed by the president. Lose 25 percent. (I)
5. It is 1925. You have experienced five straight years of falling farm prices after enjoying prosperity from 1915–1920. Lose 50 percent. (I)

Laborers

1. A rather new system of buying has come into common use in the twenties—installment plans (with high interest rates). You and your family have foolishly bought quite a number of things on this plan. Your wife becomes very ill, your wages are not rising, and your creditors start to hound you. The finance company comes to pick up the new car, refrigerator, radio, and toaster. Lose 33 percent. (I)

2. You are miserably poor, untrained, poorly motivated, and have become a "drifter," moving from one grubby job to another. After Lindbergh flies across the Atlantic, you become enormously excited about aviation. You join a group of barnstorming flyers who perform dangerous aerial stunts at country fairs etc. It is a rough life, but a prosperous one. Gain 75 percent. (S)
3. More and more families are buying automobiles. The car is fast becoming a way of life in America. Henry Ford boosts wages to five dollars a day for laborers in your division of his plant in Detroit. Gain 25 percent. (I)
4. You are a skilled laborer in a radio plant. You have scrimped and saved and managed without any luxuries in order to buy stocks regularly. By skillful buying and selling on margin, you have made a small fortune playing the market. Gain 90 percent. (I)
5. You used to be a foreman in a tire factory in Akron. You were making pretty good money and enjoying a decent standard of living. You became very concerned about many of the poor laborers working for you whose incomes were pitifully small. You secretly join a group making plans to form a Labor Union. This is discovered by your company. You are fired and put on a blacklist. Lose 60 percent. (I)
6. You used to be a Negro sharecropper from Georgia. During World War I you moved to Chicago and got a job in a munitions plant. The factory is now making only rifles. You are the first one fired. Getting a new job is very difficult because of the color of your skin. Lose 75 percent. (I)

Activists

1. You own a newspaper in a small town in Tennessee in 1925. You write an editorial praising Clarence Darrow for his attack on the "narrow fundamentalism of William Jennings Bryan" at the Scopes trial. You also criticize the Klu Klux Klan, which is growing in strength in some regions. Your home and newspaper are both bombed. Lose 85 percent. (I)
2. In 1925 you write a book describing the big changes in American morality—you deal with prohibition, the flapper, organized crime, new entertainment—and the results on American society. It is a best seller. Gain 40 percent. (I)

3. You are a liberal history professor at a small Midwestern college. In your classes, you constantly preach against the politicians in Washington who seem to favor the big businessmen while the farmer and the laborer remain poor. Because of this, you are fired. The word gets around that you are "dangerous" to have on a faculty and you find it difficult to get a new job. Lose 70 percent. (I)
4. You become very unhappy with the wildness of Americans in the "Roaring Twenties" and leave the country. You join a group of other American artists living in Paris and paint a lot of art that does not sell. Lose 50 percent. (I)
5. You were a strong backer of the Eighteenth Amendment, but you are alarmed at the effect of prohibition on the country. You write a book that related the great rise in organized crime to the Eighteenth Amendment. It meets with modest success. Gain 25 percent. (I)

Women

1. You are a former suffragette who worked very hard to get the vote for women. You feel strongly that women should have more rights. You quit a job that gives higher pay to men who do the same work you do. Lose 25 percent. (I)
2. For the first time in history, makeup is widely used—lipstick, rouge, and powder are very popular with the women of the twenties and thirties. You organize a cosmetics company and make a fortune with your lipstick motto: "Help your lips say yes!" Gain 80 percent. (I)
3. Your husband, a Chicago policeman, is killed by Al Capone's mob. You suddenly have seven children to support, and you have only a seventh grade education. Lose 80 percent. (I)
4. You are a liberated "Jazz Baby" with silk stockings, short skirts, painted lips, and dangling cigarette. You become a celebrity, singing songs in speakeasies up and down the Atlantic Coastal cities. Gain 50 percent. (I)
5. The popular movies of the early twenties become a positive craze as they start to make the first "talkies." You go to Hollywood with a head full of dreams. You are one of the very few lucky ones who "makes it big" as a screen star. Gain 100 percent. (S)

Pressure Cards—Second set (The 1930's)

Bankers

1. The Federal Reserve banking system started under Wilson is expanding and growing more powerful. You give up your position as vice president of a large city bank to accept a government position on the Federal Reserve Board. You advance rapidly in your job and in your salary. Gain 75 percent. (S)
2. Because you are a skillful scholar of high finance, you realize that small banks will not be able to survive very well in an age of big businesses. Therefore you allow your small town bank to be merged into a giant banking firm. You hate to see your independence disappearing, but you do make a small profit. Gain 10 percent. (I)
3. You are a small town banker in Oklahoma. Your depositors are mostly farmers in the dust bowl area. Most of these people give up their land after ten years of drought and head for California—broke. You have to declare bankruptcy and close your doors. Lose 90 percent. (S)
4. Your small town bank is not prospering because the farmers are in economic trouble. Also, too many of your savings account depositors are investing money in the stock market rather than putting the money in your bank. Lose 20 percent. (I)
5. You give a series of lectures on economics at a nearby university and warn your audience about the dangers of the fast rate of expansion in American business. These warnings are headlined in a local newspaper and your depositors lose faith in your bank. Many people withdraw their funds. Lose 40 percent. (I)

Businessmen

1. You have a factory that makes electric fans. Business has been so good that you have expanded and gone into debt to build new factories. You produce so many electric fans that the demand for them falls off. You can no longer sell your fans at a fast rate. You lay off workers and close two of your factories. The bank demands that you pay your loans. You take a large loss. Lose 75 percent. (S)

2. Your company has developed a new product called nylon. As a junior executive of the company, you promote this miracle fabric for use in making women's stockings. The project is an immediate success, and you are granted a well deserved raise in salary. Gain 25 percent. (S)
3. You are a small grocer who has been "holding on" very bravely for the last five years in competition with the new large chain stores. You finally go bankrupt when the A & P opens a beautiful new store one block from your little grocery store. Lose 80 percent. (I)
4. You use scientific management techniques to improve the efficiency of your assembly line. This has cut the cost of the refrigerators that you manufacture and thus you have increased your profits. Gain 100 percent. (I)
5. You hire a very capable and creative advertising manager. He advertises your soap through a series of stories on the radio, thereby creating the "soap opera." Your sales increase dramatically. Gain 50 percent. (I)

Farmers

1. The Congress has passed laws providing for very high tariffs in order to protect manufacturers from competition from Europe. Because Europeans cannot sell anything to us, they are unable to buy farm products from the United States, thus affecting your income. You have written many letters to your Congressmen protesting this, but they do not take any action. Lose 25 percent. (I)
2. You have had several years of poor crops on your farm in Oklahoma because of the dust bowl. You are unable to pay the mortgage on your farm, and the bank takes over your property. You leave for California where you will have to become a migrant worker. Lose 80 percent. (S)
3. A long lost uncle dies in Australia. You discover that he had been quite successful as a sheep rancher. He remembers you in his will, and your receive a sizable inheritance. Gain 60 percent. (S)
4. Since your life in the Appalachian Hill country was very poor in income, even though rich in freedom, you finally decide that you must give up your farm and try something else. You

move to a Northern city. There you get a poor paying, but steady job. Gain 10 percent. (I)

5. You are a cattle rancher in the Midwest. You tire of struggling to make ends meet. You call a meeting of many other cattlemen in the area and propose that you combine your efforts and your capital to start a meat packing plant in Omaha. Your venture succeeds. Gain 40 percent. (S)

Laborers

1. You are a mechanic in a gas station in a large city. You want to find a better life for yourself and your family. Because credit is easy and there is a growing demand for good auto mechanics, you manage to obtain a loan and open a garage in a small town. You work very hard and manage your money carefully, thus enjoying eventual success. Gain 40 percent. (S)
2. You have worked very hard for many years as a meat cutter in a meat packing plant. You have managed to keep your family going, but you have no savings. You get a disease called polio, which leaves you badly crippled. Medical science can offer you little relief; your medical and hospital bills are staggering. You soon become destitute and end up begging for coins on a street corner. Lose 90 percent. (S)
3. You work on an assembly line in an automobile plant. You figure out a way to improve a very important gadget on the motor. You are rewarded with a substantial bonus. Gain 25 percent. (S)
4. You have worked at a shoe factory for many years. Suddenly, with no warning, you receive with your pay check a pink slip that says, "Termination of Employment." A new type of sewing machine has been invented that will replace you and 25 other workers next Monday morning. No longer will the company's moccasins be hand stitched. Twenty-six men are the victims of technological advancement. Lose 50 percent. (I)

Activists

1. You believe so much in the necessity for the Tennessee Valley Authority Project that you give up a highly paid job in

private industry to help organize the fight for this legislation. Your new job as a government official pays you quite a bit less. Lose 35 percent. (S)

2. You have a deep concern for the problems of the aged during the depression. As a young executive aid to President Roosevelt, you spend long hours making speeches and writing pamphlets to convince the nation of the value of a Social Security Program. When the law is finally passed, Roosevelt rewards your efforts by giving you a rather important position in the Social Security Administration. Gain 35 percent. (S)
3. You are a struggling young lawyer who becomes concerned about the corruption in government that you are seeing at all levels—police, judges, and other official agents accepting payoffs, bribes, etc., from the mobs. You are appointed prosecutor of a Midwestern city and build up a tough investigative force that is free of corruption. Your career advances rapidly. Gain 60 percent. (S)
4. You run for governor of Iowa on a reform platform—you promise to set up a vigorous campaign against bootlegging and to strictly enforce the prohibition laws. However, the year is 1932, and the presidential candidate, F. D. Roosevelt takes a stand against prohibition and calls for the repeal of the Eighteenth Amendment. You are overwhelmingly defeated. Lose 40 percent. (S)
5. You are a poorly paid schoolteacher in a small town. You become very concerned about the future of American young people just out of school who are unable to find work. You become one of the backers and promoters for the Civilian Conservation Corps. Eventually you are rewarded with a management position in the Corps. Gain 60 percent. (S)

Women

1. You are a member of an acrobatic act that has enjoyed considerable success for many years in vaudeville. As the movies become more sophisticated during the thirties, vaudeville gradually disappears from the theaters. You find it very difficult to get bookings, and your income is reduced. Lose 40 percent. (S)

2. Your father died many years ago, leaving you a sizable inheritance. According to state law, this money had to be turned over to your husband. Your husband totally dominates your household. For many years, he has given you very little money and forced you to account for every penny that you spent. He suddenly has a fatal heart attack, and for the first time you come into control of your own affairs, including your money. Gain 100 percent. (S)
3. Like an increasing number of women in the 1920's, you are divorced. You are fortunate enough to find a job, since certain office jobs require women's skills and talents. Gain 10 percent. (I)
4. You struggle very hard during the early years of the depression to earn enough money to put yourself through college. After five years of sacrifice, you finally earn a degree in teaching. You get married shortly after your college graduation, and then find that no one will even consider hiring you, not even for substitute teaching, because your husband holds a job. Because of the depression, the policy becomes "one job only for each family." Lose 30 percent. (S)
5. You have unusual success in the twenties as a woman who owns a glamorous speakeasy. Your talents as a singer, along with your great charm, attract customers from the New York City area in large numbers. However, in the thirties when prohibition is repealed, most of your customers desert you and return to the "respectable night clubs." Lose 40 percent. (S)

Pressure Cards—a Final Word

Be sure that both you and your students are very much aware of the fact that these pressure cards are not just a game. They are fun to work with, and the students enjoy them immensely. But, more importantly, they present a pretty accurate picture of the times, and they should provoke a lively and interesting classroom discussion. Don't let the "Russian roulette" aspect of the game overwhelm the learning value of this activity.

OTHER SURPRISES (S)

Four times during the unit, without warning, I collect income tax. After all, the graduated income tax is a fact of life and is an ordeal that students should experience first hand.

I take liberties with this tax for the sake of simplicity. I tax the student each time on his total wealth, rather than on his gains. We go through this exercise together in class, totaling three things to establish the student's wealth—value of stocks owned, balance in the savings account, and the balance on the WIPS balance sheet. I use the following scale for computing the tax. Each student then enters the tax as an item on the WIPS balance sheet and calculates his new balance.

Total Wealth	*Tax in WIPS*
0-100	5
101-250	20
251-500	60
501-750	80
751-1000	100
1001-1250	120
1251-1500	140
1501-1750	180
1751-2000	230
2001-2250	260

The next unpleasant surprise hits the students' paychecks. The WIPS they earn throughout the unit on quizzes and assignments represent their paychecks for work on the job. On the fifteenth day of the unit, the students submit to me a paper worth a possible twenty-four points on their grades. As I grade these papers, I put a red sticker on one-fifth of the papers and a yellow sticker on one-fifth of the papers. I return these papers on the sixteenth day and explain that unemployment has struck! Each student with a red sticker is "fired" and can gain no more WIPS through tests and assignments. Each student with a yellow sticker receives a 20 percent cut in pay, and any further WIPS he earns must be calculated accordingly. Students groan, growl, and complain so much about income taxes and unemployment that they begin to sound just like their parents!

TELEHELP (S)

I would submit that the average teenager in the average suburban school has no conception of the word "hardship." The poverty, unemployment, and misery endured by many people during the 1930's are beyond the comprehension of most of our young people.

While preparing this simulation unit, I found myself looking for a way to focus on some of these hardships suffered by many people. I particularly wanted the students to glimpse the feeling of hopelessness that was prevalent among the unemployed. I also wanted to personalize "case histories" so that the students could relate to them.

This led me to devise a project that I chose to call Telehelp. The class members are divided into six small groups. Each group represents an office staff that operates a fictional government agency that has been set up during the depression. People with problems supposedly can reach this agency by telephone—hence the name, Telehelp.

A tape was prepared for this exercise containing six separate case histories. Each of these simulated phone calls is introduced on the tape by the sound of a ringing phone. As each case history is described on the tape, the groups in the classroom discuss the problem and attempt to arrive at a solution.

To assist students in reaching a decision, each group is provided with a handout containing five alternative solutions for each case history. Students are asked to put these options in order, from the "most reasonable" to the "least reasonable" by numbering them. Since none of the options is really satisfactory, this tends to emphasize again the frustration felt by the unemployed.

I have not come up with a scoring system for this project that satisfies me. Presently, I give points according to consensus—i.e., on each case history I award points to the two teams that agree most closely on their choices of alternatives. Obviously, there cannot be "right and wrong" answers.

I find that this exercise serves my purpose well. It does lead to discussion of the personal problems suffered during the Great Depression. I include the script for the Telehelp tape, along with the alternative solutions offered to the students.

Script for Telehelp—Problem Solving—Simulation Unit[1]

No. 1

Hello, is this Telehelp? I understand that you help people with problems. My name is Heinz, Henry Heinz. I'm 44 years old, a university graduate. I worked as a construction engineer for a large firm for 15 years. I've been out of work for two years and can't find any kind of job. I was put out of my apartment three months ago because I couldn't pay the rent. I managed to make a shelter at the city dump, building a bed out of old auto parts and other junk. I've left this shanty every day to tramp the streets looking for work. Last night I settled down on my junk bed, under a blanket that a fireman had given me. I had a few rolls for supper that some neighborhood kids brought to me. Then a policeman came by and arrested me for vagrancy. I'm told I can't live at the dump anymore. I'm at the police station now. What shall I do?

No. 2

Hello, Telehelp? It's really too late to help me, but maybe you can help my family. My name is Emily Wallace. My husband has been out of work for 13 months. We've been getting some free food and milk from the city for a long time. We just got the news that we're one of 11,000 families to be dropped from the free food list because the city is having a "thrift drive." As soon as I hang up this phone, I intend to take the three littlest children and myself into the kitchen and turn on the gas. That will be four less people to go hungry. Maybe you can figure out how to help my husband and the two older boys to survive.

No. 3

Hello, Telehelp? My name is Miller, Jim Miller. I don't want charity; I want a job—any job. I'm an industrial chemist with two college degrees. I've only had three weeks work in the last two and one-half years. I've lost my home, and my wife and two children have moved in with my in-laws back in Milwaukee. I've drifted around the country for over a year looking for work everywhere. I haven't even written to my family because I'm too ashamed—I don't even have an address to give them. I won't take charity, but I want work—any kind of work. Can you help me?

---

[1]Cases are taken from *The New Deal*, copyright 1968, Xerox Corporation, Xerox Education Publications

No. 4

Telehelp? My name is Miss Wheaton. I'm a school teacher in the Chicago school system. I live with my widowed mother, who is an invalid. She is totally dependent on me for her care. In the last two years, I've only received about three weeks pay and I'm completely out of money. Last week the teachers finally got so angry that we went out on strike. We marched to the mayor's office and demanded our pay. Some of our people started smashing up the furniture, then the police started smashing us and three teachers ended up in the hospital. We still don't have our money. What are we to do?

No. 5

Hello, Telehelp? My name is Mrs. Lundborg. I live on a farm in Minnesota with my good husband, Lars, and five strapping fine sons. We've all worked for years under a sun that blisters you from May to September, and we've frozen like granite from Thanksgiving till spring, and now we have nothing but trouble to show for it all. The drought has ruined our land—farm prices are so low—and we just got the news that the bank is going to take over our farm because we can't pay the mortgage. Please help us.

No. 6

Hello, Telehelp? My name is George Kennedy. I'm calling because of 250 angry desperate people. All of us are people who have lost our homes because we couldn't pay the mortgages. We built a shanty town on the Hudson River in New York City, using scrap lumber, refrigerator crates, and anything else that we could find. We've been living in 60 unheated shacks, helping one another. We called our shantytown "Hardluck on the River." We've been clean and orderly, made rules and laws, and even elected a mayor. However, the city government sent a wrecking crew to clear away our shantytown and they leveled it to the ground. It seems that some citizens complained that it was an eyesore. We have nowhere to go. Somebody's got to do something.

Alternatives—Telehelp—Simulation Unit

Directions: Arrange the alternatives in the order of their desirability, rank them 1 to 5.

No. 1

1. Stay at the dump—set up a barricade to keep people out.
2. Move to another dump or vacant lot.

3. Prepare to defend yourself and your squatter's shack with a shotgun.
4. Move onto the street and camp in front of someone's home or apartment.
5. Move in with friends or relatives, even though this creates a disruption.

No. 2

1. Beg in the streets and scavenge in dumps.
2. Steal secretly.
3. Organize groups to protest by stealing openly from grocery markets.
4. Quietly starve.
5. Organize a protest on the steps of city hall.

No. 3

1. Find a busy city street corner and beg.
2. Rob a bank.
3. Move in with your wife's relatives.
4. Write letters to your congressman demanding a Government job.
5. Make a plan to take the mayor of your town as a hostage and demand radio time to make your protests known.

No. 4

1. Sponsor an organized movement for all teachers to quit teaching entirely until funds are available.
2. Start a movement to charge each family a fixed amount each week to pay for teachers' salaries.
3. Set up a system for parents to supply board and room for all teachers.
4. Smash all the windows in the school to dramatize the anger of teachers.
5. Continue your teaching for no pay and ask friends and relatives to support you.

No. 5

1. Put your belongings on an old farm truck and set out for California to get jobs as migrant workers.

2. Storm the bank that plans to foreclose your mortgage and steal enough cash from them to cover the mortgage.
3. Arm your sons and prepare to defend your land.
4. Move to a city slum and have your sons join the bread lines to get food.
5. Set fire to your farmhouse so that the bank can't have it.

No. 6

1. Find out the names of the citizens who complained and set up tents in their front yards.
2. Move your shantytown to a new location on the river—five miles upstream.
3. Rebuild your shantytown on the spot and prepare to defend it with clubs and rocks against anyone who comes to tear it down again.
4. March on the city hall that ordered your shantytown destroyed and smash the entire place.
5. Set up a new shantytown in the city's loveliest park.

INTERVIEWS (I and S)

The interview is an excellent tool that should be used often in any social studies program. When the interview assignment is carefully planned by the teacher, and skillfully carried out by the pupil, the result can be an unusually valuable learning experience.

Preparations for an interview should include the following:

1. Interview questions should be constructed by both the student and the teacher.
2. Good interview questions should be questions that cannot be answered by a simple "yes" or "no." The object is to inspire the person being interviewed to express himself fully.
3. Avoid questions with built-in bias. Do not ask, "Can you give reasons why F.D.R. was a good president during the depression years?" Do ask, "How would you evaluate F.D.R.'s performance as president during the depression years?"

4. Students should be aware of the need to think fast during the interview in order to add questions on the spot if the dialogue seems to call for them.
5. A student should never go into an interview uninformed on his subject. If he is scheduled to interview someone on the subject of the depression, he should first do considerable reading for background information.
6. The interviewer should be prepared to take notes rapidly and thoroughly so that he will be able to write a good report on the interview.
7. Good manners on the part of the interviewer should be stressed.

There are several benefits to be gained from this experience. This is a learning activity in which the student is actively involved. The process of setting up the interview and carrying it out tends to help develop the student's poise and self-assurance. Since most people with enough experience to be interviewed are mature adults, the interview can help to stimulate communication between generations. I have found that many older people enjoy this kind of exchange with young people.

I include the interview assignment as structured by Interact, along with additional questions constructed by my own students. I also include an interview conducted and written by one of my students.

DEPRESSION INTERVIEW (I)

Take notes as you interview one adult born no later than 1925—preferably no later than 1920. Ask the following questions and add several of your own. Write up the interview with care and be prepared to share the results with the class.

1. What is your most vivid memory of the Great Depression of 1929 through 1941?
2. During these years did you have any contact with any of the following: farmers, people on relief, vagrants, bank failures, people who lost badly on the stock market. Please comment a bit about any of these.
3. Can you remember any way that the Depression affected education?
4. What do you think of the way President Roosevelt tried to

solve the problems of the Depression? In the long range, were his actions helpful or harmful to the United States and our way of life?

5. Do you remember what you were doing in April 1945, when you first heard that F.D.R. had died? What was your *first* reaction? Why did you have this reaction? Do you think that some Americans reacted differently than you did?
6. In evaluating the accomplishments of American Presidents, where would you rank F.D.R. within a group of the "20 best Presidents we ever had"? Why?
7. In your opinion, what factor or factors finally ended the Great Depression?

Additional Interview Questions suggested and used by students (S)

1. What did you like or dislike about the 1920's?
2. Did you listen to F.D.R.'s fireside chats? How did you like them?
3. What did you think about the prohibition issue?
4. What do you remember about clothing styles during the 1920's and 30's?
5. How did you feel about women getting the right to vote?
6. Describe the music of the twenties. How did you like it?
7. Do you remember the first talking movies and your reactions to them?
8. How did you feel about going off of the Gold Standard?
9. What can you tell us about people who hid their money under mattresses, and in the sugar bowl, etc.?
10. What were the cars like in this period? Do you recall the cost of automobiles? Or the condition of the roads in those days?
11. Why did labor unions grow in the 1930's? Did you favor them?
12. What kind of entertainment did you have during the depression?
13. Can you think of any positive results of the depression?

14. Before World War II were you aware of any Nazi organization going on in this country?
15. Is there anything that you would like to add about the 1920's and 30's?
16. Would you care to comment about the experience of doing this interview with me? Do you feel that this is a good way for young people to learn?

Interview by Beth Holan with her grandparents (Mr. and Mrs. Drahas)

BETH: What is your most vivid memory of the Great Depression of 1929–1941?

GRANDMA AND GRANDPA: Our most vivid memory of the Depression is not having the money we would have liked to have. Another thing is there was no work to be found. Everyone was out of work until President Roosevelt set up the W.P.A. I (Grandpa) got a job from the W.P.A. digging ditches for $60 a month.

BETH: During these years did you have any contact with any of the following: farmers, people on relief, vagrants, bank failures, people who lost badly on the stock market. Please comment a bit about any of these.

GRANDMA: After the banks failed, my father took his money out. He later gave some to the Crown Hill Cemetery and lost that, too. So I guess we were in contact with a bank failure.

BETH: Can you remember any way that the Depression affected education?

GRANDMA AND GRANDPA: We don't think there was any effect on education because kids still had to go to school regardless of the situation.

BETH: What do you think of the way President Roosevelt tried to solve the problems of the Depression? In the long run, were his actions helpful or harmful to the United States and our way of life?

GRANDMA AND GRANDPA: We think he did a good job. He saved the nation from Depression. His actions were *very helpful*. He formed the W.P.A., giving a lot of people jobs.

BETH: Do you remember what you were doing in April, 1945, when you first heard F.D.R. had died? What was your *first* reaction? Why did you have this reaction? Do you think that some Americans reacted differently than you did?

GRANDMA AND GRANDPA: We were listening to the radio when the announcement that F.D.R. had died came on. We thought that since he saved us from the Depression, now that he was dead we would go into another one. I think there were Americans that didn't like him. My neighbor (Grandma) was not shocked. Her son was drafted so she hated him for that. Also the Germans hated him, although we are Germans we liked him.

BETH: In evaluating the accomplishments of American Presidents where would you rank F.D.R. within a group of the "20 best Presidents we ever had"? Why?

GRANDMA AND GRANDPA: We rate him *Number one!* We rate Hoover the worst because he was the one who got us into the Depression. Why we ranked F.D.R. number one because he helped people through the Depression and because he created the W.P.A.

BETH: In your opinion, what factor or factors finally ended the Great Depression?

GRANDMA: Boy that's a tough one. I think maybe the ending of Prohibition. Because again they started making booze and they needed more and more people to help, so that created jobs and money.

BETH: What did you like or dislike about the 1920's?

GRANDPA: I liked everything about the 1920's. Especially the big parties I used to go to on Saturdays. I liked the movies. I would say that was the best time of my life. I didn't dislike anything.

GRANDMA: I loved everything. The movies—everything. I didn't dislike anything.

BETH: What do you remember about clothing styles during the 1920's and 30's?

GRANDMA: The women wore these long tight dresses and big hats. I can remember trying to raise my leg to step on the trollies—boy was that hard.

GRANDPA: The clothing was *hideous*! We wore long raccoon coats, but I didn't have one. There were cuffs on the pants back then.

BETH: How did you feel about women getting the right to vote?

GRANDMA: I was all for it! The first time I voted was in 1934. I remember voting for F.D. Roosevelt. I remember taking your mom to the voting booths with me and waiting in line to vote.

BETH: Describe the music of the 1920's. How did you like it?

GRANDPA: I really wasn't into dancing, but that music is good. It's sort of like rock-and-roll.

GRANDMA: That kind of music I like.

BETH: Do you remember the first talking movies and your reactions to them?

GRANDMA AND GRANDPA: It was Al Jolson in ''Mammy.'' It was like they were right in that room with you. We both thought it was *delightful*!

BETH: Did people really hide their money under mattresses?

GRANDMA: You better believe it! Nobody trusted the banks.

BETH: What were the cars like in this period? Do you recall the cost of automobiles? Or the condition of the roads in those days?

GRANDPA: I bought my first car in 1926. It cost me $495. It was a Ford Model T. The cars were all black with rumble seats. They had running boards, and were very high. It seemed you were sitting in a truck instead of a car. Some old cars still had the wooden tires. Our car was very uncomfortable—the seats were terrible. The roads were very narrow—only allowed two cars to drive on. They were made of either asphalt or brick. On the roads they would put a little oil on them to keep them from getting dusty. When it rained, the dirt roads would be muddy and a lot of people got stuck.

BETH: What kind of entertainment did you have during the Depression?

GRANDMA AND GRANDPA: Most of our entertainment we had to make. Or we could go see a movie that cost 25 cents. The roller skating rinks stayed open and so did Euclid Beach.

BETH: Before World War II were you aware of any Nazi organization going on in this country?

GRANDMA: There were these people who lived next to my dad's house, who belonged to that organization. I talked to his wife, but we never talked to the father.

BETH: If you had a choice would you want to relive the 1920's or just stay in this time period?

GRANDPA: I'd like to live in the 1920's again, it was the best time of my life!

GRANDMA: I want to stay right here!

BETH: How did things differ then than they do now, for example: houses, food, etc.?

GRANDPA: The houses were built better than they are now. They were built to last. They were cheaper, too.

GRANDMA: Back then you got more for your money. In the 1920's I paid 5 cents for a pint of milk and 9 cents for a quart of milk. Now I pay 40 cents a quart for milk. And you still get the same amount.

BETH: How did your parents feel about the Depression? Were they worried about not having enough money?

GRANDMA: They weren't really that worried. After Grandpa's mom and dad died they came to live in our house. We had 10 people living in a three bedroom house. Most people in that house worked so we had enough money to support all of us.

BETH: I had a great time interviewing my grandparents. And my grandparents loved talking about it. They sat there about three hours telling me all their stories. I really had fun!

LEGISLATION (I and S)

Those of us who lived through the depression years will long remember the great volume of legislation that was part and parcel of the New Deal. The three R's were no longer reading, 'riting, and 'rithmetic. They became known as relief, recovery, and reform and were heralded as a part of the program that was to bring us out of the worst depression in our history. Most of this legislation was, and still is, highly controversial, and serves very well as a subject for debate in the classroom.

In my view, four laws loom above all others in this massive legislative program in their impact on our history. They are:

1. Agricultural Adjustment Act (AAA) introduced the practice of government support for the farmers.
2. Tennessee Valley Authority (TVA) paved the way for many huge projects sponsored by the Federal Government.
3. Social Security Act provided a compulsary pension plan for older people.
4. Wagner Act strengthened the power and effectiveness of labor unions.

Our simulation unit would not be complete without a project involving this important legislation. For this purpose, I allow two days for "Congressional Committee hearings." Two of the above laws are debated on each of the two days.

If you have used the Civil War Debates in your class, you will find your students swinging into the debates on New Deal legislation with skill and enthusiasm. This provides an excellent opportunity for learning more about the committee system used by our Congress.

The following procedures are used in setting up the simulation exercise for any one of these four "bills":

1. Appoint a student to serve as the sponsor of the bill. This sponsor must be prepared to introduce the bill and explain it to the committee.
2. Set up a congressional committee of five. One of these five members acts as chairman and presides over the hearing. The function of this committee is to discuss the merits and drawbacks of the bill, listen to comments from the audience, and finally

Bill	*Date*	*Sponsor*	*Committee Chairman*	*Other Committee Members*
Tennessee Valley Authority				______ ______ ______ ______
Social Security				______ ______ ______ ______
Wagner Act				______ ______ ______ ______
Agricultural Adjustment Act				______ ______ ______ ______

vote on the bill, supposedly to determine if it will proceed to either house of Congress.

3. All other students in the class will assume the roles of citizens at the committee hearing. Any of these citizens may request permission to speak before the committee in order to represent a particular pressure group. For example, farmers might speak in favor of the AAA; laborers will be pushing the Wagner Act, etc.

A bit of simple arithmetic will rather quickly demonstrate the fact that by the time committees and sponsors are set up to handle four proposed laws, most members of the class will have the opportunity to play the role of congressman once and the role of interested citizen three times. To avoid confusion, I distribute handout sheets to all students. These provide an easy method for recording student assignments on the project.

ALPHABET SOUP (S)

A nation grows in population, size, industry, technology, wealth, and power. Because of this growth, the nation's problems become increasingly complex. This necessitates a corresponding growth of the government, which presents a whole new set of problems. Government itself becomes cumbersome, bureaucratic, inefficient, and sometimes corrupt. I suggest all of this as a pattern that I wish students to explore.

Reflect for a moment on the expansion of government power that started in the last half of the nineteenth century. At that time, and in retrospect, legislative control certainly was necessary. I cannot dispute the need for the Sherman Anti-trust Act, the Interstate Commerce Act, The Pure Food and Drug Act, the Federal Trade Act, etc.

It is an easy leap from this to the growth of government in the 1930's. The problems caused by the depression seemed to necessitate government action. And the government acted! The result was "Alphabet Soup," a confusing array of government programs designed to bring about Relief, Recovery, and Reform. Historians still disagree when evaluating the effectiveness of these New Deal Programs. I know of few who would dispute, however, the observation that big government is here to stay, whether or not it was, in fact, spawned by the New Deal.

This kind of analysis may seem like a pretty rich diet for junior high students. Nevertheless, I want to get my students involved in some solid discussions about our government in terms of power and complexity. For this purpose I use this Alphabet Soup exercise as a means of securing some factual background. It is a game situation, using six teams. Each team is given a sheet with the alphabet names for New Deal programs. The challenge is to see which team can most successfully find the proper names for these programs, along with an explanation of each one. This game can serve as a starting point for class discussion. The results are also useful for review for the New Deal test.

ALPHABET SOUP

Write a sentence explaining each of the following. Be sure to include the exact words represented by each of the capital letters.

1. New Deal
   Program of Relief, Recovery, and Reform to end depression
2. NIRA
   National Industrial Recovery Act
3. AAA
   Agricultural Adjustment Administration
4. PWA
   Public Works Administration
5. WPA
   Works Progress Administration
6. NRA
   National Recovery Administration
7. CCC
   Civilian Conservation Corps
8. FERA
   Federal Emergency Relief Administration
9. NYA
   National Youth Administration
10. SEC
    Securities and Exchange Commission

11. NLRA
National Labor Relations Act

12. TVA
Tennessee Valley Authority

13. CWA
Civil Works Administration

14. HOLC
Home Owners Loan Corporation

15. CIO
Congress of Industrial Organizations

16. AF of L
American Federation of Labor

17. UMW
United Mine Workers

18. Fireside Chats
F.D. Roosevelt's radio talks to the American people

19. Bank Holiday
Banks closed by F.D.R. for four days to avoid a panic

20. Farm Credit Administration
Loaned money to farmers

21. The first 100 days
First 100 days of F.D.R.'s term

22. The Blue Eagle
Symbol of recovery from the depression

TESTING (S)

During this unit, no matter how special or exciting it may be, the world continues to spin on its axis; the sun rises in the east each day, and the teacher continues to give tests!

For ease in converting grades into WIPS (see charts on pages 197, 198, 199), I do my testing in units of twelve. Topics and point values follow:

1. Twelve point quiz—women, liquor, and crime
2. Twelve point quiz—the Great Depression and Labor Unions

3. Twenty-four point test—the Presidents of the twenties and thirties

4. Twenty-four point test—the New Deal

These quizzes and tests are announced well in advance. A study sheet is distributed early in the unit. The students are on their own to cover the text reading and the many other available books that might be helpful on the testing.

At this writing I have data on this project for only two years. If two years can establish a trend, I can report that test grades are higher on this unit than they are on others. This is probably due to the competition among the students for WIPS.

Study Sheet—the twenties and thirties (S)

1. ***Prohibition***—KNOW
   The exact years when it started and ended, the Eighteenth and Twenty-first Amendments, the Volstead Act, the resulting rise in crime, speakeasies, hijacking, bathtub gin, Carrie Nation, organized crime, Al Capone.
2. ***Women***—KNOW
   Rapid changes in their lives during the 1920's and the reasons for these changes, Nineteenth Amendment, flappers, roaring twenties, Charleston.
3. ***Depression***—KNOW
   The President in office when it started and when it ended, the stock market crash, buying on margin, overexpansion, the year of the crash, causes for the Depression.
4. ***Unions***—KNOW
   A.F. of L. and the CIO and their merger, the Wagner Act or National Labor Relations Act and the provisions, other large independent unions, reason for the rapid growth in union membership in the 1930's, minimum wage, child labor, John L. Lewis, Sam Gompers, Teamsters, Railroad Brotherhoods.
5. ***The Presidents of this period***—KNOW
   Sequence from Wilson through F.D.R., their parties. Be able to identify: New Freedom, New Deal, Keep Cool, return to normalcy, two chickens in every pot and a car in every ga-

rage, corruption in high places, fireside chats, Teapot Dome scandal, Al Smith, RFC Disarmament conferences, Hoovervilles, war relief programs.

6. ***New Deal***—KNOW
Background, other parties or movements that contributed to it, the "Three R's," effect on labor, relief and reform measures as follows: NYA, CCC, WPA, PWA, AAA, Farm Security Administration, Farm Credit Administration, closing the banks (bank holiday), FERA, SEC, CWA, NRA, Social Security Act, utilities, end of the Gold Standard, HOLC, insured bank deposits.

STUDENT INITIATIVE

I guarantee it! If you offer your students a simulation unit that is well planned and well executed, the students are going to add some original touches of their own. Such innovations will probably come as a surprise. Be prepared to think fast, examine your options quickly, and make wise decisions on the spot. All of this takes a bit of doing, even for the experienced teacher.

Some student additions to the unit could put your entire program in jeopardy; in other cases they could prove to be the best learning experiences of the year. I can best make my point by relating an experience I had this past school year.

On the third Friday of the four-week simulation program on the Twenties and Thirties, I was served notice in writing (in the middle of a class period) that my five class bankers (one for each class—see page 204) were going on strike. This strike was set to start on Monday unless their pay was raised from fifteen WIPS a day to thirty WIPS a day. Here are the options that quickly went through my mind:

1. I could easily make a rule that ''bankers'' did not strike, only laborers went on strike, thus avoiding the problem.
2. I could fire all five bankers and replace them. I knew that many volunteers would quickly seek these jobs.
3. I could refuse to permit this strike on the basis of lack of time. Only one week of the unit remained.

4. I could take the strike seriously and let the students experience a simulated strike situation. But—there could be some risk in such an action. The five class bankers had in their possession all of the banking records. These were vital to the successful conclusion of the unit just one week hence. In addition, I had no idea how a simulated strike might work out. It could result in a sticky situation.

After fifteen seconds of deliberation, I announced to the class, "I have just received in writing an official notice that the class bankers will go on strike Monday unless their pay is doubled. It so happens that this threat reaches me on the very day that we will be debating the Wagner Act (National Labor Relations Act, see page 246). If this act is passed in three of my five classes, I will be required by law to recognize unions and will be compelled to negotiate with the striking bankers. If the Wagner Act fails in three of my five classes, however, I shall fire all five of my class bankers and hire new people to take their jobs."

The Wagner Act was passed by four of my five classes. By the end of the day I sent notice to the bankers that I could not meet their demands because of the depression and that if they went on strike, we would set up negotiations immediately.

The strike did indeed start on Monday. All banks were closed, and students in all classes were unable to make withdrawals or deposits. The stock market was open as usual. The following steps were taken in preparation for negotiation:

1. Striking bankers were instructed to choose a team of three to represent them.
2. I chose two students to work with me as a negotiating team. I deliberately chose people whom I knew to be management oriented.
3. Our assistant principal was invited to serve as the mediator. He happened to be a person who had actually experienced negotiations between our teachers' association and our school board.
4. The negotiation session was set up for Tuesday during one of the lunch periods.
5. Students not directly involved in the negotiations were invited to drop in from lunch period and study hall to observe the experience.

On Tuesday we went through the whole bit. Management called for binding arbitration because of the urgency of a quick settlement. Labor (the bankers) responded, "No way!" The mediator separated the two groups and proceeded to talk privately with each group. Both teams came back to the table for further discussion. The discussion became heated. A few personal remarks were exchanged, and feelings definitely got involved. Further caucuses were called. Management finally offered a raise of five WIPS a day as a "final offer." Labor agreed to take this offer back to their members for a vote. The mediator instructed all five striking bankers to be in his office before school the next morning.

On Wednesday morning the bankers met. After a heated discussion, the chief negotiator reported to the mediator that they agreed to the raise of five WIPS a day.

As I met with each class that day, I called upon a student who had been directly involved in the negotiations to report to the class on the results. I asked each of these students to share with us his or her feelings about the entire experience. One sensitive and thoughtful young lady explained the procedures and the outcome and then went on to say, "This was a really neat experience. You can't learn what a strike is all about by reading a book, but you surely find out in a hurry when you live through negotiations. If we had to decide all over again, I don't believe we'd vote to strike. We got so upset with management's negotiators, and I even found myself getting angry with my fellow bankers because I thought they were unreasonable. If we could get this hassled and mad over something that doesn't even exist (WIPS), think what the real thing must be like."

As a teacher, I shared the young lady's feelings. This was a fantastic learning experience for all of the students and led to some mighty productive discussion in the classroom.

I add a postscript to this story. The banks opened on Wednesday as the bankers came back to work. It was interesting to observe that in each class, students quietly lined up to withdraw all of their WIPS from the banks and transferred them back to the WIPS balance sheet. It was a real, and spontaneous, "run on the banks" and again reflected human nature. This incident led to further class discussion. Most students agreed that they had withdrawn their WIPS because they'd lost faith in the bankers.

I relate this entire incident in order to make a point. Be creative, imaginative, resourceful in setting up your programs. Get your students actively involved in the learning process. If they respond by matching your creativity with ideas of their own, be prepared to react immediately before a golden moment slips away. Seize any reasonable suggestion quickly and with enthusiasm. You will find your class caught up in a learning situation with built-in motivation that will sustain itself. I can think of nothing in the world of education that is more gratifying or more exciting than being a part of such a learning process.

As I reflect on the value of this kind of learning I realize, with true humility, that two of the most exciting things that I have ever seen in my own classroom were initiated by students. I speak of the Civil War Debates (see Chapter 6) and the Bankers Strike of 1979 that I have just described. The bottom line, however, is the fact that the teacher must provide the climate where such exciting learning can take root. Provide it!

TWENTIES AND THIRTIES DAY (S)

This idea, happily, came from the students, and it is a fitting finale to the unit. It needs little explanation.

On the twenty-first and final day of the unit, most of my students come to school dressed in the costume of this period. The girls choose, almost exclusively, to come as flappers with the straight knee length dresses, long strings of beads, fringe and frou-frou in abundance, and plenty of makeup. The boys come in a variety of outfits—knickers, old fashioned garb designed for riding in open cars, goggles and all. Many go the Al Capone route, complete with a slouch hat and ''violin case.'' Some students come dressed as poor people in the thirties in drab, dingy outfits that show evidence of much wear. The Teacher? Well, of course, a liberated jazz baby of the twenties; the students would scarcely settle for anything less.

Whatever the costume, it is a fun day for all of us. Not much serious work takes place on this day. We total WIPS scores, determine the ''top ten champions,'' and evaluate the unit. This leaves time for nonsense—a Charleston act, some music of the twenties, or other appropriate amateur entertainment.

I wish to conclude this unit as I started it, by expressing again my appreciation to the writers of *PANIC*—Interact, P.O. Box 262, Lakeside, California 92040. I understand that this company currently has over 80

The "Twenties and Thirties Day" takes full advantage of students' high levels of interest, imagination, involvement, and learning, as these photos attest. Shown above, in the front row, are Ted Groth, Kris Urban, Tina Fiocco, and Lee Derry; standing (from left to right) are Diane Harboth, Mark Thonnings, Brian Barth, Cindy Caldert, Michele Stech, Sandy Kostantaras, Pam Peterson, and Chris Urbanski.

In the lower photo, Mark Jacubec and Rex Cassidy kneel in front of Darin Kolakowski, Kim Kroenke, John Varga, Rita Krueger, Ingrid Schaefer, and Sue Pele.

simulation units on the market. My readers might find it helpful to send for their catalog.

Next comes a challenge! It is time to set aside this approach to learning through games and shift gears very suddenly. This unit is followed by a traditional, and very serious, unit on World War II. However, before leaving the simulated Twenties and Thirties, I must share with you my "bible" for that unit. The follow-pages recapitulate the daily activities for the entire unit. I follow this schedule zealously, and it works!

Daily Schedule—Simulation Unit—21 Days

1st Day Explanation of the Unit

1. Distribute to each student:
   Name Tags
   WIPS Balance Sheet
   Grading system sheet
2. Give a choice of one of six banks (named after teachers).
   a. Introduce banker for each class
   b. Starting pay for bankers—30 WIPS daily
   c. No interest given on Saturdays nor Sundays
3. Play the tape of the annual business report.

2nd Day Further explanation. Banks and stock market opened for the first time. A long business period is necessary as this is the first experience with business transactions.

1. Explain stock market and names of stocks (offer only three).
2. Explain sample slips for savings deposits and withdrawals, WIPS checks, and stock certificates. Business done in multiples of five only.
3. Play tape of the first daily business report.
4. Open stock market and the banks.

3rd Day Scavenger Hunt No. 1—30 items. Allow three periods of five minutes each.

1. Distribute study sheets and explain testing.

2. Put students in groups according to occupations. Conduct a scavenger hunt.
3. Go over the results. Declare the winners and assign WIPS as follows:
   First place—75 WIPS
   Second place—50 WIPS
   Third place—25 WIPS
   All others—10 WIPS
4. Play tape for second day's stock report.
5. Issue dividends for stocks.
6. Open stock market and banks.

4th Day Scavenger Hunt No. 2—30 items. Allow three periods of five minutes each.

1. Very carefully teach how to determine total wealth for income tax purposes—then collect taxes as follows:

0–100 WIPS—	5 WIPS	1001–1250 WIPS—	120 WIPS
101–250 WIPS—	20 WIPS	1251–1500 WIPS—	140 WIPS
251–500 WIPS—	60 WIPS	1501–1750 WIPS—	180 WIPS
501–750 WIPS—	80 WIPS	1751–2000 WIPS—	230 WIPS
751–1000 WIPS—	100 WIPS	2001–2250 WIPS—	260 WIPS

2. Give scavenger hunt—groups by professions.
3. Go over it and declare winners. Assign WIPS (see 3rd day for scoring).
4. Tape for 3rd day's stock report.
5. Open stock market and banks.

5th Day Scavenger Hunt No. 3—30 items.

1. Scavenger Hunt in Regional groups. Change these groups as needed to achieve numerical balance.
2. Go over the results and assign WIPS as indicated in Day 3.
3. Fourth day's stock report.
4. Pay dividends—add to WIPS accounts.
5. Open banks and stock market.

6th Day Study session with partners to prepare for quiz on women, liquor, and crime. First 12 point quiz.

1. Catch up day—give individual help to straighten out accounts while they are studying.
2. Have students get out study sheets. Distribute answer sheets and explain.
3. Allow study time.
4. Give quiz—collect papers and grade them for grade points and WIPS.
5. Fifth day's stock report.
6. Open stock market and banks.
7. Raise pay for bankers to 50 WIPS per day.

7th Day Independent Study—General Statements.

1. Return quizzes and have students record WIPS.
2. Distribute General Statements Sheets.
3. Allow most of period for this—24 points.
4. Stock market open for both 6th and 7th day's reports.
5. Calculate dividends and add to the students' WIPS.
6. Open banks and stock market.

8th Day Set One—Pressure Cards.

1. Distribute Interview Sheets and explain assignment for 15th Day.
2. Explain the need to study the four laws for legislation for 17th and 18th days.
3. Have the drawing for Pressure Cards and record results in students' records.
4. Stock market report for the 8th day.
5. Stock market and bank open.

9th Day General Statements—Reports made.

1. Have students report orally their findings on General Statements. Collect and grade—both grade points and WIPS.

2. Income Tax collection—see lesson for 4th day.
3. Stock report for 9th day.
4. Calculate dividends and add to WIPS accounts.
5. Open stock market and the banks.

10th Day Film strips on the 1920's and 30's

1. Return General Statement papers and record WIPS.
2. Show film strips.
3. Stock market report number 10.
4. Open stock market and the banks.
5. Assign AAA and Wagner Act for the 16th day.

11th Day Study session in groups for Depression and Labor Unions.

1. Have students study for Quiz No. 2 in regional groups—12 points.
2. Give quiz—collect papers and grade—points and WIPS.
3. Announce Legislation assignment due on the 16th and 17th day (12 points each day).
4. Interrupt with the business report—market crashes!
5. Banks open but stock market remains closed.

12th Day Telehelp.

1. Have students in occupational groups.
2. Play the tape of case studies. Have each group arrange alternatives in order of preference.
3. Two winning groups are chosen by consensus. WIPS—75 apiece for the two top groups. 25 WIPS for third place—10 to all others.
4. Banking report No. 1 is given.
5. Stock market open—banks are closed.

13th Day Study session in regional groups. The Presidents of this period.

1. Set up the legislation days in detail.
2. Group study for tests—24 points.
3. Stock market open—banks still closed.

4. No business report today.
5. Give tests—score in WIPS and grade points.

14th Day Set two—pressure cards.

1. Income tax collection—see lesson for 4th day.
2. Return tests and record students WIPS (before taxes).
3. Draw Pressure Cards and record on students' records.
4. Have the second bank report—banks still closed.
5. Open stock market.
6. Interviews are due tomorrow.

15th Day Interviews.

1. Banking and stock report right away. Compute and get banking records up to date. Open stock market at same time.
2. Have students report verbally on the results of their interviews.
3. Collect papers and grade (24 point assignment).
4. Remind students that legislation is due on AAA and Wagner Act on 17th day.

16th Day Open day for study.

1. Discuss Costume Day for the 21st day.
2. Business report for the 16th day.
3. Open stock market and banks.
4. Unemployment strikes—cut one out of every five by 20 percent—put one out of every five out of work. This means it affects WIPS earned on assignments. Bankers' pay cut to 10 WIPS per day.

17th Day Legislation; AAA; Wagner Act.

1. Return interviews and record WIPS.
2. Set up Congressional Committees—one person from each occupational group—each gets 25 WIPS for serving.
3. Students make speeches for and against the bill.
4. Committee votes on bill.

5. Papers are handed in to be graded—12 points.
6. Business report—17th day—banks and market open.

18th Day Legislation; Social Security; Tennessee Valley Authority.

1. Return graded speeches and have them record WIPS on students' records.
2. Announce WIPS results for the two bills yesterday as follows and have them recorded:
   a. If AAA passes it must be paid for in taxes.

0–100	.... Lose 5 WIPS	Businessmen	.... lose 50
101–250	.... Lose 10 WIPS	Bankers	.... lose 50
251–500	.... Lose 40 WIPS	Farmers	.... gain 100
501 and up	Lose 60 WIPS		

   b. If AAA fails—Farmers lose 50 WIPS
   c. If Wagner Act passes:
      All people with less than 500 WIPS—gain 25
      Bankers lose 50 WIPS
      Businessmen lose 100 WIPS
      Laborers gain 100 WIPS
      Activists gain 100 WIPS
   d. If Wagner Act fails all laborers lose 50 WIPS
3. Set up new Congressional Committees—each gets 25 WIPS for serving.
4. Students make speeches for and against each bill.
5. Committee votes on bill.
6. Papers collected for grading—12 points.
7. Business news—open bank and stock market.

19th Day Alphabet Soup.

1. Return graded speeches and have WIPS recorded.
2. Announce effects from the two bills as follows:
   a. If Social Security passes:
      All with less than 500 WIPS gain 25. Women gain 100. Activists, Laborers, and Farmers all gain 25. Businessmen and bankers each lose 75.
   b. If Social Security fails, women, activists, laborers, and farmers each lose 25. Businessmen and bankers each gain 50.

c. If TVA passes, tax cost the same as for passing the AAA—see 18th day. Also a bonus of 100 WIPS for all southerners.
d. If TVA fails, penalty of 50 WIPS for southerners and farmers.

3. Collect income tax—see plan for 4th day.
4. In occupational groups—contest in filling out the Alphabet Soup lists.
   First prize—75 WIPS
   Second prize—50 WIPS
   Third prize—25 WIPS
   All others— 10 WIPS
5. Bank and stock market take a day off.
6. Return legislation papers and record WIPS.

20th Day Study Session in regional groups for test on the New Deal—24 points.

1. Allow study time for the test.
2. Give test and score in grade points and WIPS.
3. Final Stock Market report—close out the stocks and the bank accounts. Put all points in the WIPS Balance Sheet.

21st Day Twenties and Thirties Day; Costume Day.

1. Return tests and record the WIPS.
2. Make final calculations of all wealth and record on the blackboard.
3. Evaluation of the unit.

9

Bringing It All Together

EVEN THOUGH IT MAY SOUND LIKE A RE-RUN, IT IS TIME to take a backward look. We have examined hints, tips, and techniques, handouts, testing and grading, current events, and several special major programs. All of this is offered as practical material that should be helpful in day-to-day classroom procedures. It would seem that I have achieved what I set out to do.

There are some loose ends, however, that demand attention. Whirling around in my head is a series of words and phrases that we often tend to dismiss as "educational jargon." Some of these words are dully overworked and dimly understood. Some of them we resist as the product of "ivory tower" theorists. These terms deserve a closer look and some thoughtful contemplation.

OBJECTIVES

WEBSTER: *That toward which effort is directed; an aim or end of action; goal.*

As teachers we may become weary at the very thought of including objectives for all our programs, projects, and lesson plans. However, I would submit that carefully thought out objectives are fundamental in a good teaching program. I borrow from the old chicken and the egg cliché, "Which comes first, the objectives or the program?" Begin with the objectives, by all means. Decide first precisely what you are attempting to achieve with any given unit of study, then determine the most effective way to meet that goal. Not one bit of classroom planning should be purposeless, drifting, nor haphazard. Nor should it be designed merely to fill time.

Whatever your objectives for the year, a project, or simply a day's lesson, they should be shared with the students. They should also be reinforced by frequent discussion in the classroom. Students usually respond to such sharing by exerting greater effort. They need to know that assignments given by teachers have clear-cut, valid purposes.

You will notice that I have hammered at objectives throughout this book. Sound objectives are the first step in developing any worthwhile educational program.

CURRICULUM

WEBSTER: *A course; especially a specified fixed course of study, as in a school or college, as one leading to a degree.*

Program planning has been the major thrust of this book. The definition above reminds me of the awesome responsibility that educators have in this direction. In the last analysis, it is primarily the function of the classroom teacher to be certain that the "course of study" has undisputed worth in "leading to a degree."

At the risk of committing academic hara-kiri, I feel obliged to express some strong views on the subject of curriculum. I do recognize the fact that each school system must provide some structure, some basic guidelines for the classroom teacher to follow as he plans his own teaching programs and procedures. This is necessary, though not always desirable, in order to comply with board of education policies, as well as state and Federal regulations. The key word in providing this structure is "broad." If the teacher is fenced in by curriculum guidelines that are too detailed, it could have a stifling effect that would discourage creative planning by the teacher.

I also find myself questioning the traditional course of study required by most school boards. It seems to me that its greatest value is to the person who wrote it. I will concede, however, that a course of study can be of use to a beginning teacher if it goes beyond an outline of the textbook.

I also take a dim view of curriculum committees that seem to be constantly convening, only to "spin their wheels." As I consider the opinions set forth here, I readily admit that they reflect the thinking of a strong individualist who becomes impatient with the "committee" approach to education.

In my view, a good curriculum director is one who spends much of his time visiting classrooms, where he can observe the educational process first hand. He should be available to offer assistance, guidance, and encouragement to individual teachers as they develop the programs that can be most effective in their individual classrooms. He should also do everything possible to disseminate information on techniques, materials, and programs that have proven to be unique, interesting, and successful. His work must focus on the classroom, not the central office.

MOTIVATION

WEBSTER: *To stimulate active interest in some study through appeal to associated interests or by special devices.*

This is a tough one! How does a good teacher "stimulate active interest" in an American history course? What kinds of "special devices" will result in a learning situation that will keep the kids actively involved? How should a teacher proceed if the students are bored and listless and unresponsive? Above all, how does anyone teach another teacher how to motivate students?

I'm not at all sure that I have answers. As I ponder the questions already raised, I come up with further questions. Are there workable rules for motivation? Is this a skill that can be learned, or is it, in fact, a special talent? An art? Does the personality of the teacher become an important factor?

All I can do is list some things that I see as contributing to the development of a classroom situation where students are willing and eager to learn:

1. The teacher should have a positive approach and sincere enthusiasm for any unit of work that is used.
2. Explanations and directions should be given clearly and thoroughly, both orally and in writing.
3. Goals and objectives should be shared with the students.
4. Evaluation of students' work should be fair, thorough, and prompt, with emphasis on positive factors.
5. Difficulty of the work should be determined by the capability of the class. Within that framework, however, standards should be set by the teacher that can challenge and inspire the students.
6. There should be a variety of activities and frequent change of pace in the classroom.
7. Honest praise should be used wherever possible.
8. Students should feel that the teacher likes and respects them. Rapport between students and teacher should be carefully established and constantly nurtured.
9. To all of the above I suggest adding a sense of humor and bits of nonsense along the way.

I suppose that educators could produce countless rules for motivation. When all is said and done, good motivation is a highly individualized process, and each of us must find our own way.

DEDICATION

WEBSTER: *To set apart formally or seriously to a definite use, end, or service; as to dedicate one's life to study.*

This word seems to conjure up a vision of an old fashioned spinster lady, complete with long black dress, adorned very properly by white collar and cuffs. She carries a wooden pointer and wears her hair in a tidy bun. This stereotyped lady is, of course, serious, drab, and stern. Her sole interest in life is teaching.

I really cannot believe that the Mr. Chips or Miss Dove type of teacher is the best for modern schools. Those of us with many interests and varied experiences bring an extra dividend into the classroom. But I do hope that the word "dedicated" does not become an outmoded adjective in education. We have a great need for such teachers.

Today's dedicated teacher is one who:

- Teaches because he or she has chosen this field above all others and would choose it again, regardless of the number of attractive available alternatives.
- Spends time reading in order to stay up to date in the field of education in general and in his or her academic subject in particular.
- Seldom puts in a mere eight-hour-day or a five-day-week—is willing to give whatever time is necessary to do the job well.
- Really likes people, and has a particular affinity for the age level of his or her own students. I would be miserable teaching kindergartners, and I know of teachers who would climb the walls if they were assigned to teaching junior high school students.
- Supports the school and the community, is willing to help other staff members, and cooperates with the school principal in order to help keep the school functioning smoothly.
- Seeks self-improvement on the job, tries new methods and programs, and is willing to listen to evaluations from students and from superiors.

I am not naive enough to feel that I have just described the average teacher. The criteria enumerated here give us a very idealistic view of a teacher. But I have come to know a few such teachers, and I feel enriched because of my friendships with them. What is far more important is the fact that they enrich the lives of their students.

PROFESSIONALISM

WEBSTER: *Conduct, aims, qualities, etc. characteristic of, or peculiar to, a profession or professional men.*

Tackling this word bears some resemblance to sticking my head in a buzz saw. As I approach this topic, I ask you to "hold your fire." I fully intend to cover both sides of the coin. That might not offer me much protection. People with either view of this controversial word may end up taking pot shots at me.

School boards, administrators, and the general public have every right to expect professional behavior from their teachers. Teachers, like it or not, do serve as model figures for their students. This is an especially critical factor with young teenagers who are trying to establish identities. Our manners, speech, work habits, self-control, grooming, dress, and a host of other personal qualities should reflect our professionalism in the classroom.

Professionalism certainly demands from teachers a very strict code of ethics regarding confidential information about individual students. It is most assuredly proper and constructive and professional for teachers to discuss a youngster's personal and family problems with guidance counselors, principals, and school psychologists with a view toward assisting a troubled child. It is quite a different, and most unprofessional, act to gossip about that same child over lunch in the faculty room, or worse yet, over the bridge table in the community. It has been my observation that such gossip is usually accompanied by simplistic solutions and harsh judgments of students, parents, and teachers that are not only shallow, but very unfair. Most of us in education today are very aware of the unbearable family situations that some students face. Such students do not need nor deserve the added burden of community or school gossip. I hasten to add that I believe that this type of unprofessional behavior is very rare among teachers. It is of such vital importance, however, that I feel the need to cover it thoroughly in this book.

The question of students' personal problems opens up another aspect of professionalism. I consider it unprofessional, counterproductive, and in some cases, downright dangerous for a teacher to pry into the personal aspects of a student's life without invitation, even though it be under the guise of such "progressive programs" as "rap sessions," "values clarification," etc. In making such a strong statement, I realize that I am flying in the face of some strong, modern trends in education. This I must do; some of these trends concern me deeply.

If a student feels comfortable confiding personal feelings and problems to a teacher, that student will take the initiative if the teacher has always maintained an open door policy. Even then, a teacher needs to proceed with caution. If the problems are severe enough, the most constructive and professional move the teacher can make is to arrange a contact for the student with a school psychologist or psychiatrist who is really well qualified to handle such problems.

Another area where professionalism becomes important is in our relations with the parents of our students. When a parent comes to school to raise questions about an incident concerning his child, that parent is usually reasonable and cooperative. There are occasions, however, when the parent arrives at school tense, angry, and obviously wanting a piece of the teacher's hide. We must remember that the parent lives day in and day out with that volatile teenager whom we see for only one period a day. Adolescence is crisis time, and the parent occasionally reacts to a crisis emotionally.

The teacher needs to approach any conference or phone call with parents in a spirit of cooperation and reasoned calm. If it seems advisable, try to include a guidance counselor or the principal in any conference that promises to be difficult. You will usually find such colleagues to be supportive and helpful.

Now, let us examine the other side of the coin. It is of equal importance. The teachers have every right to expect to be treated as professionals by the school board, the administration, and the general public.

Let us begin with the paycheck. Teachers certainly should receive "professional pay." They should not be the last ones to advance financially when a new wage-price cycle adds to inflation. Nor should they have to fight against school boards and a reluctant public for a fair wage. An atmosphere of constant confrontation cannot result in a good educational system.

I have already commented on the importance of teacher professionalism in terms of contacts with the parents. The parent, too, has a responsibility to treat the teacher with the courtesy and respect that is due to a well-educated, dedicated, professional educator. It is especially important for the parent to support the teacher when dealing with a problem that involves his own child. If a parent feels inclined to back his child in a disagreement with a teacher, he should proceed with caution and investigate thoroughly before committing himself. I deplore some of the divide and conquer tactics that have been used successfully by some students as a means of defying adult authority. I am concerned about the recent trend toward "students' rights and responsibilities" that has been promoted by some parents. I feel that there has been too much emphasis on the "rights" and not enough on the "responsibilities."

I hasten to point out that the vast majority of parents do support the teachers. I also wish to emphasize the fact that unprofessional treatment of students by teachers is very, very rare.

The most flagrant examples of lack of respect for today's teachers are the incidents where students attack the teachers, physically or verbally. Abusive language, violence, or even a belligerent attitude simply cannot be tolerated. Whenever I hear of such incidents repeatedly in a school district, I clearly view it as a situation where school board members or administrators simply are not doing their jobs.

One last thing should be touched upon in terms of professional treatment of teachers. All of us in the profession find trivial things in the day to day routine that are irritating. Taken separately, they are of little consequence. If these small pressures are multiplied, however, they can create low morale on a school staff.

As a professional educator do you have:

- Free access to supplies from a central supply room, or are materials doled out upon request?
- A measure of freedom to leave the building for such things as doctor and dentist appointments?
- A reasonable system for obtaining students' confidential records when needed? (Government restrictions on this matter do not respect the professionalism of teachers.)
- A private life that is your own, with no restrictions imposed by community or school board? (Providing, of course, that you show discretion in keeping your private life relatively private.)

- Support from your superiors when you find it necessary to discipline a student?
- Consistency in interpretation and enforcement of school rules in the central office of your school?
- A reasonable degree of academic freedom in planning and carrying out your courses?
- A situation where staff members of both sexes are paid equally, treated equally, and given equal responsibility?

Now that I have managed to alienate teachers, parents, administrators, the general public, the Civil Liberties Union, and probably the United States courts, I will gladly lay aside this difficult topic of professionalism. I move on to less controversial subjects with the hope that some readers remain with me!

EVALUATION

WEBSTER: *To ascertain the value or amount of; to appraise carefully.*

As I view it, there are three levels of evaluation of the classroom teacher. The first, and most obvious, is evaluation by superiors. This process can, and should, include the principal, assistant principal, department chairman, curriculum director, and on occasion, the superintendent. Such evaluations, of course, should be as objective as possible, and usually are. They should also be rather frequent, so that the final evaluation for the year is based on a number of samples. Evaluation sessions should be unannounced; a scheduled visit would tempt the teacher to stage a show. An unexpected visitor to the classroom can be rather unnerving, even to the experienced teacher, but it does give the observer a more realistic view of the daily classroom procedures. I have found evaluation reports to be valuable. From them I have gained new ideas for programs, suggestions for new techniques, and awareness of bad habits that needed to be broken.

Beginning teachers should certainly welcome the constructive criticism that comes with evaluations early in their careers, and they should never approach the experience defensively. Just as teachers are expected to give report cards to their students, they are expected to receive their own "report card" from their superiors.

A second type of appraisal is self-evaluation. This should be a relatively constant process. Admittedly, self-evaluation is rather subjective, but a teacher can learn much about their classroom performance by this kind of awareness. Do your test results approximate a normal curve? Are your students attentive and alert? Are written assignments done with care and submitted to you promptly? Do you make it a point to do less than 50 percent of the talking in your classroom? Are you raising questions that lead the students to think, or are you making pronouncements that they are expected to memorize? Do you repeatedly review the educational goals for the various activities that you use? There we are—back to objectives again!

The third level of evaluaton consists of some kind of feedback from the students to the teacher. A number of professional appraisal forms have been devised for the purpose of teacher evaluation by students. These are usually available in the principal's office, guidance department, or professional section of the school library. Such forms may or may not tell you everything that you wish to know. I have found it helpful to devise forms of my own that are tailor made to provide student reactions to my own programs.

I include two of these evaluation forms as samples. The first one consists of three pages. The first page includes questions about the entire history course. Many of the activities referred to on this page are described in this book. The second and third pages concern only the unit on the twenties and thirties (Chapter 8). The second evaluation form, two pages in length, relates only to the Individualized Instruction Unit (Chapter 7).

By all means, construct evaluation sheets that are appropriate for your own particular classroom activities. You will find them to be valuable when planning future programs.

EVALUATION SHEET—AMERICAN HISTORY COURSE

Do not write your name on this paper. Period ______

1. Check one: ______ Boy ______ Girl

2. What was your first semester grade in American history?
______A ____B ____C ____D ____E

3. How do you feel about school in general?

_______ Like it very much _______ Like it

_______ No strong feeling _______ Dislike it

4. How do you feel about your American history course?

_______ Favorite subject _______ Like it very much

_______ Like it

_______ No strong feeling

_______ Dislike it

5. How would you rate the teaching performance of your American history teacher?

_______ Excellent _______ Good

_______ Fair _______ Poor

6. Rate all of the things listed below in terms of their learning value and helpfulness to you. Use "E" for Excellent; "G" for Good; "F" for Fair; and "P" for Poor.

_______ Teacher's lectures and stories

_______ Passaround Tests

_______ Civil War debates

_______ Vocabulary

_______ Political cartoons

_______ Current Events reports on national and world groups

_______ Daily Outline on the board

_______ Bulletin Board displays

_______ Mimeographed handouts

_______ Teacher's explanations or answers to questions

7. Estimate as accurately as possible the *average* amount of time that you have spent on homework in American history each week. Count all time *outside* of the history classroom _______.

8. Place the number 1 in front of your favorite of the following three programs. Place the number 2 in front of your second choice and 3 for third choice.

_______ Civil War Debates

_______ Individualized Instruction Unit

_______ Stimulation Unit on Twenties and Thirties

EVALUATION SHEET—TWENTIES AND THIRTIES SIMULATION

Do not write your name on this paper. Period ____

1. How do you feel in general about this unit?

   ______ Like it very much ______ Like it
   ______ No strong feeling ______ Dislike it

2. Do you feel that this unit should be repeated next year?

   ______ Yes ______ No

3. Would you like to see more than one unit done with simulation next year?

   ______ Yes ______ No

4. While doing this unit, how much time did you spend on history outside of the classroom as compared with the traditional approach?

   ______ More time ______ About the same
   ______ Less time

5. While working on this unit, did you find yourself discussing history with your family?

   ______ More than usual ______ About the same
   ______ Less than usual

6. Did you receive advice from family members on your financial investments?

   ______ Yes ______No

7. How did you feel about each of the following activities on this unit? Use "E" for Excellent; "G" for Good; "F" for Fair; and "P" for Poor.

   ______ Investing in stocks and banks
   ______ Scavenger Hunts
   ______ General Statement papers
   ______ Pressure Cards
   ______ Telehelp
   ______ Interviews
   ______ Legislation Debates
   ______ Alphabet Soup

8. Do you feel that Pressure Cards should be used?

   ______ On a pre-announced day
   ______ With no previous warning

9. Do you feel that Pressure Cards should affect:

_______ Your total wealth _______ WIPS Balance Sheet only

10. Check the WIPS balance that you had at the end of the unit:

_______ Net Loss _______ Net Gain

11. The twenties and thirties were a period in our history when people in general

_______ A. felt they had little control of their destinies.
_______ B. felt defeated, angry, frustrated, or fearful.
_______ C. felt the extremes of good and bad fortunes.
_______ D. at times found life to be tense and frantic.
_______ E. often felt that life "just wasn't fair."

Put a check mark in front of any of the feelings you actually experienced while "living through" this unit.

To what level of intensity did you experience any of these feelings?

_______ very strongly _______ slightly
_______ moderately _______ not at all

12. Are there any comments that you care to make on:

A. The history course in general?

B. The Simulation Unit on the twenties and the thirties?

C. The American history teacher?

13. In general, do you prefer in American history:

_______ The traditional approach, that is, texts, discussion, etc. _______ Special projects and programs

EVALUATION SHEET—INDIVIDUALIZED INSTRUCTION UNIT

Do not write your name on this sheet. Period _____

1. How did you feel about this unit in general?
   _______ Like it very much _______ Like it
   _______ No strong feeling _______ Dislike it

2. Would you recommend that this unit be used again next year?
   _______ Yes _______ No

3. How do you feel about being able to choose your own homework schedule and testing time?
   _______ Like it very much _______ Like it
   _______ No strong feeling _______ Dislike it

4. How do you feel about being able to take a second test when you wish to?
   _______ Like it very much _______ Like it
   _______ No strong feeling _______ Dislike it

5. How about the amount of time given to this type of approach to history?
   _______ Not enough _______ Just right
   _______ Too much

6. How would you rate the degree of difficulty of the project activities?
   _______ Too hard _______ Just about right
   _______ Too easy

7. During this project have you discussed your American history course with your family?
   _______ More than usual _______ Less than usual
   _______ About the same as usual

8. During this project how much time have you spent on American history *outside* of class?
   _______ More than usual _______ Less than usual
   _______ About the same as usual

9. How did you feel about the film strip operation as a learning activity?
   _______ Liked it very much _______ Liked it
   _______ No strong feeling _______ Disliked it

10. In terms of the contract that you signed at the beginning of the project, did you:

_______ Make your goal exactly
_______ Go over your goal
_______ Fall short of your goal

11. How would you rate the materials supplied to you for this project by the school library?

_______ Excellent _______ Good
_______ Fair _______ Poor

12. Check one:

_______ Boy _______ Girl

13. Are there any further comments that you care to make?

RESOURCE PEOPLE ON THE STAFF

WEBSTER: *A new or reserve supply or support . . . something in reserve or ready if needed.*

You will find on most school staffs a number of people who most assuredly do serve as a source of "support" or "something in reserve." These resource people can be of substantial help to the classroom teacher.

I have already discussed the importance of the school librarian (see Chapter 2). The library skills that can be learned in a good history course will probably be more useful to the student than his knowledge of history.

In addition to the librarian, there are many other specialists. Their functions in the educational process are paramount. Let us examine a few situations that call for assistance:

- Discipline problems, the disruptive child. Turn to the assistant principal for help; in many schools, discipline is his primary function.
- Reading problems. Your reading teacher is ready and willing to assist.
- Learning disabilities. Do you have special tutors on your staff for this function?
- Hearing, vision, speech problems. Refer these to the school nurse. Do you have a speech therapist in your district?

- The child who never takes part in class discussion, the child who comes alone to class each day and has no friends, the worry-wart, the tense or fearful student, the class clown.

It is very important that you recognize these problems. You need to know the members of your classes as individuals. You also need to have some awareness of each child's total school experience. After teaching history six periods daily, I begin to feel that history is the focal point of the lives of my students—a totally ridiculous assumption.

When you come to recognize individual problems, you should seek help and support. Your school principal, a guidance counselor, or a school psychologist will either reinforce what you are doing or point you in a new direction.

These staff specialists are all there to help the child and to give assistance to the classroom teacher. Take the time to consult them and to work with them on a partnership basis.

BASIC OR PROGRESSIVE?

WEBSTER: ***Basic****—Of or pertaining to the base or essence; fundamental; as a basic fact.*
Progressive*—Characterized by, devoted to, evincing or pertaining to progress, or continuous improvement . . . making use of new opportunities, inventions, methods, or the like.*

I find it interesting that the word "basic" can be defined in such a simple manner, while the definition for "progressive" requires so many words. I offer no conclusion; I simply suggest that it merits some thought.

In my view, we must teach the basic facts, the fundamentals, of any subject. This needs to be our top priority in setting up curriculum. I consider the following to be basic in an American history course.

1. The students should master the basic vocabulary, identification of famous and interesting people, and sequence of significant events.
2. They should be able to recognize major patterns and themes through each period of our history, as well as the factors that influenced the flow of events.
3. Our students must be given a thorough foundation in our system of government—its structure, function, and principles.

4. They should be aware of our foreign policy thoughout history, including the issues involved in our wars.

Beyond all of this, students need to master a variety of basic learning skills that are related to the study of history. These basics in learning skills are every bit as important as the subject oriented basics listed above.

All students should be working to improve:

- Sound study habits—note taking, outlining, organization of time and materials.
- Competency in the use of our language—spelling, punctuation, grammar, and writing papers.
- Reading skills, comprehension, and speed.
- Poise and confidence in public speaking—formal speeches, class discussion, argumentative skills.
- Library skills—use of catalog file and Readers' Guide—familiarity with reference sources.
- Analytical thinking—decision making, forming convictions.

I have just described what I consider to be the basics in history. Your choices may differ. Whatever you choose as your basics, they should represent the very heart of your own program and you should set up your objectives accordingly.

Next we must deal with the word "progressive." How about "progress or continuous improvement"? Of course! That must be a constant goal for any teacher. How about "new opportunities, inventions, or methods"? Proceed carefully, please. Under the guise of innovation, change, and progress, educators have been saddled with a number of programs that have turned out to be disasters.

In this book I have described several programs that can certainly be considered to be progressive. By all means, use such programs and devise similar programs of your own. Such special programs do add interest, fun, and a change of pace to any curriculum. They also serve to motivate the students and often result in better classroom performance. However, it is my opinion that the programs I have described (debates, games, individualized instruction, simulation, etc.) should not be attempted—particularly by a new teacher—until the students have had several months of traditional work. By this time teacher-student rapport has been developed. Classroom procedure and control are established. In addition, the students have already mastered many basic facts and learning skills related to history.

In the growing controversy between advocates of basic education and progressive programs, let us choose the "best of both worlds" to accomplish our objectives.

CONCLUSION

SEVERANCE: *The end!*

The time has come to bring this book to a close, and I find myself decidedly ambivalent about doing so. I'm very aware of several unexpected personal benefits that have come to me because of this writing. I have been forced to examine thoroughly my goals, my values, and my classroom procedures. It has also been necessary for me to face my own teaching faults and weaknesses. I have learned quite a bit about the publishing business, and that's a whole new world to me. And much to my surprise, I've discovered that I have more than one book in me; I am already plotting a second one.

My hope, of course, is that this book will prove to be of equal value to the reader. In spite of the direct and candid manner in which I have expressed deep convictions on the subject of education, I do not presume to have all the answers. But I would submit that I have raised most of the questions. Therein lies the greatest possible value to the reader. The questions raised in this book need to be faced and answered by teachers.

People in our profession may disagree on philosophy, programs, and educational theory, however, we all should agree on one thing. Teaching is a great profession, and an important one. We should all take pride in the work that we do, and do everything possible to improve the profession.

I share with you one final surprise discovery that I made during the writing of this book. While writing is both pain and pleasure, the end result of this book has brought much joy to me. I can only conclude that life does not begin at 40. It begins, in fact, at 60.

Index

1 2 3 4 5 6 7 8 9 10—RRD—87 86 85 84 83 82 81